Russia 1848–1917

Jonathan Bromley

Series Editors
Martin Collier
Erica Lewis
Rosemary Rees

Heinemann

HEINEMANN ADVANCED HISTORY

Heinemann Educational Publishers
Halley Court, Jordan Hill, Oxford, OX2 8EJ
a division of Reed Educational & Professional Publishing Ltd
Heinemann is a registered trademark of Reed Educational & Professional
Publishing Ltd

OXFORD MELBOURNE AUCKLAND
JOHANNESBURG BLANTYRE GABORONE
IBADAN PORTSMOUTH NH (USA) CHICAGO

© Jonathan Bromley 2002

Copyright notice
All rights reserved. No part of this publication may be reproduced in any material form (including photocopying or storing it in any medium by electronic means and whether or not transiently or incidentally to some other use of this publication) without the prior written permission of the copyright owner, except in accordance with the provisions of the Copyright, Designs and Patents Act 1988 or under the terms of a licence issued by the Copyright Licensing Agency Ltd, 90 Tottenham Court Road, London W1P 0LP. Applications for the copyright owner's written permission to reproduce any part of this publication should be addressed to the publisher.

First published 2002

ISBN 0 435 32718 6
04 03 02
10 9 8 7 6 5 4 3 2 1

Designed, illustrated and typeset by Wyvern 21 Ltd

Printed and bound in Great Britain by The Bath Press Ltd, Bath

Index compiled by Ian D. Crane

Picture research by Liz Moore

Photographic acknowledgements
The author and publishers would like to thank the following for permission to reproduce photographs:
David King: 7, 43, 66, 69, 72, 88, 117, 124, 126, 132, 146, 162, 166, 208, 215
Hulton Getty: 14, 16, 24, 51, 131, 204, 214, 216
Stedelijk Museum, Amsterdam: 5

Cover photograph © Mary Evans Picture Library

Dedication
In memory of my father (5/2/1908–30/10/1986) and my mother (9/8/1919–16/12/2001).

CONTENTS

How to use this book   vi

AS SECTION: NARRATIVE AND EXPLANATION

Introduction   1
1 Alexander II's inheritance in 1855   13
2 Alexander II, 1855–81   23
3 Conservatism and modernisation under Alexander III and Nicholas II, 1881–1905   58
4 The dawn of modern Russia?   94
5 The collapse of imperial Russia, August 1914 to March 1917   128

AS Assessment   **151**

A2 SECTION: HISTORIOGRAPHY AND ANALYSIS

Introduction   159
1 The historiography of late-tsarist Russia   160
2 Reforming late-tsarist Russia   175
3 Opposition in later-tsarist Russia   195
4 The wider context   211

A2 Assessment   **225**

Bibliography   230

Index   232

HOW TO USE THIS BOOK

This book is divided into two distinct parts. The first part – Narrative and explanation – is designed to meet the requirements of AS level History. This section offers an analytical narrative to explain the course of Russian history in the second half of the nineteenth century and the early-twentieth century, up to the revolution of February/March 1917. There are summary questions at the end of each chapter to challenge students to use the information in order to develop their skills in analysis and explanation, and to reinforce their understanding of the key issues. The first half of the book will also provide a solid foundation for the more analytical work expected at A2 level.

The second part – Historiography and analysis – explores the historiography of late-tsarist Russia and provides a thematic, analytical approach, addressing the key questions confronting students at A2 level. Both the exploration of historiography and the extended analysis will enable AS students to deepen their understanding of the subject matter.

At the end of both the AS and the A2 parts there are assessment sections which have been designed to provide guidance for students to meet the requirements of the new AS and A2 specifications when answering examination questions.

It is hoped that the book will also be useful to the general reader who wishes to appreciate the contradictions, strengths, weaknesses and, above all, the enormous possibilities of pre-revolutionary Russia.

AS SECTION: NARRATIVE AND EXPLANATION

INTRODUCTION

The introduction falls into two parts:

- a general introduction to Russia and the Russian Empire, and
- a more specific introduction to Russia in 1848.

RUSSIA AND THE RUSSIAN EMPIRE

Russia is, and always has been, mysterious. It is the largest country in the world. It occupies one-sixth of the world's land surface (making it 91 times larger than Great Britain) and has eleven time zones. From the permafrost in the Arctic circle to the sub-tropical climate of the Caucasus, and from the Baltic Sea to the Pacific Ocean, it should really be several countries. Yet under the **tsarist** empire and its successor, the **Soviet** Union, it was, in most respects, just one. Since 1991 this imperial tradition has come to an end but the Russia of today, which has recently lost many fringe territories, is still recognisable as the creation of the tsarist regime.

Some of the keys to understanding Russia and Russian history are:

- size and diversity, which made the country insecure
- its development into a military state
- poverty in some of its regions
- the impact of reaching its natural frontiers
- involvement with other areas and countries.

Size and diversity. For the last 300 years or so, Russia's size

KEY TERMS

Tsar (male) and **Tsarina** (female) These titles, used by Russian monarchs from the fifteenth century, come from 'Caesar'. The first tsar to name Russia an 'empire' was Peter the Great (1696–1725).

Soviet (meaning 'council') The key word in the title Union of Soviet Socialist Republics (USSR) given to Russia in 1922, after the revolution. The USSR lasted until 1991.

has been due to a lack of firm, defensible frontiers in the northern Eurasian land mass. Russia's natural frontiers are: the Baltic Sea to the north-east; the Black Sea, the Caucasus and Central Asian mountains to the south; the Pacific Ocean to the east (see page 6).

Russia has no clearly defined land frontier in the west, a particular weakness. As all early Russian rulers found, if Russia did not control this enormous area, it was vulnerable to invasion – and it was invaded, repeatedly.

Russia's development. Size and insecurity determined Russia's development into a centralised, expansionist military state. From the seventeenth to the twentieth centuries, Russia's greatest success was achieved by **autocracies**, tsarist and communist, both of which prided themselves on military strength and **centralised power**.

Poverty of the land in the central and northern regions. To support a growing population and to escape repression in the central areas, Russia had to expand southwards and south-eastwards towards the steppe, the fertile black earth region of the Ukraine and northern Caucasus – hence the Russian historian Klyuchevsky's (1908) remark that, 'the history of Russia is the history of a country that colonises itself'.

The impact of reaching its natural frontiers. Russia reached most of its natural, geographical frontiers to the east, south and north (none existed in the west) at the end of the eighteenth century. In doing so the tsarist state had unavoidably absorbed a host of diverse, non-Russian peoples (see pages 3 and 4) – including Poles in the west, Caucasian peoples in the south and Tatars in the south-east – making it a complex, potentially unstable multi-national empire.

Involvement in European affairs. As Russia expanded westwards and needed to secure a western frontier, it became deeply involved in Europe and European politics. Poland was at the heart of this involvement, with Russia taking control of Poland's eastern and central regions.

Involvement in other areas. Similar expansionism on

KEY TERMS

Autocracy Term used to describe the Russian system of government, at least until 1905. It means rule by a sole and supreme ruler, appointed by God.

Centralised power When power is concentrated in one place with no devolution of authority to regional or local government.

Major nationalities in late-nineteenth century Russia (from 1897 census)

	Numbers (million)	%
Russian Group		
Great Russians	55.7	44.2
Ukrainians (Little Russians)	22.4	17.8
Belorussians	5.9	4.7
Baltic Group		
Lithuanians	1.7	1.3
Latvians	1.4	1.1
Estonians	1.0	0.8
Caucasian Group		
Georgians	1.4	1.1
Armenians	1.2	1.0
Turkic (Azerbaidjani) peoples	2.0	1.6
Other Caucasians	1.0	0.8
Central Asia		
Kirghiz (Uzbek, Turkmen, Kazakh)	4.0	3.2
Others		
Poles	7.9	6.3
Finns	3.6	2.9
Jews	5.0	4.0
Tatars	3.7	2.9
Germans	1.8	1.4
Miscellaneous (including other Finnish peoples, Romanians and Bashkirs)	6.3	5.0
Total	126	100

Notes to table
1. The 1897 census used a classification for nationalities different from the one used today. 'Kirghiz' was used as a catch-all for several nationalities, and Azerbaidjanis were lumped together with other Turkic peoples. This table includes the 2.6 million Finns in the Grand Duchy of Finland, who were not included in the 1897 census.
2. The total number of identified national groups in the Russian Empire was over 100, many of them with unique languages and origins which made (and make) them impossible to group.
3. The Russian group made up 67% of the total population.

Density of settlement varied enormously. The Ukraine was the most densely populated rural area. At the other extreme the Kirghiz peoples were nomadic herders, covering a huge area, much of which was unoccupied at any one time.

Source: H. Seton-Watson, 1952

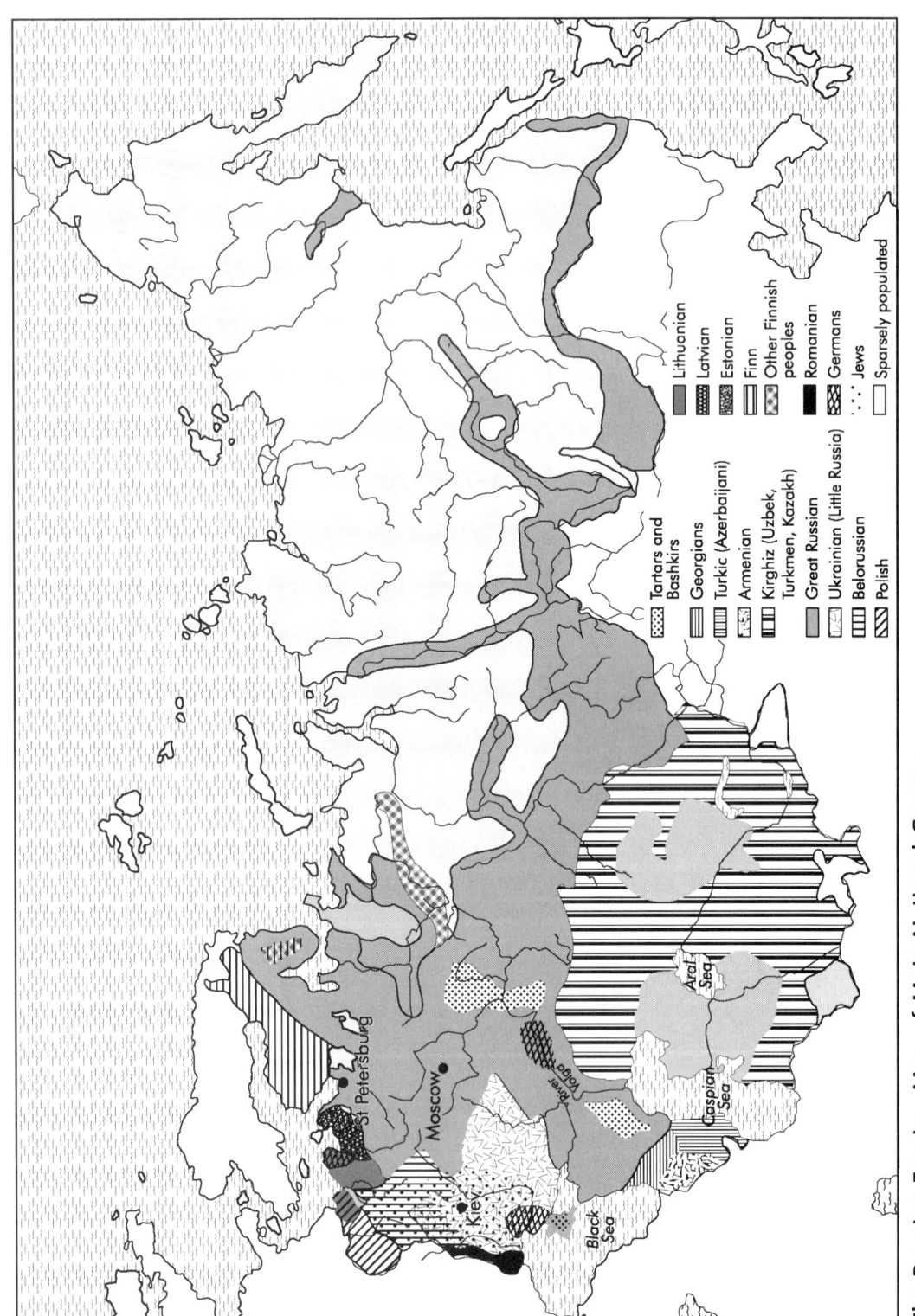

The Russian Empire: Map of Main National Groups.

Russia's southern and eastern frontiers brought wars with Turkey (1853–6 and 1877–8) and Japan (1904–5). By this time (around 1850 to 1917), Russia was anxious to secure access to the Mediterranean and an ice-free Pacific port as governments realised the importance of uninterrupted access to international trade routes.

- These strategic, geographic considerations are of central importance in understanding why the Russian state behaved as it did.
- They are also essential to understanding why it regularly took major risks in going to war, regardless of leader.
- Additionally, these factors had a profound influence on Russia's internal development, as the text below explains.

Internal development

Russia's political system was an autocracy for most of the period covered by this book. The country's social system was founded on **serfdom**.

Attitudes of serfdom. Although in legal terms serfdom was abolished in 1861, its effects were felt for many years

KEY TERM

Serfdom Prevalent in many regions of Russia, this tied agricultural workers (peasants) to the land by a binding contract between serf and serf owner (landowner), in which the serf had a defined role (agricultural labourer, domestic servant). Serfdom was not, therefore, as barbaric as slavery, a slave being a personal possession of the owner.

Kasimir Malevich's depiction of peasants in *Taking in the Harvest* (1911) – Ancient culture, modern art.

Introduction 5

The Russian Empire, 1848–1917: Natural geography

afterwards. The attitudes and habits it had bred were hard to escape for the vast majority of Russian peasants until well into the twentieth century.

Restrictions of serfdom. For the serf, serfdom was more or less inescapable. It bound families to a particular village for generations and ensured that most of Russia's rural population would remain illiterate and uneducated.

Autocracy and serfdom. Autocracy and serfdom were obviously linked. The ignorance, superstition and isolation of Russia's rural population meant that the peasants never really questioned the autocratic system.

- Peasants believed that the tsar or tsarina had been appointed by God.
- Peasants thought that the tsar or tsarina was on their side and would be able to right their wrongs.
- Peasants believed that a visit to the Winter Palace would bring justice in any petty local dispute.
- Peasants believed that the tsar knew every last detail of peasant life hundreds of miles from the capital St Petersburg and would set things right.

This last idea did not disappear with the abolition of serfdom in 1861. In fact, Tsar Nicholas II (1894–1917) made a point of encouraging it in his attempt to reassert the ancient and unique traditions of the Russian monarchy.

The Winter Palace in St Petersburg, the main residence of the Russian royal family, the Romanovs.

Introduction

Russia and Europe

Russia's insecurity and expansionism made military organisation and technology a vital requirement. From the sixteenth century western Europe led the world in both fields and Russian rulers began a 'necessary', if uneasy, relationship with the West. **Peter the Great** set a new course in this respect, moving the capital from Moscow to St Petersburg, and westernising Russia's military establishment and state organisation. Russia's importance in Europe continued to grow after Peter. His westernising approach seemed successful and established Russia as a major European power.

Russia and Asia

At the same time as Russia moved into Europe, the Russian Empire was also expanding to the south and east, giving it an Asiatic, as well as European, orientation. Although Peter the Great adopted western ideas that were directly useful to increase Russia's power, he ignored others like the rule of law and civil liberties. Ironically, this resulted in autocracy and serfdom being strengthened, rather than reformed, emphasising Russia's eastern and Asiatic characteristics.

The twin dilemmas of tsarist Russia, 1848–1917

The size, growth and success of the Russian Empire made it increasingly complex and contradictory. As Europe entered the industrial age in the mid-nineteenth century and the pace of social and economic change quickened, Russia's rulers were confronted with a double dilemma.

- In external policy – should they continue Russia's traditional relentless expansionism and make the state more diverse and difficult to manage?
- In internal policy – should they start to modify or even abandon the autocracy–serfdom formula that had set most of Russia's economy and society in stone, but had at least brought some order?

The pressures of modernisation and industrialisation made ruling Russia in the period 1848–1917 a daunting task. It is no surprise that all of its rulers in this period could be seen as inadequate in some or several respects.

KEY PERSON

Peter the Great (1672–1725) Tsar of Russia 1682–1725. He attempted to reorganise Russia using western ideas – modernising the army, founding the Russian navy, encouraging education and building a new capital, St Petersburg, closer to western Europe.

The revolutions that engulfed Russia in 1905–6 and again in 1917 would appear to indicate that the Russian government had failed to cope with these dilemmas. It is tempting to blame this failure entirely on the tsars themselves. But while it is fair to say that the men ruling Russia in this period were not the country's greatest rulers, it is equally fair to say that the tasks confronting them would have stretched the most capable of politicians.

RUSSIA IN 1848

The key theme in the second part of this introduction is 'revolution or evolution?'. We will look at the following:

- Russia's circumstances in 1848.
- The emergence of Russia as a European power.
- Nicholas I.
- Cultural developments.

The central question of modern Russian history is whether Russia could have avoided the revolutionary upheavals that hit much of Europe in 1848 and Russia itself in 1905 and 1917. The threat of modern revolution, first seen in France in 1789, defined politics throughout Europe between 1848 and 1917, and the success of the **Bolshevik** revolution in October 1917 redefined politics for much of the world for the next 70 years. With the fall of the **communist** Soviet Union in 1991, the history of late-tsarist Russia has taken on even greater importance as Russians seek to return to their pre-communist roots. Historians have to consider:

- whether the Russian revolutionary upheavals of 1905 and 1917 were inevitable, or
- whether tsarist Russia had the capacity to evolve and modernise without political violence and extremism.

Russia's circumstances in 1848

The year of European revolutions, 1848, is a good point at which to begin a study of late-tsarist Russia. In that year, when much of central and southern Europe was thrown into political turmoil and conservative monarchies seemed on the verge of extinction, Russia was thrown into stark

KEY TERMS

Bolshevik (meaning 'those in the majority') The name of Lenin's Marxist party, which took power in Russia in October 1917.

Communist Following the ideas of Karl Marx, communism projected the ideal of a classless society, free of exploitation, brought about by a workers' revolution.

relief. It did not suffer a political upheaval in 1848 and, like Great Britain, which also remained stable, appeared not to be part of the European political mainstream.

Russia's ruler, Tsar Nicholas I (1825–55), remained true to the **conservative** principles of the **1815 settlement** after the French revolutionary and Napoleonic wars. He introduced more stringent **censorship** and internal espionage. He also played an important role in helping to suppress the Hungarian revolution in 1849.

The emergence of Russia as a European power

For a full understanding of Russia in 1848 one needs to take a broad perspective. Russia had come to dominate eastern Europe over the previous 150 years by a mixture of good fortune (the decline of its rivals Poland, Turkey and Sweden) and inspired leadership – principally from Peter the Great (1682–1725) and Catherine the Great (1762–96).

Peter the Great. Peter established the unique blend of traditional Russian autocratic (see page 2) government and modernisation along western lines that underpinned Russia's transformation from an isolated, vulnerable, inward-looking medieval state into a major European power. This transformation was secured by an unbroken string of military victories from 1709, culminating in the defeat of Napoleon in 1812–14. However, Peter also strengthened what was to become the major obstacle to Russia's continuing progress in the nineteenth century – serfdom (see page 5). Although several of his successors tinkered with the mechanics of serfdom, their fear of anarchy and rebellion, should it be abolished, meant that it remained the key element in Russian society. Serfdom had the effect of making the vast majority of the population static and impervious to change.

Catherine the Great. At the other end of the social scale, under Catherine Russia acquired a Europeanised upper class, a class that absorbed the latest ideas from western Europe in the French Revolutionary and Napoleonic period (1789–1815) and continued to do so thereafter.

Nicholas I. Hence Russia in 1825, when Nicholas I came

KEY TERMS

Conservative In nineteenth-century Russia, conservative principles meant upholding the monarchy, Church, nobility, their power and their privileges.

Censorship Government control of, and interference with, all politically sensitive publications, characteristic of tsarist government.

KEY EVENT

1815 settlement In 1792 the French Revolution set off an almost unbroken series of wars in Europe that lasted until 1815. France's enemies – Great Britain, Austria, Prussia and Russia – were then able to impose a conservative peace settlement, which aimed to control France and more generally suppress revolutionary movements – including national liberation movements.

KEY TERMS

Napoleonic wars (1803–15) A series of wars in Europe, conducted by Napoleon I, aiming for French conquest of Europe.

Decembrists They were Russia's first modern revolutionaries. Mostly army officers from the upper nobility, they were fired by idealism from the French Revolution and complained about Russia's backwardness, especially its autocracy and serfdom. Their attempted uprising was poorly organised but, because it came from within the army, greatly alarmed Nicholas I and triggered a wave of repression.

> **KEY PLACE**
>
> **Siberia** Northern part of Russia which has long and extremely cold winters. Used for prisons and labour-camps.

> **KEY TERM**
>
> **Bureaucracy** Russia's state system (the autocracy) was essentially a bureaucracy, meaning that Russia was run by centrally appointed officials. The bureaucracy worked on a strict, military 'table of ranks'. Rank soon became an indicator of social status rather than ability. This encouraged pettiness and incompetence. Although these charges were often fair, it must also be appreciated that tsarist bureaucrats were thin on the ground. In 1851 in proportion to population the Russian bureaucracy was only just over one quarter of the size of that of Great Britain.

to power, was confusing and contradictory in social terms but unquestionably a great power in military terms.

Nicholas, the youngest brother of Tsar Alexander I (1801–25), was a military man. He took the throne in dramatic circumstances in 1825 when Russia might have had its own 1848-style revolution and his military experience in the **Napoleonic wars** proved very useful.

Nicholas's succession was challenged in December 1825 by a conspiracy of army officers known as **Decembrists**.

- A military stand-off between rebel regiments and troops loyal to the heir to the throne, led by Nicholas himself, took place in the centre of St Petersburg.
- The rebels, who wished to modernise and westernise Russia by ending the autocracy and abolishing serfdom were, in principle, similar to the European liberal revolutionaries of 1848.
- However, their military challenge was a failure and the rebellion swiftly collapsed.

Nevertheless, Nicholas had had a great shock. Traitors to tsarism had been lurking in the centres of tsarist power – in other words, the officer corps and the upper nobility. Five traitors were executed and 116 sent to **Siberia**, 31 for life. The Decembrist conspiracy gave Nicholas I a deep-seated fear of revolutionary opposition and of the ideas that they had picked up in the West. As a consequence, he resorted to police methods, internal espionage and **bureaucracy**.

In 1826 Nicholas established the Third Section of the Imperial Chancellery, the main task of which was to root out potential traitors. Russia was, therefore, set firmly on a conservative path well before 1848. This conservatism was reinforced by the ruthless suppression of a Polish national uprising in the Russian-ruled part of Poland in 1830. It emphasised Nicholas's denial of nationalism as well as liberalism.

Nevertheless, there was a political logic in running the empire as one unit and maintaining one political system – hence the tsarist manifesto of conservatism ('autocracy, orthodoxy and nationality') put forward by the Minister of Education, Sergei Uvarov, in 1833. Nicholas adhered to this manifesto for his entire reign. As a consequence, there was no thought of:

- political reform to redistribute the autocrat's political power
- cultural reform to dilute the Orthodox Church's role as the state's means of ensuring loyalty and a common cultural identity among the people at large
- making any concessions to non-Russian nationalities.

Cultural developments

Russia was not static in 1848, although the political system appeared so on the surface. Even in politics there was some change, the most important being Nicholas's decision effectively to free the state peasants in 1837 and later to set up commissions to investigate the possibility of doing likewise for privately owned serfs.

In cultural terms, Russia was developing fast. Russian intellectuals (notably authors like Alexander Pushkin, Nikolai Gogol and Mikhail Lermontov), sparked off a lively period of debate about Russia, its backwardness and its relationship with the West. Such free thinking naturally caused Nicholas serious problems. He personally censored some of Pushkin's work, and the ludicrous extent of Russian bureaucracy and censorship was humorously attacked by Gogol.

Although Gogol himself became a conservative supporter of the tsarist system around 1848, the obvious discord between the tsarist autocracy and intellectuals was to lead to a growth of criticism and alienation that bred opposition to the regime among students and university teachers.

In context, therefore, the impact of the 1848 revolutions confirmed, rather than seriously challenged, existing trends in Russian politics and society. Nicholas became even more conservative and repressive but continued to preside over a stable, if rather backward, empire. However, the ultimate effectiveness of his rule was to be tested severely in the **Crimean War**.

KEY TERM

Orthodoxy When the early Russians converted to Christianity in the tenth century they chose Orthodoxy, not Roman Catholicism like the Poles. Orthodox Christianity was based in Constantinople (now Istanbul). When Constantinople fell to the Turks in 1453 Russia began to assume the role of leader and protector of Orthodox Christians under Turkish rule. Orthodox Christianity puts far greater emphasis on ritual and simple, unquestioning faith than western Churches.

KEY EVENT

Crimean War This arose from the instability and rivalry among the European powers caused by the weakness of the Ottoman Empire (Turkey). The major encounters took place on and around the Crimean peninsular on the northern coast of the Black Sea. Russia went to war with the Ottomans in 1853. Britain and France joined the Ottomans in 1854, forcing Russia to make peace on its enemies' terms in 1856. This was a heavy blow to the prestige and international standing of the Russian Empire.

CHAPTER 1

Alexander II's inheritance in 1855

This chapter looks at the threats to Nicholas I's regime, both at home and abroad, after 1848. It considers:

- the threats to Nicholas's regime
- how Russia ended up at war in 1853
- the death of Nicholas I and the end of the Crimean War
- Alexander II's inheritance.

Nicholas I's Russia appeared as strong as ever in 1848–9. There was no threat of revolution in Russia and Nicholas was able to use the Russian army to suppress the revolutionary movement in Hungary. However, complications in foreign policy led to Russia going to war with the Ottoman Empire in 1853. Great Britain and France joined on the Ottomans' side in 1854. This, the Crimean War, proved disastrous for Russia, revealing the weaknesses that lay behind the impressive façade of Nicholas's regime.

HOW SERIOUS WERE THE THREATS TO NICHOLAS I'S REGIME (1825–55)?

As we have seen from the introduction (see pages 10–12), Nicholas I's conservatism was deeply held and, from his standpoint, well justified. In the later years of his reign the stability he had given Russia was sorely tested, first by the 1848 revolutions and then by the Crimean war.

Russian reactions to the 1848 revolutions

In March 1848 Russia's conservative allies – Austria and Prussia – succumbed to student-led revolutions in imitation of the revolution in Paris in February. Both regimes were forced to make unpalatable concessions. From Nicholas's point of view, it was as if the Decembrists (see pages 10–11) had succeeded in both Vienna and Berlin. The upshot of the Viennese revolution was the chaotic disintegration of Austria.

Nicholas I, tsar until 1855 when he died during the Crimean War.

KEY TERM

Slavs The term used to describe the peoples of eastern and central Europe with a common tribal origin and similar languages. As well as Russians, Slavs include Belorussians, Ukrainians, Poles, Czechs, Slovaks, Bulgarians, Croats, Slovenes and Serbs.

KEY PLACE

Poland Caused Russia endless problems in the nineteenth and twentieth centuries. The Poles were the strongest Catholic Slav nation and natural rivals, culturally and geographically, to the Russians. In 1815 the eighteenth-century 'partition' (division) of Poland between Russia, Austria and Prussia was resumed. As a consequence, the Poles made a bid for independence and took up arms against the Russians in 1830–1. The revolt was brutally suppressed by Nicholas I's army, deepening the two nations' mutual hatred. General Bem, one of the leading officers of the 1830–1 revolt, escaped to the West. In 1848 he helped the Hungarians, partly in the hope that their revolution would spread to Poland.

- A new German national state took its first steps under the Frankfurt Parliament.
- Piedmont–Sardinia tried to create a new Italian national state.
- Most frightening of all for Nicholas, a **Slav** congress was held in Prague in an attempt to liberate all non-Russian Slavs in Austria and elsewhere – another challenge to the Russian repression of **Poland**.
- Finally, a revolution in Budapest promised an independent Hungary, which would share a border with Russia. Even worse, its army was led by a Pole – General Josef Bem.

Fearing that this revolutionary disease would spread to Russia, Nicholas took immediate countermeasures. He mobilised his army in March 1848, saying he would meet his enemies wherever they appeared, and occupied the Danubian Principalities of Moldavia and Wallachia in June

> **KEY TERM**
>
> **Intelligentsia** A term invented by Russians to describe the section of the educated class that viewed intellectual debate and the spreading of new ideas as its most important activity, its reason for existence. Centred on the universities, the media and sections of the professional classes, the intelligentsia became unusually prominent in Russian politics in the late-nineteenth century mainly because Russia lacked a numerous middle class. The intelligentsia was often associated with radical political ideas, imported from the west, then adapted to Russian conditions (see 'populism', pages 51–4 and 'marxism', pages 80–1). However, many members of the intelligentsia were neither radical nor revolutionary.

> **KEY PERSON**
>
> **Fyodor Dostoevsky** One of Russia's most famous writers. He made his name on his return from exile with a series of novels, including *Crime and Punishment*, *The Devils* and *The Brothers Karamazov*. In his later life Dostoevsky rejected western politics and became a firm advocate of Russia's unique spiritual mission, centred on the Orthodox Church. This aligned him with conservatives like Pobedonostsev (see page 59).

and August respectively. This put Russia in a position to intervene in Hungary on its eastern frontier. Nicholas's claim that the Hungarian revolution was not a Hungarian national movement, but a Polish plot against the Russian state, was his justification for invading Hungary, first with a small force in March 1849 and then in overwhelming strength in June.

The Hungarians, attacked simultaneously from the west by Austria, surrendered in August 1849.

Fortunately for Nicholas, only the Hungarian revolution had proved durable. All the others failed to put up significant military opposition to the Austrian and Prussian armies, which had remained loyal to their sovereigns, and the liberal experiments were crushed. Even Paris had succumbed to counter-revolution by 1852.

Domestic affairs: politics

If Nicholas's fears for a general European revolutionary conflagration proved unfounded, they did little to assuage his principal anxiety – a new outburst of political opposition within his empire. Foreign news was heavily censored in March 1848. Russian subjects were forbidden to travel and those abroad were requested to return, although ironically this only served to spread the news of the European revolutions to the **intelligentsia** within Russia.

The Buturlin Committee. On 2 April 1848 Nicholas gave permanence to his heightened fear of revolution and subversion by establishing a new three-man committee known as the Buturlin Committee. It remained in being until Nicholas's death in 1855, and extended censorship from the more obvious political and philosophical challenges to the regime to anything academic that could slightly be considered politically subversive.

The Petrashevsky Circle. The first and most important victims of the paranoia referred to above were the members of the Petrashevsky Circle. Mikhail Petrashevsky's group, which included the writer **Fyodor Dostoevsky**, bore little relation to the European revolutionary movements of 1848 but simply subjected the tsarist regime to critical

Fyodor Dostoevsky, a Russian novelist whose most famous works included *Crime and Punishment*, written in 1870.

discussion. In 1845 and 1846 Petrashevsky had published his *Pocket Dictionary of Foreign Words Which Have Entered the Vocabulary of the Russian Language*, a title intended to get what was essentially a discussion of modern social and political ideas past the censors. The ruse did not work for long; volume two was banned shortly after publication. Petrashevsky followed this up with a pamphlet advocating looser restrictions on merchants and some serfs – hardly radical, but in February 1848, not well timed.

The outcome. The Ministry of Internal Affairs put the Petrashevsky Circle under surveillance for a year so that the quality of its findings would score a point over its rival, the Third Section (Nicholas's internal espionage service, set up in 1826). Then, in 1849, a re-run of the Decembrist prosecution was launched. Given that the Petrashevsky Circle was, in reality, little more than an idealistic student group it is staggering to discover that 252 people were questioned, 51 were exiled, and 21 were condemned to death.

The death sentences were commuted at the end of the year, but only after those condemned had been subjected to a **mock execution**. Instead, the defendants were given long penal sentences (Petrashevsky himself died in Siberia in 1866).

Domestic affairs: serfdom and the economy

Economic progress was limited in this period. The most obvious reason for this was the maintenance of serfdom as the prime source of labour and means of social organisation.

Differences between Europe and Russia. The year 1848 had seen the last remnants of serfdom eliminated in central and western Europe, one of the few concrete achievements of the 1848 revolutionaries. This left Russia as the only European state still to retain serfdom. However, the gulf between the West and Russia in this regard was actually much deeper.

- In most European states serfdom had either been entirely abolished, or remained only in small pockets from the second half of the eighteenth century.
- In Russia, despite Nicholas's reform of the state peasants in 1837 (see page 12), the majority of the working population remained privately owned serfs.

Attempted reform. Nicholas's government, anxious to avoid economic stagnation, introduced reforms to alleviate serfdom in the early 1840s but, so stringent were the requirements that, of 22 million privately owned serfs, only a few hundred families were able to free themselves.

The main reason why serfdom was so long-lived and deeply rooted in Russia was because it served the economic interests of the **nobility** and the political interests of the tsarist state.

KEY TERMS

Mock execution A punishment in which the condemned were put on 'death row', prepared for execution then reprieved at the last minute.

Nobility Russia's landowning and, before 1861, serf-owning class. Catherine the Great's Charter of the Nobility (1785) had confirmed these essential rights and, in addition, had given the nobility the right to travel abroad and take a foreign (European) education. Hence although the nobles were first and foremost a vital support for the autocracy with a vested interest in the stability autocracy claimed it could provide, they were also a source of criticism as new European ideas such as liberalism and socialism became fashionable.

- Serfs were, in the final analysis, the noble's private property, so any reform of the system would require compensation, hard to achieve in a state with low tax revenues and extensive military commitments.
- Furthermore, the state depended on the nobility as the prime source of the officials needed to maintain government, law and order, and to staff the officer corps in the army.

Nicholas I's position. If natural social and economic change could not bring serfdom to an end, as it had in the West, the government would have to force the issue and come up with a complex, risky and potentially costly reform package. This explains why Nicholas I was actually in favour of ending serfdom, but simply lacked the political conviction and context to push through such a dramatic reform. Proof for this view lies in:

- his reform of the state peasants in 1837, and
- the committees set up in 1844 and 1846 (the latter chaired by his son, the future Alexander II) to investigate the possibilities of reforming serfdom.

Therefore, there is every reason to suppose that, had Nicholas survived defeat in the Crimea (see page 12), he might well have tackled emancipation, as his son, Alexander II, was forced to do after 1855.

The economic impact of serfdom. One of the reasons serfdom faded out in the West was that it hindered economic progress. Nicholas I was well aware of this and of the serious danger of Russia being left behind economically, technologically and militarily. Railway construction, the most important breakthrough, was proceeding rapidly in western Europe. Nicholas consequently authorised Russia's first major railway project, a line linking St Petersburg and Moscow. This was completed in 1851. However, Russia was making a start at a time when comprehensive railway networks were already being constructed in Britain, France and the German states. In more general terms, industrial progress was hampered by the social immobility caused by serfdom and by a simple lack of funds.

> **KEY TERMS**
>
> **Landless proletariat** A nineteenth-century term for a lower class with no land or property, unlike most peasants. The landless proletariat therefore had no stake in the existing order and was likely to be rebellious or revolutionary. Landless proletariat was most often used to describe the urban working class created by industrialisation.
>
> **Ottoman/Sultan** Turks from the Ottoman tribe ruled Turkey and its huge empire, known therefore as the Ottoman Empire. The Ottoman head of state was the Sultan.

> **KEY PERSON**
>
> **Napoleon III, Louis Napoleon Bonaparte (1807–72)** Nephew of the great French general and Emperor of France (1804–14) Napoleon I. Louis Napoleon won a landslide victory in the French presidential election of 1848. With only a four-year term of office, he staged a successful *coup d'état* in 1851 to prolong his power, making himself Emperor Napoleon III with the creation of the Second Empire in 1852. (Napoleon I's son Napoleon II had died in 1832.)

> **KEY PLACE**
>
> **Holy Places** Christian shrines in the Ottoman province of Palestine, such as those in Bethlehem and Jerusalem.

Further pressures on Nicholas. Finally, Nicholas feared what was termed the **landless proletariat**. Despite the fiasco of 1848, they posed the most menacing threat of revolution. To say that the later years of Nicholas I's rule lacked reform is fair. But this judgement fails to appreciate the political pressures, real and imaginary, under which Nicholas worked. It also fails to appreciate that in its essentials (political and social stability, foreign and military power) the tsarist state seemed, at least outwardly, to be perfectly healthy.

Foreign affairs: the Crimean War

The background to the war. In 1849 and 1850 Nicholas had helped to restore Austrian power and the status quo in Europe. He then convinced himself that Austria would support Russia in the great powers' struggle for influence over the **Ottoman** Empire. Thus, when France's new ruler **Napoleon III** provoked Russia over the control of the **Holy Places**, Nicholas responded forcefully.

The failure of diplomacy. Prince Menshikov, Nicholas's envoy to the Ottomans, then provoked Stratford Canning, the British ambassador in Constantinople, by demanding that Russia should have rights to protect the Ottomans' Christian subjects. Canning urged the Ottomans to resist the Russians which resulted in the failure of subsequent diplomatic moves to defuse the crisis.

War broke out between Russia and the Turks in October 1853. In November 1853 the Russians destroyed the Turkish fleet at Sinope. This helped to persuade Britain and France to fight with the Turks from March 1854.

THE INVASION OF CRIMEA

The invasion of the Crimea by Britain and France in September 1854 and the subsequent campaigns culminating in the siege of Sevastopol in 1855–6 were caused by misunderstandings and by the momentum generated by sending an Anglo–French expeditionary force earlier in the year. This force either had to be recalled or used. The failure of diplomacy resulted in it being used, but even then the war was limited. Russia was only prepared to commit about one-quarter of its armed forces, and the Anglo–French force was only capable of achieving a tactical victory in the Crimea. There was never any serious intention on the part of the allies to attack the Russian interior.

The outcome of the conflict

Given these restrictions on both sides, the outcome of this conflict was predictable. It was fought on a scale and in a location that made the most of the more advanced weaponry of the Anglo–French forces. Some Russian guns captured in the Battle of Alma (1854) dated back to 1799. Anglo–French artillery and firearms represented post-industrial technology and had a greater range, greater accuracy, and a higher rate of fire.

More than anything, these advantages proved decisive. The more specialised, technological nature of modern warfare showed that backward, peasant Russia was poorly equipped to survive in the second half of the nineteenth century.

THE DEATH OF NICHOLAS I AND THE END OF THE CRIMEAN WAR

In February 1855 Nicholas, despite having a cold, insisted on reviewing troops in a temperature of minus 23 degrees Centigrade, and contracted pneumonia. Some days later he became one of the few later Russian tsars to die of natural causes.

What the Russians thought of Nicholas

Despite his unpopularity with radical intellectual critics and foreign enemies, Nicholas was genuinely respected by the majority of Russians for his firmness of purpose and overriding sense of duty, a respect possibly magnified by the reverses in the war. His funeral witnessed a real display of public affection.

How Nicholas's succession was affected by the war

The succession (in March 1855) came at a point when defeat in Crimea was only a matter of how long the besieged garrison in Sevastopol could hold out. International humiliation forced the new Tsar Alexander II

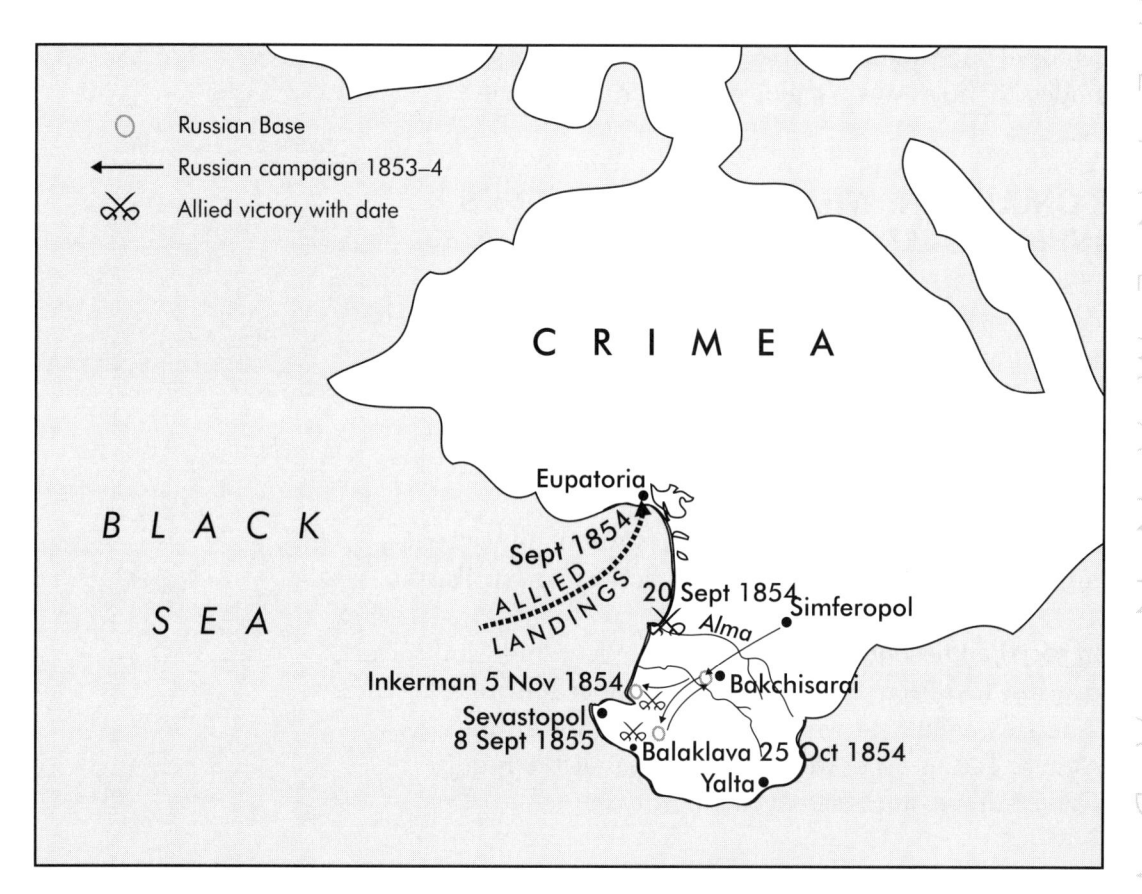

Military campaigns in Crimea, 1853–5.

to address the fundamental reasons for defeat in order to recover his empire's prestige. He thus embarked on the epic reform of the emancipation of the serfs, setting Russia on a new, more liberal, course.

The impact of the Crimean War on Russia

The Crimean War, although a limited one, was important for Russia. Russia's southward expansionism had been checked. In the Treaty of Paris of March 1856 the new Tsar Alexander II was forced to remove all Russian military establishments from the Black Sea and, with the formation of an independent Kingdom of Romania, to give up hope of taking over the Danube delta. Such a reverse, the most serious for Russia since 1700, forced a complete reassessment of Russia's social and economic structure.

Reasons for defeat

Nicholas I's conservatism had been, in a sense, self-defeating. At the time of his funeral the Russian Empire was on the point of suffering a humiliating reverse at the hands of the western European powers. Lack of reform under Nicholas was a major reason for this defeat.

CONCLUSION: WHAT WAS ALEXANDER II'S INHERITANCE?

Alexander II's inheritance from his father, Nicholas I, can be summarised as follows.

In international affairs: a nation on the verge of defeat, isolated in Europe and therefore dangerously weak.

In politics: an intact autocracy; repression of all western-influenced political thinking and practices within Russia.

In social and economic policy: Russia's economic and social progress had been extremely limited under Nicholas I, especially compared with the rapidly industrialising western European powers. Serfdom was at the root of Russia's increasing relative backwardness.

SUMMARY QUESTIONS

1 What were the main problems facing Nicholas I in 1848?

2 Why was Nicholas I so conservative in domestic affairs from 1848 to 1855?

3 Why did Nicholas I go to war in 1853?

CHAPTER 2

Alexander II, 1855–81

This chapter looks at what Alexander II's reforms achieved, whether they caused more problems than they solved, and whether they improved the chances of evolutionary social, economic and political development in Russia.

HOW SHOULD ALEXANDER II'S REIGN BE CHARACTERISED?

Alexander II's reign was a pivotal period in Russian history. The young tsar, faced with defeat in the Crimea, had to modernise Russia – starting with the abolition of serfdom. In itself a momentous change, this reform also opened up the possibility of Russian development on western European lines, socially, economically and politically. Such development directly threatened the bedrock of Russian politics: the autocracy. Alexander II's reign was, therefore, a difficult balancing act. On the one hand, he felt it necessary to conserve autocracy, out of respect for tradition and the need for political stability. On the other, he needed to reform certain aspects of Russian society and the Russian economy in order to bring about modernisation.

NEW EMPEROR, NEW PROBLEMS

Unlike many of his predecessors, Alexander II had been heir to the throne for most of his boyhood and earlier adult life. Therefore, he had been better prepared for his role as autocrat than many of his predecessors. His reign was to be characterised by two significant events – the emancipation of the serfs in 1861, and his assassination 20 years later. The first gave him the title 'Tsar Liberator'. The second showed that Russian politics had entered a new and violent phase and made him a martyr, both to liberals and conservatives.

Alexander II, the 'Tsar Liberator', painted in 1858. He became emperor in 1855 and was assassinated in 1881.

Alexander's achievements

Assessing Alexander II's achievements as ruler is made difficult by his elusive, complex personality. Certainly he was no Peter the Great, nor even a Nicholas I. He lacked their single-mindedness. Nor was he a Catherine II. One historian, David Saunders (1992), has concluded that 'he was not very bright'; others have argued that he had a split personality.

Alexander's role

The problems of assessing Alexander's role are

compounded by the uniqueness of the crisis in Russia's external and internal affairs which he faced in 1855–6. His was, by most historians' reckoning, the most difficult inheritance of all.

The changes required
At the beginning of Alexander's reign, Russia was at a crossroads.

- It had suffered defeat in the Crimean War.
- There was peasant unrest caused by Nicholas's decision to recruit a militia in January 1855.
- The Crimean War had caused the government great financial problems – a debt burden of one billion roubles.

If tsarism were to survive and Russia were to maintain itself as a great power, major changes had to be made. Could Russia modernise and retain tsarist rule?

HOW WAS EMANCIPATION OF THE SERFS TACKLED?

As we have seen from Nicholas I's reign, the emancipation of the serfs had not been far from the mind of the government for at least 50 years. It was, after all, a fundamental anomaly for Russia to retain serfdom when it had died out in western and central Europe. These areas were now experiencing the social and economic dynamism that were the keys to wealth and power in the dawning industrial age and a free labour market was an obvious, essential requirement. Russia had to tackle serfdom or flounder in the wake of its European competitors.

Despite the good intentions of Nicholas I, shown in the reform of the terms of contract for state peasants in 1837 and the various committees set up to discuss the condition of the peasantry in the 1840s, little real progress had been made towards emancipation by 1855.

The obstacles to emancipation
Two huge obstacles remained.

- Hostility of the gentry and nobility to the destruction of serfdom.
- The centrality of serfdom to the organisation of the Russian state and Russian society before 1861.

Hostility to the destruction of serfdom. The first obstacle was the general hostility of the gentry and nobility to the destruction of serfdom. They feared chaos and unrest in the short term and, in the long term, loss of status and wealth. Although several leading Slavophile thinkers were opposed to serfdom, **Slavophilism** could be used to reinforce these arguments.

In 1848 the writer Nikolai Gogol argued that serfdom and illiteracy suited Russian conditions best, that it represented a community of interest between landlord and peasant rather than exploitation of the latter by the former. Loss of wealth and status meant that any scheme of emancipation would have to compensate the serf-owning class. Given the state of Russia's finances and the general backwardness of the country's economy, it would be difficult to find a scheme that would make compensation possible. Without it, emancipation could not be contemplated, because the tsarist regime relied too heavily on the gentry class to alienate it.

Centrality of serfdom. The second obstacle concerned the centrality of serfdom to the organisation of the Russian state and Russian society before 1861. Although only half the peasantry was privately owned by this date, the principle of serfdom pervaded most walks of life. Russian society was legally classified as having three social groups:

- noble
- town dweller, and
- peasant (serf).

This classification explains how the culture of serfdom was not confined to the village. Serfdom was both a cornerstone of Russian culture and an organising principle of Russian society. The serf owner was his serfs' policeman, attorney, judge and jury. He was also their recruiting officer. Should serfdom be abandoned, all of these

KEY TERM

Slavophilism Used to describe the fashionable idea of seeing the Slavs, and especially Orthodox Slavs, as different from and, in some ways, superior to western Europeans. They objected to the call of westernisers for Russia to follow a western path of development, wishing to remain true to Russia's orthodox roots. Most Slavophils were politically conservative.

functions would have to be transferred to new institutions. A wholesale institutional reform of Russia could not be avoided.

The implications of such dramatic and extensive change on a society that had seen nothing like this before were deeply worrying. The precedent of pre-revolutionary France embarking on similarly momentous reforms in 1786 and being engulfed by revolution three years later was not lost on the conservative opponents of emancipation.

The momentum for change and the land issue

Defeat in the Crimea and a new tsar meant that the political climate changed dramatically. Alexander II, faced with a crisis, looked for new ideas. In order to hear or read these, he began to free the press.

- Nicholas I's Buturlin Committee, his harshest measure of censorship, was dissolved in December 1855. This was the first example of liberal reform, a process that continued with the pardoning and reform of the surviving Decembrists, the Polish rebels of 1830–1 and most of the Petrashevsky Circle.
- Freedom to travel abroad became more widely available after 1856, as did more relaxed censorship.
- By 1858 the Russian press was free.

The effect of change. These changes affected the climate of the debate on serfdom and, most importantly, exposed conservatives to arguments for a more liberal form of emancipation. The single most influential journal in this respect was **Alexander Herzen**'s *The Bell*. This was widely available after 1856 and was even read by the tsar.

The liberal cause. Herzen supported those who wished to press for full emancipation. This meant not just freeing the serfs from the landlord's power, but giving them land so they could set up as small proprietors rather than remaining economically bound to the landlord. Supported by **Nikolai Miliutin**, a high-ranking ministerial official who was the chief political influence on Alexander II's reform-minded aunt Grand Duchess Elena Pavlovna, such proposals gathered momentum. An outbreak of peasant

---

KEY PEOPLE

Alexander Herzen (1812–70) Became Russia's leading liberal/socialist thinker after his permanent exile from Russia in 1847. His journal *The Bell* established him as Russia's liberal conscience. Herzen's concern for freedom and individual rights made his ideas a pointed contrast with those of some of Russia's later socialists.

Miliutin brothers Nikolai (1818–72) and Dmitrii (1816–1912) are the most famous examples of 'liberal' ministers under Alexander II. Nikolai was a prime mover in the emancipation process. Dmitrii superintended the later military reforms. Both believed that the future of the Russian state was best assured by incremental, pragmatic reforms, which would bridge the dangerous gulfs in Russian society. Such arguments appealed to Alexander II in his more 'liberal' phases.

disturbances in Estonia in 1858 further strengthened the liberals' cause as Estonian peasants had been granted emancipation in 1818–19, but without land.

Alexander's position. Alexander himself seemed pliable. His famous speech to the Moscow nobility in March 1856 is a classic example of selective historical quotation. He made the remark 'It is better to abolish serfdom from above rather than wait until it abolishes itself from below' after saying that he had 'no intention of doing so immediately'. In 1857, Alexander did open up the process by circulating to the provincial gentry the proposals of General Nazimov for emancipation without land. Although in general he allowed the process to take its own course, the fact that he was prepared to be this flexible makes him different from his father.

Finalising emancipation. Perhaps the crucial contribution to finalising emancipation was made by the tsar's trusted friend and adviser, Yakov Rostovtsev. Rostovtsev was the pivotal man in the secret committee set up to look into emancipation in December 1856. For eighteen months he was inclined towards conservative emancipation on the lines of the Nazimov proposals. But by August 1858 he had moved to the Miliutin camp. Miliutin's campaign in *The Bell* and the Estonian disturbances appeared to have changed his mind. Rostovtsev's influence was to change the mind of the tsar himself.

Proposals and laws. An 'editing commission' was drawn up under Rostovtsev in 1859 to pull together the proposals of the provincial gentry (some hostile to the whole process) and draft them into workable laws. With the job half done, Rostovtsev died in February 1860. His successor Count Victor Panin diluted these proposals. In essence Panin opposed the immediate granting of land to the peasants and, although maintaining the principle of land transfer, made it a more lengthy and expensive process for the peasants.

THE EMANCIPATION STATUTES

On 19 February 1861 the emancipation statutes were finally issued.

- Serfs were given personal freedom in principle but had to remain serfs for two years while charters were drawn up.
- Serfs were to remain 'temporarily obligated' until the landlord agreed to begin the process of transferring any land apart from the peasant's dwelling place and garden (which the landlord could not refuse to sell).
- If, or when, the land transfer process began, the peasant bought the land by paying redemption dues over 49 years at 6 per cent interest to the government. The government in turn compensated the landlords by issuing them with interest-bearing state bonds.
- The economic terms of the settlement were advantageous to landlords, so most went along with the scheme.
- Over the next 20 years 85 per cent of former serfs became the legal owners of the land they worked.
- However, the landlords retained much of the best land, especially in the south. Overall, in the initial implementation of emancipation, the peasants lost about 20 per cent of the land they had worked before 1861.
- When and where land was transferred, the nobles were well placed to fix high prices.

COULD THE GOVERNMENT HAVE DONE MORE?

Although the emancipation statutes were a disappointment to Russia's more liberal thinkers, it would be churlish to criticise them too harshly.

The aim of reform

The aim of the reform was to break serfdom, but to minimise the social, economic and political disruption that would ensue. Above all, emancipation had to be practical, to be financially and politically affordable. Therefore, to overcome the objections of the landowners and to enlist their co-operation in this vast experiment was a huge achievement. It was hardly surprising that the landowners should control most of the economic levers in this process.

It would have required a huge effort (and expense) on the part of central government to impose a settlement that was more in the peasants' interests. This consideration alone dictated that the emancipation settlement had to be conservative and acceptable to the landowners.

Barriers to transformation

Perhaps the one provision of the statute that did damage Russia's future social and economic development was the strengthening of the village commune (*mir*). It became the mechanism through which peasants paid redemption dues. As a result, its role was strengthened. With this came the perpetuation of traditional farming techniques and a further barrier to the transformation of Russian serfs into individual peasant landowners, the aim of the liberal emancipators. This had to wait another 45 years until the reforms of Pyotr Stolypin (see page 76).

Emancipation as the door to modernisation

The emancipation, in its final form, was both progressive and retrogressive. In other words, it looked simultaneously to the future and to the past. It is undeniable that, for all its faults, emancipation opened the door to the modernisation of Russia, the first stage of which followed in Alexander II's subsequent reforms of the 1860s.

The logic of further reform

The emancipation of the serfs, flawed though it may have been, was a colossal and irreversible change. Because the functioning of the Russian state before 1861 had evolved around serfdom, a number of supplementary reforms were necessary, notably for the army and local government. Prior to emancipation, both army recruitment and the staffing of local government had naturally been assigned to the serf-owners.

However, the post-emancipation reforms of Alexander II did not simply fill the gaps left in the administrative and social structure of the country by the abolition of serfdom. Several went further than that and were based on the conviction of the ministerial reformers such as the Miliutins (see page 27) that Russia needed a more flexible social structure, and that western freedoms were essential to Russia's future progress.

KEY WORD

Mir The word used to describe the peasant commune. (*Mir* also means 'world' or 'peace'.) The commune was the peasant's 'world' as it, more than anything else, organised his or her life. The commune was controlled by heads of families. It redistributed land according to family size, and also organised the joint payment of taxation after 1893. Above all, the commune was backward looking. It distributed land inefficiently in narrow, very long strips and resisted new techniques in farming.

At first sight their thinking appeared to threaten the autocracy. But most of Russia's state servants accepted that only the autocracy gave Russia the structure and sense of tradition that were essential as Russian society embarked on a course of unprecedented social change.

The aftermath of emancipation

The immediate aftermath of emancipation did not look promising for the reformers.

> **KEY EVENT**
>
> **Bezdna** A large village in central Russia. It was the scene of the worst public disorder following the issue of the emancipation statutes. A local peasant named Anton Petrov read out his own popular version of the statues – that the peasants would be entirely free immediately and were entitled to all the land that they worked – which caused a riot. The authorities called in the military and suppressed the peasants ruthlessly – 102 were killed.

- First came the disorder at **Bezdna**.
- Second, the gentry of Tula and Smolensk province concluded that losing their status as serf owners entitled the nobility and gentry to greater political influence. They suggested that Alexander might grant them a representative assembly – the embryo of a parliament. The tsar rejected the idea.
- Third, in 1861 Alexander tilted the balance of his government towards the conservatives.
- Fourth, the government was confronted with its first wave of student protest.

Disappointment with the limitations of the emancipation statutes and the earlier suppression of the Bezdna peasants gave rise to intense frustration among radical students and university teachers. The effectively free press fanned the flames and, quite literally, mysterious fires broke out in the Universities of Moscow and St Petersburg, and riots in the University of Kazan in October 1861. The inevitable clampdown only increased the radical intelligentsia's hostility to the regime and became the seed-bed of populism (see pages 51–4).

WHAT WERE ALEXANDER'S FURTHER REFORMS?

The behaviour of the government was not as crude as it may first appear. Indeed, at the end of 1862 Alexander gave his stamp of approval to his more liberal ministers – principally Dmitri Zamyatnin (Minister of Justice 1862–7), Pyotr Valuev (Minister of Internal Affairs 1861–8) and Alexander Golovnin (Minister of Education 1862–7) – and set in train further monumental reforms.

Most of them came into effect in 1864. In order of importance they were the reforms of:

- the Judiciary (Russia's legal system)
- local government
- the army
- education, and
- the Church.

Reform of the Judiciary

The reform of the Judiciary in 1864 was a logical next step following the partial **codification** of Russia's laws and the founding of a legal profession under Nicholas I.

Critics of the reform. Critics, both at the time and subsequently, of the 1864 reform point out that the peasants were excluded from the new system. They had to be content with justice dispensed by their own local courts and government-appointed justices of the peace. But such criticism is misleading because, in essence, the 1864 reform revolutionised justice in Russia.

The new system. A society whose judicial system had been characterised by secrecy, corruption and inquisitorial procedure was instantly given an open western structure and system of procedure. The **Russian inquisitorial system** had been reminiscent of European witchcraft trials of the sixteenth and seventeenth century. The new accusatorial system introduced **barristers** with a British-style jury system. Moreover, trial proceedings were to be reported word for word in a government newspaper, the *Russian Courier*.

The reform of the Judiciary could be seen as the most forward-looking of all of Alexander II's reforms. Although it suffered some restrictions later in his reign, as political trials tested the mettle of Alexander's reformism and these restrictions increased under Alexander III, the system remained essentially intact until it was buried by the Bolsheviks in November 1917. For the first time Russians had the possibility of a fair trial (see page 122). This marked a crucial step in the evolution of a **civil society**.

KEY TERMS

Codification Listing, organising and fixing laws to establish a legal 'code'.

Russian inquisitorial system A prosecutor amassed evidence against the defendant with the outcome generally a foregone conclusion.

Barristers Counsellor for the defence and prosecution.

KEY TERMS

Civil society A society which is founded on respect for the rights of the individual rather than respect for the power of the state.

Zemstvo The Russian word for a local assembly, as introduced in 1864. The urban equivalent, introduced in 1870 was called *duma*.

Reform of local government

Local government reform was also a major innovation for tsarist Russia. Obviously the emancipation had created a vacuum in local government as crucial functions such as the provision and maintenance of roads and bridges, and such schooling and medical care as there was, had been the responsibility of serf owners. Some new structure now had to be devised. The options were:

- an extension of tsarist power, with the governors-general acting as local autocrats
- an extension of ministerial power by creating a new body of local bureaucrats (see page 11)
- giving power to the localities themselves through elected assemblies.

Change to a representative system. The first two options were the traditional options, the third a new departure. Yet it was the third option – elected assemblies – that was adopted. This was a very significant change in that, for the first time since Peter the Great, it endorsed the elective principle, as opposed to the autocratic and bureaucratic principles, in Russian politics. It implied that Russia could have a representative political system, spelling the end of autocracy. Why then was such a step taken?

The introduction of zemstva. The new assemblies known as *zemstva* (*zemstvo* in the singular) were a concession to the gentry. Alexander and his ministers were appeasing disgruntled former serf-owners with some local political power.

- The *zemstva* operated on two-tier system, district (*uezd*) *zemstva* sending a proportion of their members to form the higher level provincial (*guberniya*) *zemstva*. Certainly there was no intention of making the *zemstva* remotely democratic. The vote was weighted very heavily towards the local landowners. They had 42 per cent of the seats in the lower tier, *uezd* or district *zemstva* and 74 per cent in the upper tier, *guberniya* or provincial *zemstva*. The relative proportions for the peasants were 38 per cent and 10.5 per cent.

- Moreover, the *zemstva*, although elected annually, only met for long enough to elect a standing council to undertake local administration.
- Therefore, the *zemstva* were unlike modern local assemblies which, in frequent session, could act as watchdogs.

In 1865 the Moscow nobility cheekily asked the tsar for a third tier – a national *zemstvo*. This idea was firmly rejected. Alexander replied that 'such deviations from the order of things established by the laws in force can only make it more difficult for me to fulfil my plans'. After this put-down the St Petersburg nobility, who had also passed a resolution in favour of a national assembly, wisely decided not to address the emperor.

The introduction of dumy. In 1870 the *zemstvo* structure was extended to towns where the elected assemblies were called dumy (*duma* in the singular).

- The eight largest cities were given *dumy* equal in status to the provincial *zemstva*.
- Smaller cities were given *dumy* equal in status to the district *zemstva*.

Practical reasons for *zemstva* and *dumy*. The *zemstva* and *dumy* were created, above all, for practical reasons. Local government in Russia prior to 1864 had consisted of not much more than the landlord fulfilling the state's requirements for recruitment and taxation (or evading them, when possible), with the occasional foray of troops to put down peasant disturbances. So in a sense, the 1864 and 1870 reforms gave Russia the proper basis of local government for the first time. Moreover, they were cheap. Extending the bureaucracy and creating more jobs and salaries, was not a serious option given the perilous state of Russia's finances after the Crimean War (see pages 19–22).

The benefits of *zemstva* and *dumy*. The *zemstva* and *dumy* have been criticised for their inadequacies when measured against contemporary western administrative systems. However, in a Russian context, like the reform of the judiciary, they opened up evolutionary development.

KEY TERM

Duma The Russian word for an elected assembly, subsequently used for parliaments in Russia, 1906–17 and from 1991. The plural in Russian is *dumy*.

Most importantly, the *zemstva* and *dumy* had to take responsibility for local schooling, medical provision and road building. *Zemstvo* officials therefore had to engage in Russia's real social problems.

The legacy of *zemstva* and *dumy*. Although at first, as historian David Saunders points out, the *zemstvo* personnel were almost exclusively gentry whose priority was to defend their own interests, the *zemstva* and *dumy* became, from the late nineteenth century to 1917, the cradle of a new generation of more public-spirited officials, another stage in the evolution of a 'civil society' and a major political factor by 1914. It is not a coincidence that the head of the Union of *Zemstva* during the First World War, Prince Lvov, became Russia's head of state when the autocracy ended in March 1917.

Reform of the army

As well as these two reforms, the government pushed through other, less controversial measures. A top priority was the army. Some historians such as A. J. Rieber (1971) have argued that the entire emancipation and post-emancipation reform process was motivated solely by military considerations. This may be going too far, but it is obvious from the tsarist state's obsession with a strong foreign policy, and therefore its need for a strong army, that modernising Russia's army was seen as crucial.

How the army was modernised. The man entrusted with this task was Dmitrii Miliutin (see page 27), brother of the liberal emancipationist Nikolai. Miliutin wanted to give Russia a military establishment that could compete with western powers, and so avoid another war in the Crimea. Three areas had to be tackled – recruitment, organisation and education.

Russia's system of military recruitment before 1861 had been extraordinary by contemporary standards. Serfs were drafted by their owners for 25 years, effectively a life sentence. Some exceptions were made to this by Nicholas I in the 1830s when the term of military service for non-serf recruits was reduced to fifteen years. But this system guaranteed that Russia's foot soldiers would remain primitive, the recruits having little incentive to improve their education or gain a sense of professional *esprit de corps* and national purpose. The latter qualities were those encouraged by military reformers – notably General Albrecht von Roon – in Russia's western neighbour **Prussia** in the early 1860s.

Von Roon's reforms were essentially the introduction of short-term service with numbers made up by a large reserve, integrating the army with the nation rather than separating them. These reforms seemed to make sense, especially after Prussia's victories in 1866 over Austria and in 1870 over France.

Miliutin's reforms. During the period 1862 to 1874 Miliutin introduced a string of military reforms on the Prussian model. Professional military service was reduced across the board to fifteen years (six years in service and nine years in the reserves), and could be further reduced according to the level of education of the recruit (the better educated serving shorter terms). He also made these new regulations applicable to all citizens, regardless of social class, in the new statute on recruitment in January 1874. Miliutin then reorganised the regional structure of the army.

- He divided the empire into fifteen military districts to make mobilisation more efficient.
- He modernised Russia's military training establishment.
- Education for officers was overhauled with general education being the first objective rather than pure military training.

The impact of the reforms. Miliutin's reforms had a significant impact on Russian society as a whole, making the army more civilised. (For instance, recruits no longer had to have their heads shaved on being called up.) It was an exercise in social as well as military reform. Where recruitment to the army before the reforms could be seen as a life sentence to penal servitude, a new recruit could now expect to return to his town or village, and would probably be better equipped to run his daily life and contribute to his community.

> **KEY TERM**
>
> **Esprit de corps** The French term for a kind of team spirit, to defend the honour of a particular group and each of its members.

> **KEY PLACE**
>
> **Prussia (capital, Berlin)** The largest and strongest of the German states after 1815. In the midst of an industrial revolution the Prussian Minister-President, Otto von Bismarck, launched successful wars in 1864, 1866 and 1870–1 to expand Prussia into the German Empire (1871). In doing so, he seemed to have achieved the impossible: he had created a strong modern state without the Prussian upper class giving up much of their political power. Bismarckian conservatism was, therefore, an attractive model for Russian conservatives in the 1861–1914 period.

Reform of education

Miliutin's attempt, through the military, to improve Russia's educational provision was complemented by civilian educational reform.

Reasons for reform. This process was determined more than anything by Russia's universities. In the climate of greater freedom after 1858, entry quotas to the universities had been scrapped. This, combined with generous financial support, meant that increasing numbers of students came from non-gentry backgrounds and helped to generate radicalism on university campuses. At first, the political radicalism and fires of 1861–2 put the government on a conservative footing. Courses and student numbers were restricted in an attempt to strangle the subversive element and St Petersburg University was even temporarily closed in 1861. However, corresponding with the increased liberalism of reforms elsewhere, 1863–4 saw a change of approach.

New education statutes. The new minister, Alexander Golovnin (1862–7), freed the universities from their former restrictions (1863), then produced two Education Statutes in 1864:

- the first to regulate and expand elementary schools
- the second to increase the number of secondary schools (*gimnazii*) and introduce a new category of intermediate school (the *pro-gimnaziya*).

Golovnin stated that in all secondary schools 'children of all estates [social groups] are to be taught without distinction of profession or religious belief'. The elementary schools, run by the district (*uezd*) zemstva, were 'to strengthen religious and moral notions and to spread basic, useful knowledge' so that the peasantry might become literate and numerate, better able to operate as independent smallholders (private farmers). However, the statute put much emphasis on the dangers of exposing the lower classes to subversive influences through schooling. All Sunday schools had been closed down in 1862 as the **Third Section** thought that they were hotbeds of radicalism and opposition.

> **KEY TERM**
>
> **Third Section** The name of the secret police and government espionage service, 1826–78.

The outcome of reforms. This illustrates the problems that Alexander II's reformers had. Russian society had to be modernised and educated for the state to survive and prosper in an increasingly competitive European environment. Yet the upper sections of Russia's educational establishment were vulnerable to seductive, subversive western ideas. It is hardly surprising that Russian educational reform followed an erratic path.

Reform of the Church

Another major institution to be scrutinised and re-evaluated during the reform period was the Church.

Government control. Since Peter the Great, the government had taken control of the Orthodox Church, using it as a means of social control – to reinforce respect for authority, for instance – and a guardian of Russia's spiritual and moral values. The Orthodox Church made the peasants loyal to the state, in theory at least.

The reason for overhaul. In 1858 Ivan Belliustin wrote a brutal *exposé* of the poverty and inadequacy of the rural clergy which reached government circles. It sparked off a debate that led to the Minister of Internal Affairs, Pyotr Valuev, setting up an Ecclesiastical Commission in 1862. The Commission was charged with an overhaul of the Church so that it could fulfil its traditional role of instilling loyalty through Orthodoxy more effectively. In the climate of uncertainty following emancipation this was a high priority. However, the slowness of the bureaucratic process in Russian politics delayed concrete reforms until 1867–9 when the political climate had changed and the dominant influence was the highly conservative Dmitrii Tolstoy.

What the reforms did. The reforms created greater opportunities for promotion for energetic, talented priests. However, they did little to improve the life of the lower clergy or the general material condition of the Church, which was the focus of Belliustin's criticism in 1858.

WHAT WAS THE CONTEXT OF THE GREAT REFORMS?

When discussing the context of the great reforms we must consider Alexander II's economic and nationality policies.

The economy and finance

The backwardness of the Russian economy was the root cause of Russia's military inefficiency in the Crimean War. Military defeat indicated that economic modernisation was an urgent priority. The tsar and his ministers felt that they had to force the pace to give Russia a modern industrial and transport infrastructure – a 'wait and see' approach after the emancipation of the serfs would take too long. However, their options were limited by Russia's poor financial state after defeat in 1856. The government concentrated on three main areas:

- railways
- metallurgy, manufacturing and cotton
- coal and iron ore.

The railways: a background. Alexander II's government pursued a more vigorous policy of industrialisation and especially of railway building than Nicholas I. In 1861 there were 1600 kilometres of railway in Russia, and in 1878 over 22,000. Additionally, rail traffic increased more than fourfold in ten years (1865–75). The government did not want to be burdened with the cost of constructing a state railway system and encouraged the growth of private companies. However, lack of private finance forced the government to issue 1.8 billion roubles in loans for railway construction in the period 1861–76, and in the 'railway mania' years of 1870–3 to make direct investments in railway construction totalling 53 million roubles. It is clear, therefore, that railway construction was at the top of the government's political and economic agenda.

The strategic and commercial importance of the railways. This agenda was both strategic and commercial. A rail system gave the disparate empire greater coherence and immediately stimulated internal trade. The most important effect was to reduce the price inequalities between the cities of the north (principally St Petersburg and Moscow) and the main grain producing regions in the south. In the course of the 1870s the price of rye in St Petersburg relative to its price in the rye-growing regions fell by as much as 66 per cent. This effect in turn stimulated urbanisation and further industrialisation.

Metallurgy, manufacturing and cotton. In the metallurgical and manufacturing industries the emancipation of the serfs had important effects. The government-owned metallurgical industry in the Urals suffered a mass exodus of its serf labour force once workers were free. Production slumped by 30 per cent between 1860–2 and was then slow to recover. For enterprises with free labour it was a different story – especially in the cotton industry in Moscow, Vladimir and Russian Poland. Imports of raw cotton increased from 18,000 tonnes in 1863 to 85,000 tonnes in 1877 and 158,000 tonnes in 1881.

Coal and iron ore. In 1869 the Welsh industrialist John Hughes founded the New Russia Company in the Ukraine's Donets basin, an area rich in coal and iron ore. The company produced coal, pig iron and rails and it was the first step in the exploitation of the huge industrial potential of the Donbass region. However, Yuzovka and the infant oil industry on the Caspian Sea only pointed the way to proper industrialisation, the main obstacle to which was a lack of investment capital. Total foreign investment in Russia in the 1870s approached only 100 million roubles.

A system of public accounting. Underpinning these new initiatives was a vital reform of the country's finances. Minister of Finances **Mikhail von Reutern** introduced a proper system of public accounting for the first time. The state now published its accounts. Reutern abolished the ancient, inefficient system of tax farming. Under tax farming, financiers could 'farm' taxes, collecting them in whatever quantity they saw fit, giving the government only the money it required and pocketing the surplus. This was how the vodka tax had operated. Vodka tax was a key element in government finances, around 40 per cent of total state revenue. Reutern replaced the vodka tax farm

KEY PERSON

Mikhail von Reutern (1820–90) Russian Minister of Finances. He was one of many important Russian ministers who were Baltic Germans. Russia's Baltic German landowning class had a long tradition of state service, rather like the Prussian Junker landowning class in Germany. Reutern's largely competent and successful management of Russia's finances (1862–78) paved the way for rapid economic development in the 1890s.

with an excise tax (equivalent to Value Added Tax – VAT – in the UK). This had the result of the former tax farmers investing in the growth of Russia's industry. Moreover this reform benefited the peasantry as it made vodka cheaper.

The development of banks. Reutern was anxious to encourage the development of banks. A state bank was founded in 1860, followed by municipal banks in 1862 and savings banks in 1869. Nevertheless, Reutern struggled to maintain the stability of the rouble. In 1864 Russia's precious metal reserves were only 10.6 per cent of the value of notes in circulation. By 1876 Reutern had improved this to 29 per cent. Reutern's work was wrecked by the Russo–Turkish war and the same level of security for the rouble was not achieved again until 1893.

Reutern's achievement. Reutern was the first tsarist Minister of Finances to confront the problems of modernising Russia's economy in response to the spread of the industrial revolution in western and central Europe. His achievement was considerable because he had little in the way of private capital or western entrepreneurship to fall back on. The drive to modernise had to be supplied by the autocratic state. He established momentum in the vital area of railway construction, the arm of the Russian economy that was to lure French investment in the late 1880s and bring about the Witte boom of the 1890s (see pages 70–2).

THE POLISH REVOLT OF 1863 AND THE NATIONALITIES QUESTION

The policies of Nicholas I. Nicholas I had been repressive in his policies towards non-Russian nationalities and especially towards the Poles.

- The 1830–1 rising in Poland (see page 14) had seen as many as 80,000 rebels marched off to Siberia in chains.
- In 1847 Nicholas had done his best to stamp out the emergence of **Ukrainian nationalism** by arresting ten of its leaders and ordering its best-known exponent, the

KEY TERM

Ukrainian nationalism
Given that the Poles with their proud history and fierce national identity were brought to heel by the Russian monarchy, it was hardly likely that Ukrainian nationalism would get very far. The first problem with Ukraine is definition. One root of the word 'Ukraine' is 'border', in the sense of border of Russia. The Ukrainian language is very close to Russian and Ukrainians were generally referred to as 'Little Russians' in the tsarist period. Kiev, the Ukrainian capital, was the capital of the first Russian state, Kiev Rus, from around 850 to 1150. So historical arguments underscored cultural ones to make Ukrainian nationalism a marginal activity in this period, largely confined to small academic circles. There was a more general interest in Ukraine's colourful folk culture, especially its music, celebrated in Piotr Tchaikovsky's Second Symphony (the 'Little Russian') and the early ballet music of Igor Stravinsky.

poet and painter Taras Shevchenko, to take military service. This policy, although exceptionally harsh in the case of Poland, made some sense. After all, the Russian Empire was a multi-national state. If it conceded the national principle, it would at the very least start to fray at the edges. The weakness of such inflexibility was that there was bound to be a backlash if the political climate changed, as it did in 1855–6.

The results of Alexander II's intervention. Alexander II's amnesty for Decembrists, Polish rebels and most of the Petrashevsky Circle led in Russian Poland to what David Saunders (1992) describes as 'a crisis of rising expectations'. Two demonstrations in January and February 1861 commemorating the 30th anniversary of the last uprising led to five deaths and forced the tsar to appoint a Polish moderate, Marquis Wielopolski, as prime minister in 1862. Wielopolski pushed through a series of liberal reforms in education, for both Jews and peasants. However, the local gentry saw him as a Russian collaborator.

Insurrection broke out in January 1863. Poland had been deprived of its army in 1831, so a guerrilla campaign was the most that the rebels could manage, spurred on by the forlorn hope of French aid. It took the Russian army until October 1864 to root out the last of the resistance. However, once order was restored, Alexander II recognised that concessions were needed if stability in Poland was to last.

The emancipation statute for Polish peasants. Nikolai Miliutin took over from Wielopolski in 1863 and drafted an emancipation statue for the Polish peasantry that was considerably more generous in its land provision than that granted to the Russian peasants in 1861. The concessions to the Polish peasantry were an exception, however.

- In constitutional terms Poland now became part of the province of Vistulaland. In 1865 all Catholic Churchs' property was confiscated and the Church itself placed under the supervision of the Ministry of the Interior.
- In most other respects Poland lost its separate administrative status and in 1869 the University of

KEY TERM

Pan-Slavism In view of the conflict between the Russians and Poles, the idea of Pan-Slavism, some kind of union of all the slavs, may seem a little far-fetched. However, in the mid-nineteenth century in the writings of two Russians, Nikolai Danilevsky and Mikhail Katkov, it became an important new definition of Russia's European role. Both writers' views were anti-Polish, seeing true Slavs as Orthodox not Catholic. The result was that Pan-Slavism was not far from straightforward Russian imperialism and focused on Bulgaria and Serbia (both Orthodox Slav nations).

Peasant women farmers in the Ukraine in the late-nineteenth century.

KEY PLACE

Finland The Russian Empire won Finland from Sweden in 1808. Like Poland, it was more an imperial possession than a Russian province. Its Russian population was very small. The majority Finns and minority Swedes were not Slavs and did not pose the threat to the Russian state that a Polish revival would. So repression and russification were neither practical nor necessary. Power was conceded to the Finnish *diet* (elected local assembly) after 1863. However, this approach was abandoned in 1899 when Nicholas II cut down the *diet*'s power, and sparked-off a wave of Finnish resentment and protest that restored elected local self-government in 1906.

Warsaw was given a new statute decreeing that the language of instruction was to be Russian.

The Polish insurrection undoubtedly affected government policy towards the neighbouring Ukraine. A clampdown on a new wave of Ukrainian nationalism centred on the University of Kiev's Geographical Society and resulted in the latter's closure in 1876.

Other non-Russian nationalities. Elsewhere, Alexander II's policy towards non-Russian nationalities was also pragmatic rather than doctrinaire, and certainly not influenced by **Pan-Slavism**.

The situation in Finland. In 1863 Alexander summoned the *diet* (elected local assembly) in **Finland** for the first time in 55 years. The *diet* passed a language law in the same year

RUSSIAN NATIONALISM

Nationalism was, and remains, the strongest force in Russian politics. In the late-tsarist period it was used by conservatives to drum up support for the regime. It took several political forms.

- Under Nicholas I it underpinned the sense of duty and loyalty to the state that the tsar cultivated so strongly.
- Under Alexander II it led to Pan-Slavism.
- After 1881 it was the force behind russification (russianising non-Russian peoples in the Russian Empire, especially in terms of language) policies.
- After 1905 it was used to create the 'Black Hundreds', the popular street movement designed to encourage loyalty to the tsar among the lower orders.

It was, therefore, the one popular political force that the tsarist regime could draw on, and pushed it towards imperialism in foreign policy and xenophobia (hatred of other races or ethnic groups) at home.

This force in both forms soon re-emerged after 1917 to help shape the politics of the Soviet Union, most notably under Stalin. However, in 1914, many Russian peasants still had a very hazy sense of national identity. In Russia, nationalism was not yet the force it had already become in contemporary Germany, France and Britain.

that stated that Finnish should be made equal with Swedish in all public business within 20 years.

The Jewish people. Policy towards the Jews was also relatively liberal. Several categories of Jew (established merchants, degree holders, and some artisans and mechanics, for example) were allowed to reside outside the Pale of Settlement (see page 46).

The situation in the Caucasus. The **Caucasus** was a

KEY PLACE

Caucasus The southern fringe of the Russian Empire between the Black and Caspian Seas is mountainous and, in the nineteenth century as now, populated by a confusing mixture of Muslim and Christian peoples. The tsarist empire naturally favoured the Christians – mainly the Georgians and Armenians. This inclination was reinforced by Russia's long struggle in the region with the Muslim Ottoman Empire. Keeping the Muslim peoples – principally Azeris, Chechens, Ossetians and Abkhazians – under control required force and repression. However, the fragmented nature of the region meant that this was eminently practicable. The emergence of Social Democracy in Georgia after 1900 coincided with harsh russification policies to produce a strong Georgian national movement, in some ways a miniaturised version of that in contemporary Poland.

troublesome area for Russia in the mid-nineteenth century, second only to Poland.

- The essential conflict was the clash between Muslim and Christian cultures. In the nineteenth century this conflict had an external dimension in Russia's long-standing rivalry with Turkey in the Black Sea region.
- In the Caucasus the Muslim leader Imam Shamil's 25-year war against the Russians was brought to an end in 1859 with his surrender and capture. By this time all the other tribes of the north Caucasus including the Chechens had already surrendered.
- In May 1864 resistance from the Circassians on the eastern Black Sea coast was ended by General Yevdokimov. They were then offered the choice of resettlement on the plains to the north or emigration to Turkey. About half the population, some 400,000, chose the latter, a harsh example of nineteenth-century ethnic cleansing.
- As for the Christian peoples of the Caucasus, the Georgians and Armenians, they were naturally anti-Turk, anti-Muslim and thus pro-Russian.

Central Asia. Further east, Russian policy was a mixture of caution in central Asia, where the British Empire was a threat, and aggression in the Far East. Although Russian missions to the central Asian khanates of Khiva and Bukhara in 1858 were purely exploratory, in the same year and again in 1860 treaties signed with China brought huge new territories by the River Amur and the Sea of Japan into Russian hands (see page 91). This acquisitive trend continued in the 1870s with Russia's annexation of the island of Sakhalin in 1875. Rebellions in central Asia provided Russia with a pretext for military intervention. A series of minor campaigns over the next ten years saw the region fall entirely under Russian control by 1885.

HOW DID THE REFORM ERA END?

As has been seen, Alexander II's reforms in the 1860s and 1870s were at first sight a haphazard, contradictory process. Essentially they were an attempt to increase the

The main western and central regions of the Russian Empire.

1 Finland	8 Central Industrial
2 Northern	9 Urals
3 Lakes	10 Ukraine
4 Baltic	11 Central Black Earth
5 Poland	12 Volga
6 Lithuania	13 New Russia
7 White Russia	14 Caucasus

Jewish Pale of Settlement

pace of Russia's modernisation without threatening its political stability and were the product of a running battle between two groups of ministers and advisers: the one more liberal, the other more conservative.

- Liberal reformers argued that to do nothing would, given Russia's state after the Crimean War, invite distress, revolt and loss of great power status.
- Conservatives feared that the introduction of western liberal principles would ultimately have the same effect. The tsar himself, prone to switch from one point of view to the other, made the picture more confusing, for in a sense both liberals and conservatives were right.

This confusion helps to explain why the pace of reform slowed to a crawl after 1866 when a **radical** student, Karakozov, attempted to shoot the tsar. Alexander subsequently dismissed Golovnin from the Ministry of Education (1867) and replaced him with the conservative Dmitrii Tolstoy.

KEY TERM

Radical Meaning 'from the root', 'radical' in politics is used to describe people who are uncompromising, usually in their desire for change.

The swing to the right

Tolstoy (a relative of the novelist Leo Tolstoy) clamped down on the universities and tightened up entrance requirements. In 1871 it became mandatory for all applicants to have attended a *gimnazium* (see page 37) with a classical curriculum. The swing to the right was confirmed by the appointment of the following men.

- Pyotr Shuvalov, a resourceful and dedicated opponent of any reform, as head of the Third Section.
- Alexander Timashev, to replace Valuev as Minister of Internal Affairs.
- Konstantin Pahlen to replace Dmitrii Zamiatnin at the Ministry of Justice.

Only Dmitrii Miliutin at the Ministry of War and Reutern at the Ministry of Finance survived the reshuffle.

A change of political climate

These changes brought a change of political climate that lasted for most of the 1870s. As well as the ministerial shake-up, the government began to associate itself with a

Alexander II, 1855–81

more assertive nationalism in the late 1860s, most notably in its support for the anti-Polish Pan-Slav journalism of Mikhail Katkov, editor of the semi-official *Moscow News* from 1863.

Freedom of the press

The freedom of the press is another important measure of the regime's enthusiasm for reform. More or less free from 1858–62, the authorities banned radical journals like *The Contemporary* and *The Bell* in the aftermath of the university fires. However, relative freedom continued until 1866. But even after that, censorship was not as restrictive as it had been under Nicholas I and the government actually used the press to attack its radical critics.

Seeing the 1866 assassination attempt by Karakozov as a watershed is an oversimplification. Certainly, by then, the bulk of the reforms had already taken place. However, they did not dry up altogether and in 1880–1 Alexander was embarking on another important reform initiative, the consultative assembly proposed by **Loris-Melikov**. Moreover, most liberals favoured mild censorship to control the wilder tendencies of the student press.

Liberal fears

The liberals recognised that their approach to Russia's modernisation was threatened by the approach of the radicals. Both groups knew that the Russian masses were largely uneducated and might be easily manipulated. However, as we shall see, liberal fears were somewhat exaggerated.

The significance of 1866

In conclusion, 1866 represented only one of many changes of direction in the reign of Alexander II. It has acquired extra significance because it was the first time in the reform era that ideological radicalism made a direct impact on the tsar in person, and it occurred at a time when the principal reforms were in place and further reform was hard to justify.

KEY PERSON

General M Loris-Melikov
An Armenian war hero, who became the central figure in Alexander II's second liberal phase of 1880–1.

PAN-SLAVISM AND THE RUSSO–TURKISH WAR

With the reform of the army in place and the removal (in 1871) of the restrictions on Russian activity around the Black Sea enforced at the end of the Crimean War, Alexander II had greater freedom in foreign policy in the mid 1870s. Thus Alexander's foreign minister Alexander Gorchakov resumed Russia's traditional expansionism in an attempt to gain access to the Mediterranean.

Greater diplomatic freedom coincided with a redefinition of Russia's national mission as Pan-Slavism or the creation of a universal Slav (see page 14) federation. The origins of Pan-Slavism were intellectual and Slavophile (see page 26). Its two prime movers were Nikolai Danilevskii, who staged the Moscow Ethnographic Exhibition in 1868, and the journalist Mikhail Katkov.

The essence of Pan-Slavism was to emphasise the common links between the Slav peoples, regardless of their current political or religious orientation. At its most far-fetched, it envisaged a Slav empire based on Constantinople taking up where the eastern Roman Empire had left off. However, how the Catholic Slavs of central Europe were supposed to fit into an Orthodox state is difficult to understand, not least because among the Catholic Slavs were the Russians' most bitter enemies, the Poles.

In more practical terms, Pan-Slavism gave Russia a justification for interfering once more in the weakening Ottoman Empire in defence of the Ottomans' Slav Christian subjects. However, its scope meant that the Habsburg Empire which contained many Slavs (including some Orthodox Serbs), was also bound to feel threatened.

In 1875 a revolt in Herzegovina against Ottoman rule detonated further revolts in Bulgaria, and a brief attack on the Ottomans by Serbia and Montenegro. All these uprisings were crushed by the Ottomans, the Bulgarian revolt with notable savagery. Russia thus found a pretext to invade the Ottoman Empire in April 1877.

The Russian army suffered heavy losses in the five-month

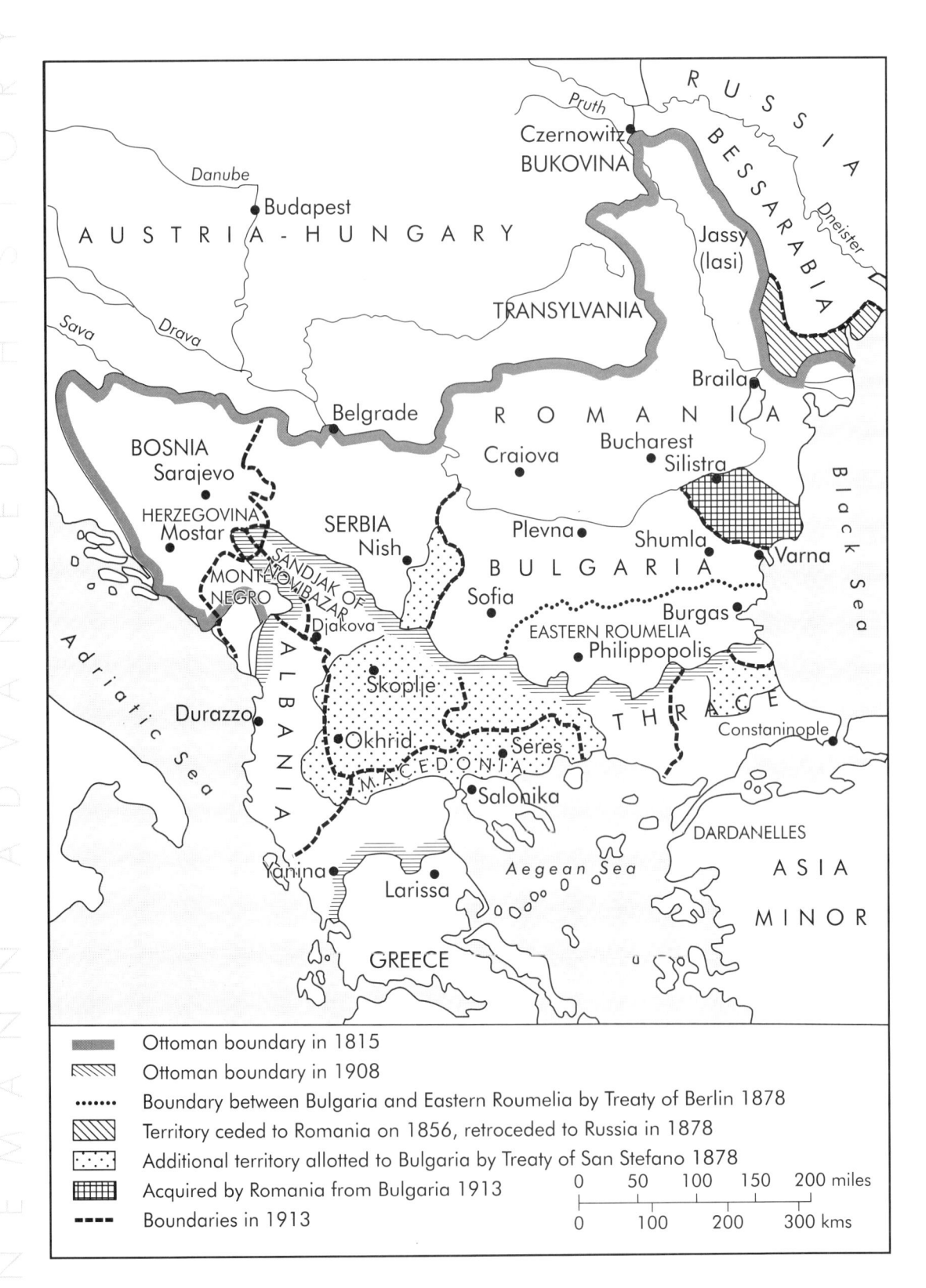

Disputed areas and boundaries in the Balkans, 1815–1913.

KEY TREATIES

Treaty of San Stefano In April 1877 Russia declared war on Turkey. By January 1878 Turkey was defeated. Russia imposed the treaty in March 1878. It secured large territorial gains for Alexander. The most important of these was the creation of a large Bulgarian state with a stretch of Mediterranean coastline.

Treaty of Berlin A major international agreement to settle the turbulent Balkan provinces of the Ottoman Empire. It also defined the limits the other European powers wanted to set on Russian expansionism. Under the terms of the treaty, Bulgaria was shorn of its southern territory, Macedonia, which was returned to the Ottomans. Serbia, Romania and Montenegro were given their independence.
Russia was still a net winner. It regained Southern Bessarabia and it acquired the important cities of Batumi in Transcaucasia and Kars in eastern Anatolia (Turkey). Although there was some ill-feeling on the part of the Russians at the time, the Treaty arrangements were broadly upheld until the Young Turk revolution (see page 113) in 1908.

siege of the fortress of Plevna in Bulgaria. But eventually it prevailed, forcing the Ottomans to sign the **Treaty of San Stefano** in March 1878.

Alarmed at Russian expansionism, Austria-Hungary, Germany and Great Britain convened a Congress in Berlin at the invitation of Bismarck, the German chancellor, which forced the Russians to climb down and accept a less generous version of San Stefano in the form of the **Treaty of Berlin** (July 1878).

After the popular campaign to support brother Slavs in Serbia in 1876, the Treaty of Berlin was something of a slap in the face. This was another example of Russia overreaching itself in foreign affairs and, unfortunately for the tsarist regime, it was not to be the last.

WHAT WERE NIHILISM, POPULISM AND THE RADICAL INTELLIGENTSIA?

The political dramas of the early 1860s produced heated debate in Russia's universities. This debate was fuelled by radical, utopian ideas from the West, mostly in the form of socialism or communism. The combination of the two gave birth to Russia's radical intelligentsia, men and women dedicated to the idea of creating a fairer, more equal society in Russia. Their dedication often expressed

A drawing showing Tsar Alexander II in his carriage, moments before being killed by a bomb, 1 March 1881.

Alexander II, 1855–81

itself in an uncompromising hatred for the tsarist regime, especially when the regime began to modernise and strengthen itself socially and economically. In the 1860s and 1870s these radicals were the first to grapple with the practical obstacles to forcing change on Russia. Their first attempts produced two movements – **nihilism** and **populism** – which have had a profound impact on subsequent politics, in Russia and the rest of the world.

Popular on the campuses of Russian universities, nihilism was blamed for the disturbances and fires that occurred in them in 1862. It marked the beginning of the radical, uncompromising extremist streak that characterised successive generations of Russian revolutionaries up to 1917. Nihilism's first important derivative was populism – a key stage in the evolution of the radical intelligentsia (see page 15) and culminated in the assassination of Alexander II by members of a populist terrorist group on 1 March 1881.

The populist spectrum. Populism threw up a variety of figures and approaches from dreamy romantics to desperate terrorists as it attempted, and failed, to bridge the gulf between progressive western ideologies – socialism and socialist revolution – and Russian reality.

The populist mentality. Populism's most remarkable achievement was the creation of a mentality of alienation and deep hostility towards the existing order. Providing the background for the development of this mentality were:

- the gulf between ideals and reality
- disenchantment with emancipation and subsequent reforms
- renewed censorship, and
- the university clampdown.

The radical intelligentsia

Nihilism's and populism's main inspiration came from the West, from the French revolutionary tradition. Paris was the 'red revolutionary' capital of Europe in the nineteenth century, and the 1848 revolution in Paris had thrown up important new revolutionary ideas and tactics. **Karl Marx**'s

KEY TERMS

Nihilism Derived from the Latin *nihil* (meaning 'nothing'). It is the term used to describe the intellectually fashionable idea of the early 1860s that a better society could only be built after existing society had been utterly destroyed. At first, nihilism was a semi-scientific ideology deriving from Charles Darwin's theory of 'survival of the fittest'. Nihilism saw no value in anything that could not be scientifically or mechanically explained.

Populism The term used to describe a broad spectrum of critics of the tsarist regime from the 1860s to around 1900. Populism was essentially an intellectual movement rather than a political movement. Populists are sometimes known in English books by their Russian name *Narodniki*. In Russian, narod means 'nation' as well as 'people' and there is no doubt that the populists were a peculiarly Russian national phenomenon. The populist state of mind had two major characteristics:
- a sense of sympathy with the plight of the common people, and
- a desire to bring about greater social equality by some form of revolution.

> **KEY PEOPLE**
>
> **Karl Marx (1818–83)** The most influential left-wing political thinker of the nineteenth century. His historical theory, based on a sequence of revolutions leading to worldwide communism, is explained on pages 80–1 (Marxism). Marx spent much of his working life in Paris and London, being an observer of revolutions in Paris and the development of capitalism (free market economics) both there and in London. His most famous works are *The Communist Manifesto* (1848, co-author Friedrich Engels) and *Das Kapital* ('Capitalism', 1867).
>
> **Friedrich Engels** Co-author of *The Communist Manifesto* (1848) and Marx's life-long collaborator. Engels became a mill-owner in Britain and gave Marx many of his ideas about the way in which class struggle between factory owners and workers was a natural product of capitalism. Engels took a larger role in the development of Marx's ideas after the latter's death. In 1889 Engels organised the Second Communist International, the first step to creating a worldwide communist movement. This lasted until the First World War.
>
> **Louis-Auguste Blanqui (1805–81)** French revolutionary politician who sought revolution not just by popularising revolutionary ideas but by conspiracy, infiltration and insurrection. He spent 33 years in prison for insurrection, and while a prisoner was elected president of the Commune of Paris in 1871.

and **Friedrich Engels**'s Communist Manifesto is the most famous, but more immediately influential for the populists was the Parisian revolutionary leader **Louis-Auguste Blanqui**. His tactics suited Russia, with its inert masses and fondness for policing and internal espionage.

Nihilism and Blanquiism came together in the *Catechism of a Revolutionary* (1869) written by Sergei Nechaev and Mikhail Bakunin. Mainly Nechaev's work, this saw the revolutionary as a blind instrument of the movement's will.

Nechaev was the most extreme of the populists, but not, in terms of numbers of supporters, the most influential. That distinction goes to **Nikolai Chernyshevsky** and Pyotr Lavrov. Chernyshevsky, through writing and imprisonment, became the populists' greatest moral authority. Lavrov was behind the first serious attempt to implement populist ideas.

In 1863 Chernyshevsky had a stroke of luck when a mistake in the censor's department allowed his subversive novel *What is to be done?* to be published. This proved highly influential in radical circles for its simple political message that ordinary people could take charge of, and improve, their own lives.

The importance of *What is to be done?* Chernyshevsky's novel is important because it defined the politics of the radical intelligentsia in four ways.

- It sympathised with the poor.
- It predicted a **utopian** socialist future.
- It advocated a simple, practical utilitarianism.
- It created the ideal of the selfless revolutionary in the book's central character, Rakhmetov.

It is no exaggeration to say that for all its weaknesses, political and literary, *What is to be done?* became the bible for Russian revolutionaries and Chernyshevsky, who lived his convictions, their saint. Lenin is one of many who were captivated.

Pyotr Lavrov. Pyotr Lavrov (1823–1900) presented a more gentle, realistic version of populism. He suggested that the only way forward was to communicate directly with the people, the *narod*, and educate them so they could understand how they could improve their lives. The first attempt to put these ideas into practice came when 3000–4000 students staged a **'Going to the people'** in 1873–4.

Trials of populists. Despite its failure, the 'Going to the people' caused alarm in government circles and Land and Liberty found itself in a new confrontational atmosphere. In 1877 the government staged a series of political trials of the populists who had 'gone to the people'.

- The first trial of 193 populists saw 28 defendants sentenced to hard labour and 90 acquitted.
- At the trial of 193, one of the defendants, Pyotr Alekseev, used the verbatim reporting of proceedings to launch a stinging attack on the regime. This tactic was used more famously in the subsequent trial of **Vera Zasulich and Sergei Kravchinsky**.

The end of Land and Liberty. Despite their evident guilt, both Zasulich and Kravchinsky were acquitted by sympathetic juries. This brought revolution no closer, however, and in 1879 Land and Liberty fell apart on the question of the use of violence, splitting into the non-violent 'black repartition' (see page 74), and the overtly terroristic group **The People's Will**.

HOW DID THE GOVERNMENT RESPOND?

The government's response was to adopt more sophisticated police measures to infiltrate revolutionary organisations under the new Minister of Internal Affairs, General Loris-Melikov (see page 48). However, Loris-Melikov also recognised the need for long-term concessions. Therefore, in January 1881 he recommended that the tsar should call what was in effect a national *zemstvo* to involve local government officials in decision making at a higher level.

KEY PERSON

Nikolai Chernyshevsky (1828–89) Established his reputation from 1854 as a radical literary critic in The Contemporary. He preached socialism in the wake of the emancipation of the serfs and, with his fellow critic Nikolai Dobroliubov, laid into the Russian writer Ivan Turgenev's Fathers and Sons for undermining the radical cause. All this brought The Contemporary an eight-month ban in 1862 and Chernyshevsky's arrest. He spent the remaining 27 years of his life under arrest or in internal exile.

KEY TERM

Utopian From the title of Sir Thomas More's book *Utopia* (1533). It depicts an imaginary island with a perfect social, legal and political system. A utopian vision was characteristic of many Russian revolutionaries.

KEY EVENT

Going to the people An attempt to communicate directly with the peasants and encourage them to overthrow what the student populists saw as an oppressive, exploitative system. The peasants, although hospitable, remained inert and uncomprehending. The populist students in 'Going to the people' simply illustrated how out of touch they were. Rural Russia's utter unresponsiveness to revolution led to further soul searchings among the populists and the formation of Land and

Russia 1848–1917

Liberty (1876). Land and Liberty sought to win over the peasants by living among them.

> **KEY PEOPLE**
>
> **Vera Zasulich and Sergei Kravchinsky** In 1878 Zasulich had attempted to murder the Governor-General of St Petersburg and Kravchinsky had assassinated the head of the Third Department, General Mezentsov. Neither was a terrorist by conviction, but their actions and the resulting publicity helped to push populism towards violence and terrorism.

> **KEY TERM**
>
> **The People's Will** This closely followed Nechaev's blueprint of 1869. It was dedicated to terrorism as a means of triggering the revolution that Populists had thus far failed to achieve. Its primary aim was to kill the tsar who, after Karakozov's attempt in 1866, had suffered three further attempts on his life. These were in April 1879, November 1879 and February 1880 (the bombing of the Winter Palace that killed and maimed ten guards and servants while the tsar was in another room).

Alexander II's approval, and his death

On 1 March 1881 Alexander II approved the Loris-Melikov proposals, which might have been the first step in the evolution towards a less autocratic, more representative system of government. Later that day, on his return from the Kazan Cathedral, Alexander was killed by the second of two bombs thrown by members of the People's Will.

CONCLUSION

In contrast to his father, Nicholas I, Alexander II had brought profound change in Russia. Socially and economically, it can be argued that Russia was far more stable in 1881 than in 1855. The same could be said of politics – except for the activities of the fanatics of the People's Will. Both in the general direction of the reforms of the 1860s and in the Loris-Melikov proposals of 1881, the tsarist regime appeared to be heading in a progressive evolutionary, westernising direction. Alexander II's achievements and failures can be summarised as follows.

Alexander's achievements

- The emancipation of the serfs was a huge undertaking, fraught with danger. In practice Russia managed to free some 40 million serfs with minimal disruption. Emancipation of the serfs was the key to all future economic and social modernisation.
- The other Great Reforms, especially those made to the legal system and local government, laid the basis for a future 'civil society' in Russia.
- Alexander II's government made the first serious attempt to modernise the Russian economy, notably by stabilising Russia's finances and embarking on the first Russian railway-building boom.
- In foreign policy Alexander II restored Russia's fortunes after the disaster of the Crimean War, despite the partial reverses of the Treaty of Berlin.

Alexander's failures

- Alexander's government veered between liberalism and repression, first encouraging criticism of many aspects of his regime, then turning on the critics.

- This in turn had the effect of pushing opposition to extremes and, ultimately, terrorism.
- Fundamentally, Alexander never attempted to resolve the contradiction between autocratic government and liberal ideas, perhaps explaining his political inconsistency.

Although there is a link between government policy and the emergence of a radical, ultimately terrorist opposition, it is also important to bear in mind that extremism and the use of terror were fashionable in many European states in the 1870–1914 period and that Russian groups were part of a wider trend.

Alexander II's political legacy

Westernising reform did not end with the assassination of the tsar. However, where it continued after 1881 it continued despite the government, rather than at the government's instigation. The Russian monarchy veered to the right after the assassination of 1881 and, in the personal politics of the last two tsars (Alexander III and **Nicholas II**), that is where it stayed until 1917. Thus, after 1881, the People's Will revived the bunker mentality of Nicholas I with a vengeance. Never again did a Russian monarch feel able to experiment or adopt as flexible an approach as Alexander II had done. After 1881 confrontational politics were often a first, rather than last, resort. This was a risky strategy as Russia embarked on a course of even more rapid and profound social and economic change.

KEY PERSON

Nicholas II (1868–1918)
Succeeded to the throne on his father's premature death in November 1894 and was ill-prepared for the responsibilities of the autocracy. Married to Princess Alix of Hesse shortly afterwards, he stuck to his father's policies and personnel for the first years of his reign. In January 1895 he made clear his opposition to diluting the autocracy by calling the idea of giving more influence to the *zemstva* 'senseless dreams'. Nicholas was not unintelligent, but proved a poor communicator, withdrawn and sometimes shy. Instinctive conservatism and slavophilism characterised most of his political decisions, both before and after 1905. He was forced to abdicate in the Russian Revolution of 1917.

SUMMARY QUESTIONS

1 Why did Alexander II decide to emancipate the serfs?

2 Why did Alexander II continue to reform after 1861?

3 Why did Alexander II's reforms slow down dramatically after 1866?

4 How substantial was Russia's economic modernisation, from 1855–81?

5 How effective were Alexander II's foreign and nationality policies?

6 Why, and with what consequences, did political opposition to the tsarist regime grow from 1861–81?

CHAPTER 3

Conservatism and modernisation under Alexander III and Nicholas II, 1881–1905

In this chapter we will be asking how effectively the tsarist state handled the pressures of modernisation. We will be examining:

- the impact of Alexander II's assassination on his successor
- New Conservatism
- russification
- economic development, industrialisation and agriculture
- opposition to the tsar, and
- the Russo–Japanese war and its effects.

It was after 1881 that the economic effects of the emancipation of the serfs became apparent and Russia underwent the early stages of industrialisation. However, the assassination of Alexander II forced the tsarist regime to be more conservative and, potentially, backward-looking. This apparent contradiction was revealed in the turbulent events of 1905–6 – the 'Revolution' of 1905.

THE IMPACT OF ASSASSINATION AND THE NEW TSAR

Alexander III was Alexander II's second son, the new tsar's elder brother Nicholas having died in 1865. Alexander had therefore been prepared for the succession for fifteen years. Father and son had their differences, most notably over Alexander II's complicated private life. The new tsar's father had had two families:

- one with his wife, the Empress, and
- one with his mistress Ekaterina Dolgorukaya, by whom he had four children and whom he married **morganatically** on his wife's death in 1880.

KEY TERM

Morganatic A morganatic marriage is one in which the father's rank is not conferred on the spouse or children.

Alexander III took his mother's side in this tangle. This helped to reinforce his conservative inclinations, especially as out-of-favour conservatives sought his attention in the Loris-Melikov years (see page 55). The new tsar was known for his conservatism before he came to the throne. The assassination of his father simply deepened his convictions. Naturally, the assassination played into the hands of conservative ministers in a more general sense. The simple, if misleading, argument that Alexander II had been too liberal and had paid for this error with his life had an obvious appeal.

> **KEY PERSON**
>
> **Konstantin Pobedonostsev (1827–1907)** Probably the most influential political thinker in Russia, 1881–1905. Capitalising on the assassination, he gave conservatism a new sense of purpose with the slogan 'Autocracy, Orthodoxy and Nationality'.

Foremost among the proponents of this heightened conservatism was the Chief Procurator of the Holy Synod, future tutor of Nicholas II, **Konstantin Pobedonostsev**. Pobedonostsev first showed his power by denouncing the Loris-Melikov proposals, gaining the new tsar's support and forcing Loris-Melikov to resign at the end of April 1881. Earlier that month five members of the People's Will who had been at the centre of the assassination plot were executed. This was the most dramatic aspect of a nationwide police crackdown on all terrorists and terrorist sympathisers involving 10,000 arrests.

THE NEW CONSERVATISM

This section takes a look at the Safeguard System, land captains, and the thinking behind New Conservatism.

The Safeguard System

The hard-line conservative approach was not simply a short-term solution. In August 1881 it was enshrined in the Safeguard System, a series of governmental instructions that amounted to two stages of a state of emergency giving the governors-general and police extraordinary powers. The Safeguard System remained to the end of the tsarist regime. It had two levels – the lower Reinforced Safeguard, and the higher Extraordinary Safeguard.

This meant that governors-general and police chiefs could:

- arrest suspects and imprison them for three months

- close down and fine the local press
- close down (under the Extraordinary Safeguard) the *zemstva* and *dumy*, and dismiss any officials in state service below the first three ranks.

Reinforced Safeguard was immediately applied to ten provinces, including St Petersburg and Moscow. During the 1905 disturbances Extraordinary Safeguard was used selectively. After 1906 Reinforced Safeguard was applied universally by Pyotr Stolypin (see page 76). So in a sense, Russia after 1881 was a kind of 'police state'. It revealed the state of mind of the conservatives surrounding the new tsar, that only by reasserting traditional Russian autocratic values could the Russian state's future be secured.

Land captains

The Safeguard System was a hint of things to come and was the first of Alexander III's 'counter-reforms' – conservative amendments to the reforms of the 1860s. The Safeguard System itself struck a major blow at the reformed, westernised judicial system, further eroded the freedom of the press, and compromised the authority of the *zemstva*.

This was followed in 1889 by the introduction of 'land captains', centrally appointed delegates of the governors-general who were able to interfere with local government. The land captains were a clear return to 'autocratic' administrative principles. Yet they did not replace the *zemstva* and *dumy*. In this sense they typified the contradictory nature of counter-reforms.

The thinking behind the New Conservatism

The new regime of Alexander III and Pobedonostsev completely rejected the creeping liberalism that the reforms of the 1860s set in motion, but they were not prepared to reverse the reforms themselves. It would have been ludicrous to attempt to re-impose serfdom in 1881 and, as the subsequent reforms of Alexander II were the consequences of emancipation and appeared to work, the term 'counter-reforms' as applied to the conservatism of Alexander III and Pobedonostsev seems overstated. In reality they constituted conservative amendments to the reforms of the 1860s.

However, there can be little doubt from the writings of Pobedonostsev that he regarded the Alexander II reforms as a grave error. The fact that he could not reverse them reveals an important point about the Russian autocracy and the limits of its power. Russian autocrats prided themselves on the strength of their government and the ability of the autocrat to impose his or her will. In this sense they could claim to be the most powerful rulers in Europe. But if power means the ability to effect change then the Russian monarchy was painfully weak and, with hindsight, all the weaker for its refusal to countenance further western-style reform after 1881.

- Socially and politically Russia still lagged behind the West.
- Administratively, the country was primitive.
- Perhaps most importantly, in relation to its size (and for a European great power), Russia was poor.

RUSSIFICATION

This section looks at the general principles and successes of **russification**, and the negative consequences.

General principles and successes

After 1881 there was a discernible change of mood and ideology. Pobedonostsev was a fierce and perceptive critic of the West and its liberal ways, and he sought to create a workable, popular, conservative ideology of his own. His starting point was Uvarov's 'Autocracy, Orthodoxy and Nationality' of 1833. Pobedonostsev updated this by putting much more emphasis on the last of the three, 'Nationality'. He admired Bismarckian Germany where **Bismarck** had successfully redirected German nationalism to conservative ends and created a dynamic, powerful industrialised state in the process.

Bismarck's success, although perhaps a model for Russia, was also a threat. So for conservatives like Pobedonostsev, an attempt to create a popular nationalism was not merely desirable, it was essential. Pobedonostsev's nationalism took the form of russification, a drive to mould the inhabitants of the Russian Empire into a single nationality.

KEY TERM

Russification Attempting to create a single 'Russian' nationality out of the multi-national Russian Empire (only 44 per cent Great Russian in 1900). It was a key policy of the tsarist government after 1881. It aimed to give the empire greater strength and coherence.

KEY PERSON

Otto von Bismarck-Schönhausen Minister-President of Prussia, 1862–71 and Chancellor of the German Empire, 1871–90. He was the mastermind behind Prussia/Germany's rise to the status of being Europe's leading military and industrial power in 1914. Bismarck's politics were unapologetically conservative (in other words, preserved as much power as possible for the ruling class of old Prussia). His success indicated that economic and military progress were not necessarily linked to liberal politics, as appeared to have been the case in Britain.

Mikhail Katkov was another enthusiast for russification. His ideal was Britain, in which a state nationality – British – had been contrived among the English, Welsh, Scots and some Irish. To transplant these ideas successfully to Russia was a huge task, given that:

- Great Russians made up only 44 per cent of the population
- there were over 100 other ethnic groups in the Empire as a whole, and
- there was a huge diversity of language, culture and economic development.

However, in some cases russification was easier than it might appear.

The Caucasian and Turkic peoples of the south and south-west were, with the exception of the Georgians and Armenians, largely illiterate and culturally backward. As primary education spread in 1880–1914 these peoples learned to read, write and speak Russian. They also had their names Russianised, as can be seen today in the surnames of many Azeris, Kazakhs and others.

The Georgian and Armenian élites, Christian and anti-Turkish were naturally pro-Russian, so russification in the Caucasus had some initial chance of success.

In Ukraine an anti-Ukrainian policy had already been established under Alexander II. This was continued, denying the existence of Ukrainians as a distinct national group, describing them instead, as was traditional, as 'Little Russians'. Thus, russification was a possibility in the south-west, especially as industrialisation brought a steady influx of Russians into eastern Ukraine after 1870.

Russian Central Asia was a special case in that it had only just been secured. It was thinly populated (mostly by nomads), and could therefore be treated as a colony. The northern steppe in modern-day Kazakhstan was steadily settled by ethnic Russians from the 1890s.

KEY PERSON

Mikhail Katkov (1818–87)
One of Russia's most prominent journalists. He fiercely promoted Russian nationalism, the suppression of Poland and Pan-Slavism from the 1860s to the 1880s.

Pobedonostsev and his Slavophile supporters could therefore claim some success.

The negative consequences of russification

However, the overall impact of russification was mainly negative.

The Caucasus. In the Caucasus social and economic change was eroding the power of the Georgian and Armenian landowning élites. Their pro-Russian sympathies ensured that popular lower-class movements founded in the 1890s – the Dashnaks (similar to the Russian populists) in Armenia, and the Social Democrats (subsequently Mensheviks) in Georgia – were strongly nationalist and anti-Russian. This situation was inflamed in Armenia by high-handed treatment from a new Viceroy of the Caucasus, Prince Golitsyn, in 1903. Paradoxically, Russia's triumphs over the Turks had weakened its hold over the Christian peoples of the region.

The Baltic Provinces. In the **Baltic Provinces** clumsy applications of russification such as imposing the Russian language on the cosmopolitan, largely German University of Dorpat and renaming it Iurev University in 1893, only helped to increase tension. The relative numerical decline of Baltic Germans continued. The proportion of ethnic Latvians and Estonians rose. A substantial Russian minority brought further complications.

Finland. In Finland the pro-Finnish, anti-Swedish policies of Alexander II continued to 1898 when Nicholas II appointed a new governor-general, Nikolai Bobrikov. Bobrikov aimed to integrate Finland into the empire by:

- abolishing its separate army
- introducing Russian as the official language of the administration
- making the Russian language more prominent in the school curriculum, and
- abolishing the Finnish State Secretariat, the Finnish component in the government of the province.

The results were disastrous. Mass protests and non-

KEY PLACE

The Baltic Provinces of imperial Russia These roughly correspond in territory to today's Baltic states, Estonia, Latvia and Lithuania. In the late-tsarist period their populations were substantially different. First, there was a substantial, powerful German minority (Baltic Germans) who formed the ruling class. Second, as the area experienced rapid economic growth, there was an influx of Russians. Riga, now the Latvian capital, was the fastest-growing city in the Russian Empire from 1900–14. As the population of the Baltic peoples rose and education spread in the second half of the nineteenth century antagonisms sharpened, culminating in bloody clashes in Riga in 1905. However, as long as the Baltic Germans remained influential (they had been prominent in the running of the tsarist state since the early eighteenth century) there was little likelihood of the Baltic peoples causing serious unrest. In the last resort they simply lacked numbers.

cooperation preceded Bobrikov's assassination by a Finnish terrorist in 1904. These protests formed the background to Finland being given virtual autonomy in 1905. In 1908, however, this was severely curtailed by Stolypin. Finland was once more reduced to provincial status.

The Poles. Perhaps the worst examples of the russification policies were the treatment of the Poles and the Jews. In the case of the Poles russification was already established under Alexander II after the 1863 rising. In 1885 it was stipulated by law that, even in primary schools only the Polish language and Catholic religion could be taught in Polish, and all other instruction had to be in Russian.

Such an onslaught on Polish culture made no sense except to Russian chauvinists (aggressive patriots) because it was totally impractical. The fact that a garrison of at least 100,000 troops was permanently stationed in Poland in this period is revealing, although some of these troops were there to protect the Russian Empire's western border.

Despite this oppression, Russian Poland was one of the most prosperous regions of the empire. By 1905, with 8 per cent of the empire's population it was contributing 25 per cent of its industrial output. The growth of a Polish working class naturally coincided with Poland becoming a seedbed for socialism, and Marxist socialism in particular.

The Polish Socialist Party (PPS) was founded in 1892 in Paris and the rival Social Democratic Party of the Kingdom of Poland in the following year, well before their Russian counterparts. Rapid social change also bred a more broadly based nationalist movement in Russian Poland, the National Democrats (NDs), led by Roman Dmowski. The NDs attracted middle-class as well as some working-class support with the party's blend of fierce nationalism, anti-Semitism and political pragmatism. Nowhere was opposition to russification more popular or better organised than in Russian Poland.

The Jews. Persecution of Jews in Russia marked a reversal of policy after the increasingly tolerant treatment of Jews under Alexander II. Russian anti-Semitism developed out of Russian nationalism and was, in the words of historian Geoffrey Hosking (1998) 'a kind of frustrated Slavophilism' whose main proponent was the Slavophile and Pan-Slav, Ivan Aksakov.

- In 1881 Nikolai Ignatiev, the new Minister of the Interior, wrote to the tsar about the menace of 'alien forces', a 'diabolical combination of Poles and Jews', the peoples most hated by Russian nationalists.
- In 1882 Jews' rights to acquire property were severely restricted and restrictions on Jewish residence, confining most Jews to the **Pale of Settlement**, were strictly enforced. Jewish entry to the legal, medical and military professions was forbidden. Jews were also denied the vote in local government elections. Strict quotas were introduced to limit how many received higher education and in most cases they were only permitted to complete part of their degree course. The result was to make many of the best educated and most able Jews fierce critics of the regime, especially as the universities were already a breeding ground for the radical intelligentsia.

It is no surprise that the revolutionary parties that emerged at the end of the 1890s attracted many Jews, notably the Marxist Social Democratic party.

Russian anti-Semitism

Russian anti-Semitism was not just restrictive, it was also violent.

1891. Two-thirds of Moscow's Jewish population were expelled.

1881–1905. This period witnessed the disfiguring phenomenon of the **pogrom** in the Pale of Settlement. The government did not have to promote such activities. It simply had to turn a blind eye to the innate **xenophobia** of Ukrainian peasants and **Cossacks**. However, it did more than this.

1902. The tsarist secret police (named the *okhrana* from 1881) went to the trouble of concocting the infamous 'Protocols of the Elders of Zion'. This was the first (and

> ### KEY TERMS
>
> **Pale of Settlement** The belt of territory in Poland, Ukraine and south-western Russia where Jewish settlement was permitted and most of Russia's Jews lived (see page 46).
>
> **Pogrom (or 'little thunder')** Organised violence, lootings, burnings and murders of Jews, most commonly in the Pale of Settlement.
>
> **Xenophobia** Fear or hatred of other races or ethnic groups.
>
> **Cossacks** A distinct sub-group of the Great Russians concentrated in the south of Russia on the steppe, notably around the Don and Volga rivers. Famous for their horsemanship and military prowess, the Cossacks struck deals with the tsarist regime to retain control of their own land and local affairs in return for military service. Because they had never been serfs, the Cossacks considered themselves superior to Russian and Ukrainian peasants. They treated non-Russian nationalities with even greater disdain. They were, therefore, the ideal tool for suppressing internal unrest. Instances of their brutality earned them a fearsome reputation.

Conservatism and modernisation under Alexander III and Nicholas II, 1881–1905

Desecrated Torah scrolls in the synagogue at Kishinev after the 1903 pogrom.

most famous) theory of a worldwide Jewish conspiracy to subvert European nations and set up a ruthless police state.

1903. The worst wave of anti-Semitic pogroms began, starting in Kishinev, Bessarabia. In just two days, 47 Jews were murdered, 400 were wounded, 700 houses were burned down, and 600 shops were destroyed.

Such policies, by playing on xenophobia, were popular with many ordinary Russians and Ukrainians, as were the measures taken against the Poles. A link can therefore be made between such policies and the fashionable anti-Semitism and **Social Darwinism** that spread among an influential section of the ruling élite in the 1890s, not least Nicholas II. However, it is hard to avoid the conclusion that although russification may have had some appeal to the Russians, its practical impact on the empire as a whole was largely destructive.

ECONOMIC DEVELOPMENT: STRATEGIES IN THE 1880S

The Russian failure in the Crimean War had illustrated the country's industrial backwardness. Although Alexander II and Reutern had made some progress in modernising Russia's economy, Britain and Germany were now forging ahead even more quickly. Russia's European rivals had

KEY TERM

Social Darwinism A social theory based on the work of Charles Darwin. It used natural selection to justify laissez-faire capitalism and so argued that only the strongest individuals and businesses would survive in commerce. By 1900 the natural selection theory was being applied to nations and races.

undergone (or were about to undergo) industrial revolutions that would transform their military capacity, not simply through increased productivity but through the gathering pace of technological development spawned by the industrial revolution.

In the wars of 1866 and 1870–1 the Prussian army made full use of new technology (rifled guns and railways) to inflict crushing defeats on Austria and France, demonstrating a military efficiency well in advance of all of the combatants in the Crimea.

If current trends continued Russia would become decreasingly effective as a military power and the security of the state would be threatened. Unfortunately for Russia, an industrial revolution on British or German lines was not possible. There were several reasons for this.

- The Russian economy was seriously retarded by serfdom and the slow process of disentangling it after 1861.
- Consequently, Russian society lacked a sizeable, educated and entrepreneurial middle class.
- The country was huge. To industrialise it would require massive investment. This simply was not available in such a poor country with such an unsophisticated economy.
- The Russian autocracy had a compulsive fear of the 'landless proletariat' (see page 19). The nightmare of the Russian regime was the combination of peasant lawlessness with concerted political protests in urban centres.

In the light of this, it is hardly surprising that Russia did not launch a full-scale drive to industrialise until the 1890s. Lack of will and resources determined that. However, Alexander II and Reutern (see pages 39–41) had taken some important steps in the right direction by emancipating the serfs, maintaining social stability, pioneering railway expansion, and setting up a more modern banking system.

The major cities showed rapid growth.

- Kiev doubled in size between 1861 and 1874.

- Moscow tripled in size between 1846 and 1897.

However, the Russo–Turkish war (see pages 49–51) showed how perilous Russia's financial stability was. Reutern resigned when the rouble declined in value in 1878. The social disruption the regime so feared soon made itself apparent. The incidence of urban strikes doubled in ten years, 1864–74, although they remained on a small scale.

PRACTICAL DIFFICULTIES OF ACCELERATING INDUSTRIALISATION

By the mid-1880s Russia had still not developed a coherent strategy to cope with the rapid advance of industrialisation in western Europe. Two practical difficulties confronted Russia's finance ministers.

- The Russian state had to spend beyond its means in order to maintain a competitive military establishment.
- The depression in agricultural prices after 1879 and the move continental Europe made towards **protectionism** forced a re-think in the Ministry of Finance which, under Reutern, had practised free trade policies.

Courses of action

Two courses of action were possible:

- either to control expenditure to create financial stability and attract foreign capital
- or to raise taxation with the same objective.

The first approach was tried by **Nikolai Bunge**, Minister of Finance, 1881–7.

The second approach was tried by his successor, **Ivan Vyshnegradsky**, Minister of Finance, 1887–92 after Bunge's policies had failed to avoid deficits. After a series of upward revisions of tariffs, Vyshnegradsky raised import duties to 33 per cent in 1891. Superficially this had the desired effect. The Russian budget achieved a surplus in 1892 and the first of a series of French loans was secured in 1888. However, the net effect of this desire for fiscal rectitude (balancing the books in taxation and expenditure)

KEY TERM

Protectionism Introducing import duties or tariffs to protect a domestic market and domestic producers.

KEY PEOPLE

Bunge and Vyshnegradsky Russian finance ministers of the 1880s. They linked the policies of Reutern with those of Witte (see pages 70–?). Their significance lies in their attempt to speed Russia's economic development by conventional, cautious means, without resorting to major foreign loans. This strategy failed to produce quick results, leaving the field open to the more radical policies of Witte.

was to put pressure on the peasantry. Grain exports, which were increased by 18 per cent as a percentage of total exports between 1881 and 1891, were a vital component of Vyshnegradsky's policies – in his words, 'we must go hungry, but export'.

The 1891–2 famine

Vyshnegradsky's export drive, combined with over-population and poor weather, made his statement prophetic. In 1891–2 Russia suffered its worst famine of the nineteenth century. It cost 1.5–2 million lives and brutally exposed the shortcomings of government policy.

The famine sparked off widespread public criticism of the tsarist regime. This, in itself, marks an important stage in the evolution of modern civil society in Russia. The government's attempts at famine relief were seen to be shoddy and slow, especially by members of the *zemstva* who tried to make up for the regime's inadequacies at a local level.

Under pressure from the Safeguard System and land captains, it was only natural that the newfound importance of the *zemstva* in the famine crisis would ignite a campaign for further liberal reform. Thus the famine crisis gave birth to a more widespread liberal 'responsible' opposition to the tsarist regime. In a sense, Russian **political pluralism** was born at this point. It would last only until the end of the civil war, some 30 years later.

KEY TERM

Political pluralism A political culture in which rival political ideas and organisations can co-exist.

Starving peasants in 1892 Russia, queuing for food at a soup kitchen in Mzhin-Novgorod.

The catastrophe of the famine cost Vyshnegradsky his job. He was replaced by **Sergei Witte**.

WITTE: HIS RAPID AND FORCED INDUSTRIALISATION, 1892–1900

Witte's fame rests on his far-sightedness, as well as his short-term success. He was one of the few Russian ministers to appreciate the sheer magnitude of Russia's problems as it tried to modernise. Hence he entitled his most important policy statement: 'Save Russia by rapid and forceful industrialisation'.

Witte's strategy

Witte sought to take advantage of Russia's late start to industrialisation in two ways.

- He saw that the western European experience of industrialisation produced an unstable first phase which brought impoverishment, dislocation and social protest. However, in the second phase, the increased wealth generated by the industrialised economy eased tensions and created a more complex, but more harmonious society.
- He also saw that Russia's late start would enable it to play technological leap-frog, to begin its industrialisation with the most modern methods and techniques, and thus achieve industrial efficiency more quickly. Witte therefore sought to compress and accelerate the first phase to minimise instability. An unforced, slow industrialisation was, in Witte's opinion, infinitely more dangerous politically and socially. He only needed to allude to the low points of Russia's history since 1861 – the terrorism of the 1870s and the recent famine – to make his case.

Witte's economic policies

Witte's economic policy built on the work of Vyshnegradsky. He recognised that healthy finances were essential to attract foreign capital. A second major loan from the French was secured in 1893 and the money pumped into capital goods projects, notably railway building.

> **KEY PERSON**
>
> **Sergei Witte** Minister of Finance, 1892–1903 and Prime Minister 1905–6. One of tsarist Russia's few outstanding statesmen. As Seton-Watson (1967) writes: 'Witte was both a brilliant organiser and a man of broad ideas.' Witte was a firm advocate of modernisation but in politics was relatively conservative, hoping to make the autocracy forward-looking and efficient.

INDEX OF ECONOMIC GROWTH
(1861=100)

	Industrial production	Agricultural production	Total population	Urban population	Grain exports	Railways (length)
1861	100	100	100	100	100	100
1871	149	111	116	212	242	618
1881	252	112	136		359	1050
1891	399	117	162		504	1395
1896	533	196	170	425	647	1795
1901	750	181	183		740	2564
1906	810	189	199		725	2891
1913	1165	309	232	696	783	3191

Source: adapted from D. Christian, 1997.

KEY TERM

The Trans-Siberian Railway It stretches 9600 kilometres from Moscow to the Pacific coast at Vladivostok. It was the single most important project of Witte's industrialisation of the 1890s. It was nominally completed in 1903, although much of the track was single, and until the 1920s Lake Baikal was traversed by ferry in summer and temporary track over the ice in winter. The Trans-Siberian Railway was as much a part of Russia's imperial expansion as of the country's domestic industrialisation. It gave Russia more leverage in the Far East as the European carve-up of China gathered momentum. Without the railway, it would be hard to explain Russia's readiness to provoke war with Japan in 1904.

Approval from the tsar. The fact that an efficient railway system offered significant military and security advantages, in addition to economic ones, persuaded the tsar that Witte's plans were worth backing. The result was a sudden but sustained dash to industrialise over the next seven years (1893–1900). The results were impressive (see the table above). However, one has to bear in mind that Russia was starting from a low base.

Initial investment. Russia's industrial revolution needed huge initial investment in comparison with smaller countries like Great Britain. In Britain's industrial areas resources such as coal and iron ore were concentrated locally or could easily be transported over the short distances involved. For Russia to begin to exploit its far-flung resources, then transport them to major population centres or make them available for foreign trade, railway building was bound to be much more expensive because of the distances involved. The **Trans-Siberian Railway** alone was more than one-third of Britain's total route mileage at the time. In this sense the spectacular growth figures are deceptive. They indicate substantial achievement but by no means allow one to say that Russia had an industrialised economy by 1900, or even by 1914.

Industrialisation after Witte. Witte's policies began an

Construction of the Trans-Siberian Railway.

irreversible process in that his approach was successfully continued by the tsarist regime after 1908, as soon as Russia had recovered from a worldwide slump (1900–4), defeat by the Japanese (1904-5), and the revolution of 1905.

Witte's social policies

Witte accompanied his industrialisation with some forward-looking social policies, in this respect building on the work of his predecessors. He recognised the need to do whatever was possible to relieve distress and consequent protest in the initial, harsh period of industrialisation.

- A factory inspectorate had been set up in 1882 and, in the same year, regulations controlling the use of child and female labour were introduced.
- In 1886 laws were passed to set up factory boards to arbitrate in industrial disputes.
- As a consequence, in 1897, Witte introduced decrees to limit hours of work for all workers to 11.5 hours (10 hours for night work) and even to permit trades unions.

To stabilise and encourage external trade, Witte put Russia on the **gold standard** in 1897, at the same time devaluing the rouble by one-third to make the currency fully convertible. This was a vital reform, which greatly increased the inflow of foreign capital (see page 73) from 40 million roubles in 1893–6 to 144 million roubles in 1897–1900.

As much of this came from loans, Russia ran up huge debts: 1.25 billion roubles in 1861 became 8 billion

RAILWAY CONSTRUCTION (average kilometres constructed per year)	
1859–60	228
1861–5	443
1866–70	1378
1871–5	1656
1876–80	767
1881–5	632
1886–90	914
1891–5	1292
1896–1900	2820
1901–5	1570
1906–10	1100
1911–15	1873

Source: P. Gatrell, 1986.

KEY TERM

Gold Standard A system by which a currency is valued and defined in terms of gold.

FOREIGN INVESTMENT IN RUSSIA, 1860–1914	
Year	Amount
1860	10 million roubles
1880	100 million roubles
1900	800 million roubles
1914	1750 million roubles

Source: Adapted from D. Christian, 1997.

PROPORTION OF FOREIGN CAPITAL AS A PERCENTAGE OF TOTAL RUSSIAN CAPITAL IN KEY ECONOMIC SECTORS IN 1914	
Sector	Percentage
Mining	90%
Metallurgy	40%
Textiles	28%
Commercial banks	43%
Overall	33% (approx)

Source: Adapted from D. Christian, 1997.

roubles in 1914. In 1900 servicing the debt took 20 per cent of the annual budget, ten times the amount spent by the Ministry of Education.

AGRICULTURE, 1881–1905

This section explains the contrast between industrial and agricultural polices after 1881. It also looks at the problems of agriculture and the eventual crisis at the turn of the century.

The contrast between industrial and agricultural policies after 1881

Witte's progressive policies contrasted sharply with the conservatism of the Ministry of the Interior. As the Ministry of the Interior was responsible for policy regarding the peasantry and therefore agriculture, this meant that the Russian economy was being pulled in two directions at once in the 1880s and 1890s. The Ministry of Interior's priority was rural peace. To this end it maintained an unshakeable faith in the peasant commune. As with the government's russification policy, there was more than a hint of Slavophilism in this (see page 26). In practice this made the Ministry largely unresponsive to new and unforeseen pressures in Russian agriculture.

Problems in agriculture after 1881

Although the emancipation of the serfs had achieved its short-term objective of managing a peaceful transition from serf to paid labour, the 1861 settlement had important shortcomings.

- There was inadequate land provision for the peasants in the first place and the terms on which peasants might acquire further land were poor.
- There was a rural population explosion. Russia's rural population more than doubled in the period 1861–1913 (74 million to 164 million). Clearly industrialisation could siphon off some of the surplus but full-scale industrialisation was slow in coming, as we have seen.

What the peasants thought. From the peasants' point of view, there was a simple solution: to be given the land (usually the best land) still held by the landowner. The Russian peasant had a hazy idea of the legal concept of private property, especially when applied to land – the notion was that the land belonged to those who worked it. This explains the widespread belief in the **black repartition**.

What the landowners thought. The landowning nobility were obviously not of the same mind but had serious problems of their own. The inefficiency of Russian agriculture, with yields in the black earth regions only about one-third of those in US prairies, was exposed in the world depression in agricultural prices after 1879, when cheap US grain imports hit the European market. Russian estates were unprofitable and, as the nobility was seriously indebted anyway, investment was low.

What the government did. The government looked to provide credit to keep the system afloat by founding a Nobles' **Land Bank** in 1882 and a Peasants' Land Bank in 1885. These did little to alleviate the pressure.

KEY CONCEPT

Black repartition A peasant fantasy of a judgement day when all land would be shared out fairly among the peasants.

KEY IDEA

Land banks Created in the 1880s to try to open the bottlenecks in land ownership and land transfer that were the consequence of the provisions of the Emancipation Statutes of 1861 (see page 29). If anything, they made the problems worse by offering the nobles a financial cushion to continue in debt, rather than an opportunity to invest in more modern farming techniques. They allowed the nobles to spin out land transfer, and run up further debts – 707 million roubles by 1904.

This critical situation was made even more delicate by Vyshnegradsky's export drive in 1888. However, he had little choice, given his financial priorities. It was simply unfortunate that, just at the time when Russia needed to export its one major marketable resource – grain – prices were depressed.

The Ministry of Agriculture's response to the 1891–2 famine

As already mentioned, the government's relief effort was poor and it led to no change of agrarian policy. In 1893 peasants were obliged to pay their taxes through the commune, creating a further obstacle to peasants who were brave enough to 'go it alone' and set up as individual proprietors. The reason for this apparently backward step was the ingrained conservatism of the Ministry of the Interior under I.N. Durnovo (1889–95). Durnovo, like Pobedonostsev, saw western policies and practices as a fatal mistake. All that his ministry was prepared to do was to ease the pressure of numbers on the land by encouraging peasants to colonise the virgin steppe of Western Siberia. This initiative was coupled with the construction of the Trans-Siberian Railway, which began in 1893.

However, the number of peasants prepared to move from the overpopulated central and southern regions was insufficient to make a significant impact. Approximately 850,000 emigrated to Western Siberia from 1895 to 1905.

The simple fact is that peasant population growth was too explosive to be easily contained, even by a combination of industrialisation and internal migration. In 1900 the net growth of population in European Russia was fourteen times greater than the population loss through migration. From 1900 to 1914 rural population growth averaged one million a year.

Agricultural crisis around 1900

The consequence of population growth was an explosion of rural unrest in the early years of the twentieth century. After a serious crop failure in 1901, 1902 saw the Russian Empire suffer its worst outbreak of rural lawlessness since the 1860s. The unrest was most serious in the provinces of Poltava, Kharkov and Saratov. It took the form of arson attacks and looting on landowners' houses and barns, with the vague aim of a so-called black repartition (see page 74). The government responded in two ways. First, it used force to restore order. Second, it began a complete overhaul of its agricultural policies by setting up a Commission on Agriculture in 1902.

Commission on Agriculture. This Commission was epoch-making for the tsarist regime: for the first time, the government faced up to the reality that increasing misery in the countryside was threatening the regime's policy of modernisation by industrialisation. The most important member of the Commission was the Governor of Saratov Province (one of the provinces worst affected by peasant unrest in 1902), **Pyotr Stolypin**.

Stolypin's proposal. Stolypin was a conservative pragmatist. He recognised that the regime had to engineer social reform among the peasants if, in the twentieth century, it was to escape eighteenth-century problems. Stolypin's proposal was that the archaic peasant commune, the *mir* (see page 30), which made the peasantry as a whole inward- and backward-looking, should be weakened to encourage peasants who showed individual initiative to set up as independent farmers, who would then, as property owners and small traders, have a stake in the tsarist regime.

The first practical result of this turnaround in the government's agricultural policy was the abolition of the commune's responsibility to pay taxes in 1903. This was the prelude to more extensive reforms after 1905.

KEY PERSON

Pyotr Stolypin Russian prime minister from 1906 to 1911. He had a major impact on Russian politics. Like the German politician Bismarck (see page 61), Stolypin was a conservative, yet a reformer. He sought to preserve the tsarist state but realised that this could not be achieved without social and economic reform. By tackling agricultural backwardness, in partnership with Minister of Agriculture Alexander Krivoshein (1906–15), Stolypin offered the regime a possible solution to its deepening agrarian crisis.

UNREST IN INDUSTRY AND THE UNIVERSITIES, 1900–5

This section takes a look at workers, how they were alienated by the government, then how the government tried to gain back their support. It also looks at protests in the universities.

Alienation of workers from the government

Unfortunately, Nicholas II's government was simultaneously beset by a crisis in Russia's fledgling industrialisation programme. Between 1900 and 1907 Russia was badly affected by a world slump prompted by a series of poor harvests in 1897–1901, rising interest rates, the Boer War, and unrest in China.

Government railway orders were cut by 10 per cent in 1899–1900, and this had knock-on effects for Russian heavy industry.

> **KEY TERM**
>
> **Syndicates** Groupings of firms in particular sectors to control production and prices.

The downturn in the trade cycle led to wage cuts, strikes, lock-outs, and the formation of **syndicates** (such as Prodameta for the metallurgical industry).

This was by no means unique to Russia. British industry suffered similar problems in industrial relations at the same time. However, in Britain the key issue was the unionised workforce lacking proper legal protection, whereas in Russia, legal issues were overridden by the government's direct and violent intervention in strikes, often with troops. The most famous examples of this were the brief general strikes in Rostov (1902) and Odessa (1903), and the Baku oil strike (1903).

The heavy-handedness of the government and its obvious bias towards the employers had the dangerous effect of turning strikes into political protests.

Attempts by the government to gain support from the workers

Heavy-handedness from local officials and ministers ran concurrently with a policy of greater subtlety from the Chief of Police, Sergei Zubatov, which included:

- the formation of trades unions, and
- the exploitation of nationalism and anti-Semitism.

Encouraging the formation of trades unions. Trying as ever to learn from the West, Zubatov came up with the idea of actually encouraging the formation of trades unions with guidance from the government so that workers' demands would be channelled in a politically acceptable, less confrontational direction. His policy rested in part on the infiltration of the unions with police agents. However, it did something to bridge the divide between the state and the working class, a divide which had proved fertile ground for Russia's Marxist agitators. It had the backing of the Grand Duke Sergei, Governor of Moscow and, briefly, of Viacheslav von Plehve, the Minister of the Interior. After the 1903 strike wave, however, Zubatov's ideas became unpopular with the government.

Encouraging nationalism and anti-Semitism. Another attempt to woo the workers back to supporting the regime was the **Black Hundreds**. They stressed Russian nationalism and anti-Semitism, and thus chimed in with the policies that the government had been pursuing since 1881 under Pobedonostsev's influence.

Protests in the universities

The universities were another source of political turbulence. Government interference with the curriculum and with university teachers' freedom to teach caused a strike among students in 1899 and set off a chain of increasingly bitter confrontations over the next five years. The fact that students were so frequently either protesting or being denied lectures encouraged some of them to participate in revolutionary politics. The wave of terrorism, which began in 1901 with the assassination of Dmitrii Sipiagin (Minister of the Interior) and continued at the rate of one prominent minister a year until 1905, only encouraged the reactionaries in the government to clamp down more firmly on the universities.

KEY TERM

Black Hundreds A monarchist populist movement that had some official backing. One of its tactics was to organise marches around working-class districts. The marchers sang the national anthem 'God save the tsar' and meted out violence to any worker who would not take part.

OPPOSITION, 1881–1905

Opposition during this period came from Populists, Marxists, Social Democrats, Socialist Revolutionaries and Liberals.

The Populists after 1881

The assassination of Alexander II made surprisingly little difference to the nature of opposition to the tsarist regime.

- Populism continued after 1881.
- Another People's Will planned another assassination in 1887.
- Liberal, moderate opposition remained, but was more marginalised in the new conservative climate.

The impact of the 1881 assassination

In terms of its political objectives, the assassination was a failure. Rather than triggering a wave of revolution, it brought a wave of revulsion. Its practical consequence was to increase the effectiveness of police activity against terrorists. That no successful terrorist campaign was mounted until 1900 is testimony to this. By making the tsarist state more oppressive, the assassination may have deepened the gulf between the people and the regime. However, the fact that the regime had become manifestly more unpopular by 1905 owes much more to social, economic, and political change in the 1890s than to the assassination.

Populism continued after 1881 because the assassination had little impact on the development of the radical intelligentsia. By and large, the radical intelligentsia retained its aloof, utopian (see page 55) state of mind. It regarded the assassination as a failed experiment that did not undermine or challenge its belief in the need for revolution as the only effective agent of positive change in Russia.

However, 1881 did force the Populists to acknowledge their split, and, among their ranks, temporarily discredited the advocates of terror. Sympathy for those who were executed confused the issue. The five Russian martyrs – Sofia Perovskaya, Andrei Zheliabov, Timofei Mikhailov, Nikolai Rysakov and Nikolai Kibalchich – had died for the cause but had failed to ignite revolution. So had their sacrifice been in vain? For many Populists the rational 'Yes' was drowned out by the emotional 'No', and the movement continued to try, with little practical success, to persuade the peasants to revolt.

In 1886 an attempt was made by a small group of students in St Petersburg University to revive the People's Will. The group manufactured some bombs to assassinate Alexander III. However, the police found out about this, and arrested the group's leaders. Five of them were executed in 1887. One of the victims was Alexander Ulyanov, a law student. His death at the hands of the authorities had a powerful influence on his younger brother Vladimir, then at school in Simbirsk. Vladimir **Ulyanov** later adopted the pseudonym '**Lenin**'.

RUSSIAN MARXISM

The most important new development for the opposition to the tsarist regime after 1881 was the introduction of **Marxism**.

What Marxism stood for
- Marxism, unlike populism, was a socialist doctrine that hinged on economic change – specifically the development of capitalism and industrialisation.
- Marxism could therefore be applied to a Russia that was beginning to embrace economic change.

Why Marxism differed from populism
- Marxism and industrialisation were both at odds with populism in that they accepted the necessity of capitalism.
- The Populists condemned capitalism because it brought inequality and was un-Russian. Industrialising Russia would take the country down a western path of development and the special, morally desirable features of Russian society, notably its sense of community fostered by the *mir* would be lost.

Why populism failed
By 1887 it was obvious that the momentum behind populism as a practical political movement was flagging. Neither terrorism nor propaganda among the peasants had produced results. Russia was industrialising and new ideas were needed to accommodate this profound change. Marxism fitted the bill.

KEY PERSON

Ulyanov/Lenin The Ulyanov family from Simbirsk were members of Russia's small provincial middle class. The genealogy of the Ulyanov family reveals an unusual ethnic mix – Russian, Kalmyk, Jewish, German and Swedish. This mixed ancestry was suppressed by Stalin and kept secret until the 1990s. Ilya Ulyanov, father of Alexander and Vladimir, was a local government official and an admirer of Tsar Alexander II. Alexander Ulyanov (b. 1866) was the second child and Vladimir (b. 1870) the third of a family of five surviving children (two others died in infancy). Both brothers were gifted children. Alexander also showed himself to be highly principled. After his arrest in 1886, he refused to make the usual plea to the tsar for clemency, which would have saved him from the death sentence. Although his brother's sacrifice had a major impact on the young Vladimir, it was but one of several influences that contributed to his conversion to radical politics. These included earlier Russian revolutionary writers like Nikolai Chernyshevsky and Sergei Nechaev, and the prevalence of radical politics in university life in St Petersburg in the 1890s.

> **KEY CONCEPT**
>
> **Marxism** The doctrine derived from the works of the political philosopher Karl Marx. His essential doctrine was as follows. The history of mankind was driven by economic struggle, the struggle between the possessing classes (the haves) and the exploited classes (the have nots). Capitalism was driven by material greed and therefore the possessing classes would grind down the exploited classes until the latter could bear it no longer. The result would be revolution and the emergence of a new political and economic order, equal and fair, with no classes and therefore no class struggle. Marx called this vision of social and economic perfection communism. Marx's ideas were very attractive to intellectuals who hated the social and political inequality that abounded in nineteenth century Europe. The downside of applying Marxist doctrine to Russia was that Russia's backwardness demanded that Russia's Marxists be patient.

Why Marxism succeeded

- Marxism provided a prospect of revolution and socialism by the study and application of Karl Marx's theory of economic and political development in which industrialisation played a pivotal role.
- Moreover, Marxism was 'scientific'. Points of Marxist theory could be debated and proved. This appealed to the intelligentsia.
- Finally, Marxism contained a utopian vision, something it shared with populism and which had great appeal to the Russian intelligentsia.

By the end of his life, Marx had changed his attitude towards the Russian Populists, and spoke approvingly of the attractions of the *mir* as a short cut to socialism and communism.

Georgii Plekhanov and the Russian Marxist Group

Georgii Plekhanov founded the Russian Marxist Group in 1883, the year of Marx's death. Plekhanov ignored Marx's flirtation with populism, taking the view that Russia had a long way to go in terms of economic and social change before revolution had a realistic chance of success. Unlike the Populists, Plekhanov saw the peasants, in political terms, as an inert mass. In the meantime, he emphasised the importance of converting fellow members of the intelligentsia to Marxist ideas and trying to popularise these ideas among the workers.

The Russian Social Democratic Workers Party

The accelerated industrialisation of the 1890s increased Marxism's appeal and in 1898 the Russian Social Democratic Workers' Party was founded in Minsk. Most of those who had attended were arrested within a couple of weeks, including Vladimir Ulyanov, a law student at St Petersburg University who had frequented local Marxist groups since 1893. Ulyanov remained in exile in Siberia until 1900 when he escaped to the West. From then on he began to use his pseudonym 'Lenin' (see page 80).

Lenin's concerns about the strategy of Marxism

The founding congress of the Social Democrats in 1898 had failed to resolve vital questions of organisation and strategy and it was to these that Lenin turned in the next few years. In 1901 he published his own *What is to be done?*, in homage to Chernyshevsky (see pages 53–4). It was a forceful analysis of the current state of Marxism and Marxist parties in Europe.

Concerns about the SPD. Lenin's greatest concern was the debate about fundamental strategy in the German socialist party, the SPD, the biggest and most important Marxist socialist party in Europe at the time. In the 1890s a movement called **revisionism** had emerged in the SPD, which suggested that the coming proletarian revolution could be achieved by reforms, by the socialists simply winning a majority in the bourgeois parliament. This meant an abandonment of the original Marxist commitment to a revolution as the only way in which the workers could take power.

Concerns about trades unions. Lenin feared that the Russian Social Democratic party was heading in the same direction. He protested strongly against any groups that diluted the party's commitment to revolution. Among these were the supporters of trades unions. Lenin condemned trades unionists as short-sighted collaborators with the bourgeoisie.

Lenin and revolutionary tradition

Lenin was forcing Marxism to bend to the Russian revolutionary tradition, to the tradition of Bakumin and the People's Will. This became even more evident in the dispute that arose at the Social Democratic Party's second congress in Brussels in 1903. Building on the ideas of *What is to be done?*, Lenin rejected the idea of a party that was responsive to, or controlled by, its membership. He suggested instead that a revolutionary party had to guard the purity of its doctrine so that it could lead the workers to revolution.

Bolsheviks and Mensheviks. In the election of the editorial board of the Social Democratic paper *Iskra* Lenin's supporters won a lucky majority. Lenin subsequently exploited this by giving his group the name 'Bolsheviks' or 'men of the majority'. He named his opponents 'Mensheviks' or 'men of the minority', despite the fact that his group was the smaller of the two. However, at this

> **KEY TERM**
>
> **Revisionism** A theory, based on Marxism, which moderates some of the principles.

stage, it would be premature to describe this as a split. The Bolsheviks and Mensheviks were really two wings of the same party.

From 1900–3 Lenin's activities were largely destructive and, in an immediate sense, harmful to his cause. They were typical of the bitter salon politics and inability to compromise, characteristic of the whole Russian revolutionary movement.

THE SOCIALIST REVOLUTIONARIES

The unruly Russian Marxists had serious competition as a revolutionary socialist party with the emergence of a single Socialist Revolutionary (SR) party from three distinct Populist groups.

What the Socialist Revolutionaries stood for

The Socialist Revolutionaries were not Marxists, although were heavily influenced by Marxism. They were a new generation of Populists.

- Like the Populists, the SRs were anxious to help the 'people' in the actual conditions in which they lived.
- The Marxists, however, saw the current state of Russia's society and economy as a transitional phase that would only lead to revolution after further economic development had taken place.

This essential difference explains both the strength and weakness of the SRs.

The Socialist Revolutionaries and the peasants

The Socialist Revolutionaries' less theoretical, more emotional view of revolution had a more immediate appeal to the peasants. They had none of the Marxists' inbuilt tendency to regard Russia's infant working class as the only real hope for a successful revolution.

The strength of the Socialist Revolutionaries

The key factor in explaining why the SRs had so much greater direct impact either than their Populist predecessors or the Social Democrats is that, around 1900, the strains of backwardness and overpopulation had brought the Russian peasantry to a state of distress and protest. This was especially the case in the Volga and black earth regions where land hunger was acute. The explosion of peasant anarchy in 1902 contrasts strongly with the relative calm on the land in the 1880s, when the Populist movement had lost momentum. The direct relationship of the SRs to these waves of protest – the party was composed of a loose association of political groupings based specifically in areas of rural unrest, on the Volga and in the Ukraine – meant that, at certain times, the party had impressive, active popular support.

The weakness of the Socialist Revolutionaries
However, the SRs' strength was also their weakness. The party's incoherence and lack of a long-term programme made it too dependent on short-term economic distress.

The political spectrum of the Socialist Revolutionaries
In political terms the SRs covered a wide spectrum:

- from moderates, who simply wanted to use the popularity of the party to campaign for western civil rights and liberalism
- to the hard men of the Combat Detachment, a dedicated terrorist operation that assassinated at least one prominent government official every year from 1902 to 1906.

The Socialist Revolutionaries and terrorism
The SRs, like the People's Will before them, used terrorism to put the government under real pressure. However, in 1902–5 this was much more effective because of its coincidence with an upsurge of peasant distress. The atmosphere of crisis created by the structural difficulties of the Russian economy was given real edge by the desperate conflict between terrorists and the inflexible police mentality of the Russian state. The pressure on Nicholas II's government helped to encourage it into a fateful foreign venture, war with Japan.

THE LIBERALS

The SDs and SRs can be seen as evolving from the intelligentsia's revolutionary opposition. A parallel evolution was that of the liberal opposition. Just as the SRs, in particular, began to put down roots in Russia's problematical social and economic situation, so too did the liberals.

What liberalism stood for

A purely intellectual movement before 1900, liberalism began to find genuine support as Russia's modernisation created an educated class outside the confines of the tsarist bureaucracy. The social impact of Alexander II's reforms encouraged the growth of the professional classes (lawyers, doctors and teachers, for instance), and Alexander III's industrialisation spurred the growth of the entrepreneurial, business middle class. These two social groups actively desired the further liberalisation of Russia on western lines. However, the development of liberalism was complicated by Slavophilism (see page 26) and its rejection of the western model, and the doctrinaire opposition of the radical intelligentsia.

The growth of liberalism

None the less, liberalism was growing. Above all, it began to put down roots through the *zemstva* (see pages 33–5) as they became established in Alexander III's local government, despite counter-reforms. The 1891–2 famine deepened and accelerated this tendency. In 1895–6 the *zemstva* revived the idea of a *zemstvo* union (not to ask for a liberal constitution but merely to put any concerns to the government), only to be ridiculed by Nicholas II in the famous 'senseless dreams' remark (about a constitution for Russia) in his 1895 coronation speech.

Shipov's moderation

In 1899 the leader of the *zemstvo* of Moscow province, D.N. Shipov, organised a *zemstvo* society called Beseda ('Symposium') to persuade the new tsar to take up moderate, legal reform. Shipov deliberately avoided calling for a parliament. His moderation did him no good. The regime increased the repression of moderate liberals as part of the general repression sparked off by the universities in

1899. By 1904 Shipov's moderation had been defeated and the majority of *zemstvo* leaders voted in favour of a parliamentary constitution for Russia.

Union of Liberation

Shipov's moderation was overtaken by the more confrontational liberal politics of the urban intellectuals **Pavel Miliukov** and **Pyotr Struve**. Using contacts in the *zemstvo* movement, Struve published a journal *Osvobozhdenie* ('Liberation') in 1902 and founded a Union of Liberation in 1903–4. The Union aimed for:

- national liberation, and
- a common programme of freedom and justice for all.

In October 1904 this was formulated as an eight-hour day for workers, land redistribution (with compensation) for the peasantry, and a Constituent Assembly, democratically elected to give Russia a liberal, constitutional regime.

Liberalism becomes revolutionary

Such a programme indicated that under Struve, Russian liberalism had become revolutionary, because it aimed to end the autocracy, and introduce an entirely new political culture.

In 1904 Struve set in motion a campaign of organised public protest. He held political banquets and formed unions for the professions. This had rapid effect. With the Russo–Japanese war going badly, Nicholas II took the advice of his relatively liberal Minister of the Interior, Svyatopolk-Mirsky, and in December 1904 promised concessions on censorship, religious toleration, and the *zemstva*. However, he refused to consider an elected assembly.

It is clear, therefore, that of the three strands of opposition after 1900 – SDs, SRs and liberals – the latter had achieved the greatest practical success.

KEY PEOPLE

Pavel Miliukov (1859–1943) The most important of Russia's liberals. A professor of History, he became leader of the Constitutional Democratic party (Kadet) after 1905, a prominent critic of the government during the First World War and one of the leaders of the first liberal government in Russia, the Provisional Government, in 1917. He fled Russia after the October Revolution.

Pyotr Struve One of Russia's most prominent social and political writers and thinkers at the turn of the century. He became an interesting model for the political future of Russia. In the 1890s, Struve started as a liberal, then joined the Marxist social democrats. But, coming to realise the limitations of orthodox Marxist class politics, he returned (via Marxist revisionism) to liberalism. Struve was consistent in his basic aims of greater equality and universal civil rights, aims which were shared by most Marxists and Populists/SRs. Struve supported the anti-Bolshevik Whites in the Russian Civil War and hence found himself in exile after 1920.

THE FAR EAST
- The decline of the Chinese Empire in the nineteenth century offered huge and tempting gains for Russia.
- 1858–60. Treaties of Aigun, Tientsin and Peking. Russia takes control of Amur River and establishes port of Vladivostok, further south than Okhotsk but still icebound in winter.
- 1875. Island of Sakhalin taken in a settlement with Japan by which the latter acquired the Kurile Islands.
- 1895. Japan defeats China and gains territory but is forced to give up claim to Liaodong peninsular (including Port Arthur, ice-free all year).
- 1896. Russia signs secret alliance with China, securing a railway concession in Manchuria for the Chinese Eastern Railway.
- 1898. Treaty with China grants Russia the lease of the Liaodong peninsular (including Port Arthur) for twenty-five years with a railway concession to link Port Arthur with the Chinese Eastern Railway.
- 1900. Chinese 'Boxer' rising against foreign powers leads to Russian military occupation of Manchuria.
- 1902. Anglo-Japanese alliance.
- 1903. Russo-Japanese talks break down over Russia's continued occupation of Manchuria.
- 1904–5. Russo-Japanese War

THE RUSSO–JAPANESE WAR, 1904–5

This section looks at the origins and course of the war. It also studies the Battle of Tsu-shima, the Peace of Portsmouth and the significance of Russia's defeat.

The origins of the war

There is no doubt that tsarist Russia was beginning to change quickly at the turn of the century and was beginning to catch up with the West. The combination of political protest and economic troubles, both in industry and agriculture, may well have dissipated in time. However, the government decided to indulge in some **sabre-rattling** imperialism to rally the people to the regime. The Minister of the Interior, von Plehve, pronounced early in 1904 (he was that year's SR assassination victim in July) that what Russia needed was a short, successful war.

Rivalry with Japan need not have led to war. However, when the Russians deliberately delayed the withdrawal of a contingent of their troops in January 1904, Japan's military leaders seized their chance.

- Japan broke off diplomatic relations with Russia on 22 January/4 February 1904 (according to which **Russian calendar** is used).
- This was followed by a surprise torpedo boat attack on the Russian fleet at Port Arthur on 25 January/7 February.

Why the Russians risked war

Why had the Russians been prepared to risk war? As is often the case, they thought that they were bound to be victorious.

First a comparison of the physical size and resources of the two countries made Russian victory seem inevitable. Second, Russia's military planners were sure that the recently completed (1903) Trans-Siberian and Chinese Eastern railways would negate Japan's logistical advantage

KEY TERMS

Sabre-rattling To threaten military action. It is usually aimed at engaging public support for foreign adventures, as well as intimidating foreign rivals.

Russian calendar Until 1917, Russia was still using the Julian calendar (devised by Julius Caesar in 46 BC) while the rest of Europe was using the Gregorian calendar (devised by Pope Gregory XIII in 1582). Dates given in this book are in the format Julian calendar/Gregorian calendar (for example, 22 January/5 February). Russia did not change over to the Gregorian calendar until after the 25 October/7 November Revolution in 1917.

Russo-Japanese war poster, showing a Russian mariner punching a Japanese mariner.

of having its main bases closer to the theatre of operations. Such were the arguments put forward by a group of imperialist enthusiasts, led by Captain Bezobrazov, which influenced the opinions of the tsar himself.

The course of the war
However, from the moment the Japanese torpedo boats first struck, Russia's strategy was in disarray. Although the attack did not cripple the Russian fleet, it showed how vulnerable it was. On 31 March/13 April 1904, when the Russian flagship *Petropavlovsk* ventured out of port, struck a Japanese mine and sank with heavy loss of life, including Russia's most capable admiral, Stepan Makarov. Russia, which should have had the superior battle fleet, now had its forces split between Port Arthur (where its ships were trapped by the enemy) and Vladivostok (which was icebound through the winter) – see the map on page 91.

The war at sea
After the failure of the Port Arthur squadron to break out in the Battle of the Yellow Sea on 28 July/10 August, the Russians decided to take a military gamble. At the end of October the Baltic fleet set off more than half-way round the world from Libau, Russia's naval base in the Baltic, to the Sea of Japan. The mission was made even longer by the British refusing the Russians passage through the Suez Canal.

After an incident in the North Sea when the Russians thought that they were being attacked by Japanese torpedo boats (which were in fact British trawlers), the Baltic fleet proceeded steadily but increasingly slowly through the Atlantic and Indian oceans. It had regular problems obtaining fuel and had to stop several times for repairs. One vital military advantage that was sacrificed was any vestige of surprise or secrecy. The Japanese knew exactly what was being sent to attack them, what condition it was in and when it would arrive.

The war on land
Meanwhile the Japanese were winning the land war. The crucial blow was struck when Port Arthur fell on 6/19 December 1905. The Russian commander, Stoessel, had conducted the port's defence incompetently. At one point

he sacrificed an impregnable defensive position and later ordered the sailors of the Pacific squadron to fight on land rather than use their naval artillery.

In February 1905 a major engagement was fought near the Manchurian city of Mukden. After three weeks of intensive fighting with total losses of 85,000 Russians and 41,000 Japanese, the Russians were forced to pull back. After the Battle of Mukden the Russian army regrouped. In fact, its reserves of manpower now threatened to turn the tables on the Japanese. However, the will to continue to fight ultimately depended on the fate of the Baltic fleet.

The Battle of Tsu-shima

The Baltic fleet arrived in the war zone in May 1905. On paper the Russian fleet was the stronger with several bigger and more heavily armed ships. In practice, the reverse was true.

- The Russian ships, built to French designs, then modified, ended up overweight. In several cases their main belt of protective armour was below the waterline.
- Even worse, their epic journey had reduced their speed to the point where the faster British-built Japanese navy could easily out-manoeuvre them.

Hence the Japanese commander, Admiral Togo, was able to prepare an ambush on what were, essentially, sitting ducks. The result was the Battle of Tsu-shima on 14/27 May 1905, which wiped out the Russian battle fleet with the loss of 12,600 men. The Japanese emerged largely unscathed. As a contest the war was over and Russia had to sue for peace.

The Peace of Portsmouth

The Peace of Portsmouth (USA) was signed in August 1905.

- It recognised Japanese control of a nominally independent Korea.
- It forced Russia to hand over the Manchurian railway leases and the lease of Port Arthur to Japan.
- It also forced Russia to surrender the southern half of the island of Sakhalin to Japan.

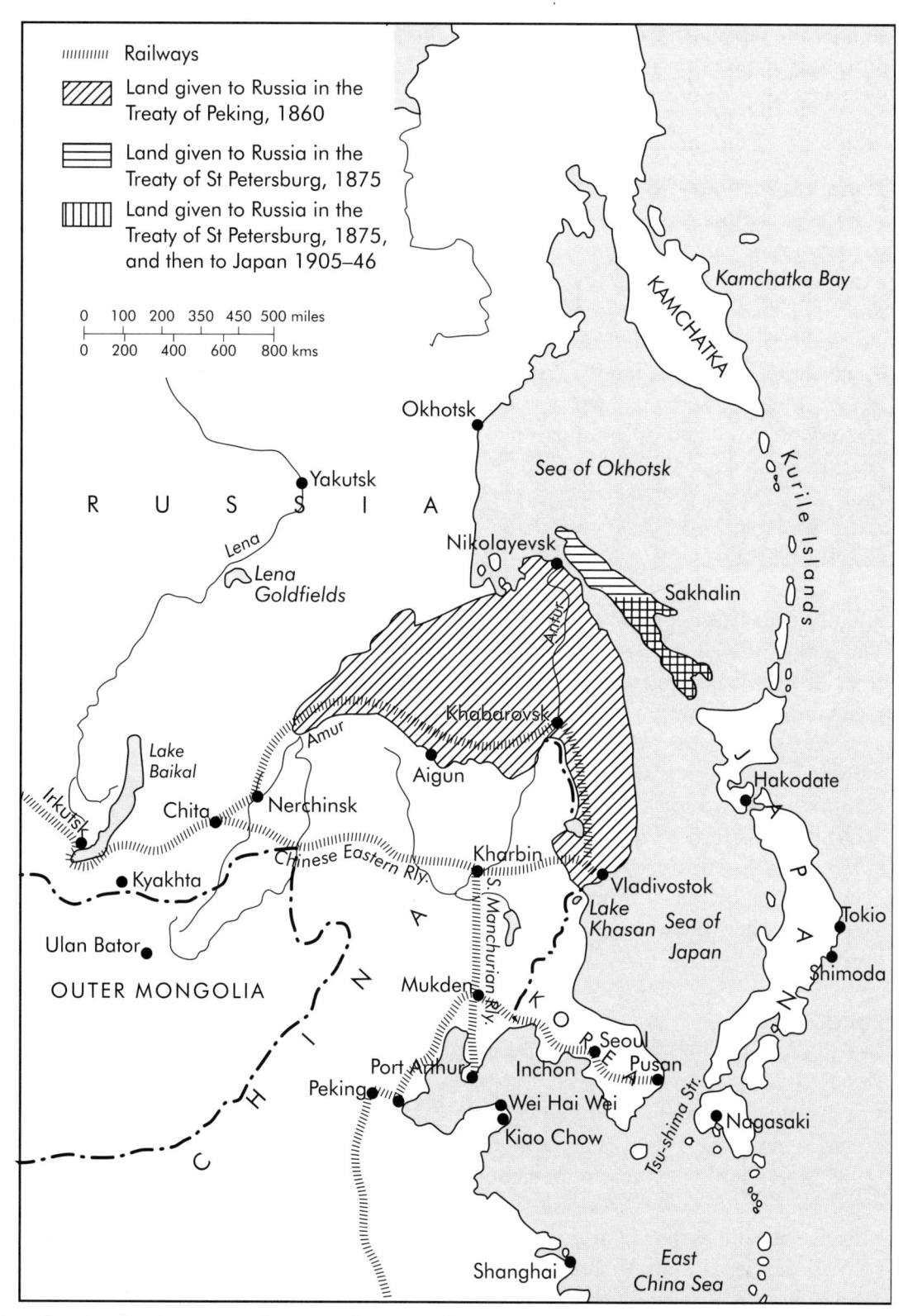

Land gains for Russia and major places in the Russo-Japanese War, 1904–5.

Conservatism and modernisation under Alexander III and Nicholas II, 1881–1905

In fact, the Japanese were the more disappointed by the peace treaty than the Russians, who might have been forced to concede more territory and made to pay an indemnity (compensation for the costs of war) to Japan.

The significance of Russia's defeat

For Russia, defeat was both serious and significant. As in the Crimea, it had over-estimated its military capability and taken on a technologically and socially more advanced state. This had dire consequences for the prestige of a political system that prided itself on its military and its expansionist foreign policy. As in 1855–6, there were serious domestic repercussions. But given Russia's much greater economic and political complexity in 1904–5 these latest repercussions were far more dangerous.

CONCLUSION

Society and the Economy

The period 1881 to 1905 saw the revolution of serf emancipation begin to pay off in terms of economic and social modernisation.

- By 1904 Russia was still well behind the western European powers in economic and social modernisation but had shown the capacity for startling change.
- However, Russia's progress was unbalanced. Agriculture was lagging behind industry and clearly needed further reform under the pressure of a rural population explosion.

Politics

In politics modernisation was at best very limited.

- A return to some of the principles of Nicholas I was accompanied by attempts to exploit modern nationalism and xenophobia to create popular support for the regime.
- Above all, the autocracy was unswervingly upheld, both by Alexander III and Nicholas II. From 1881 to 1905 no political concessions to representative government, as

had been considered in 1880–1 by Alexander II, were ever contemplated.

Opposition

Opposition remained fragmented for much of the period, but at the turn of the century it began to gain coherence.

- The *zemstva* movement and the general growth of Russia's professional classes gave liberalism real impetus.
- Russia's economic problems and infant working class gave revolutionary opposition new cause for hope at around the same time.

The net result was that Russia became, from 1900 to 1905, a political, economic and social pressure cooker. Nicholas II's response – repression followed by war with Japan – was an extremely risky strategy. He paid a heavy price for this in 1905.

SUMMARY QUESTIONS

1 What were the political consequences of Alexander II's assassination in the years 1881–1905?

2 What were the purposes and effects of the policy of russification, 1881–1905?

3 How effective was Russian industrialisation, 1881–1905?

4 How effective was Russian agrarian policy, 1881–1905?

5 How did opposition to the tsarist regime change and develop in the years 1881–1905?

6 Why did Russia risk and then lose the Russo–Japanese war?

CHAPTER 4

The dawn of modern Russia?

In this chapter we take a look at the 'revolution' of 1905 and the constitutional monarchy in peacetime, 1906–14. This short period raises several important questions. For example, to what extent were the events of 1905 actually a 'revolution'? And did these events, and the constitutional monarchy that followed, set Russia on an evolutionary or revolutionary path? This short period before the First World War is a subject of great historical debate. Broadly speaking, there are two views.

- The first is that 1905 and its aftermath represented a real break from Russia's past and, with it, hope of rapid evolution along western or semi-western lines.
- The second is that the changes in this period were superficial and simply emphasised how difficult it was for the tsarist regime to modernise.

Marxist historians take the second view further and attempt to prove that Russia's problems simply became worse and revolution was inevitable.

THE 'REVOLUTION' OF 1905

First, it is debatable whether the disturbances and political changes that swept Russia in 1905–6 constituted a revolution at all. Historian Geoffrey Hosking (1973) points out that, 'the constitutional monarchy which emerged from this turmoil carried within itself the marks of the complex and violent conflict of which it was born'. This meant that there was much that was backward-looking about the 'new' regime. For instance, the monarch continued to be described as 'autocrat' and, to avoid the liberal connotations of the word 'constitution', 'fundamental laws' was used instead. Orlando Figes (1997) comments that, after 1906, 'the newly won freedoms of the socialist parties were now lost and the old police regime was restored'.

KEY PEOPLE

Marxist historians
Historians of Russia who are guided by Marx's theory of history (see pages 80–1) fall roughly into two categories: Soviet historians who had to make Russia's history fit the Marxist–Leninist ideology of the Soviet Union, 1917–91, and western historians who were guided by Marx's approach to history (the importance of economic development and class struggle) without being held to a specific overall interpretation.

Was there a revolution?

It is important to discuss whether the changes of 1905–6 did constitute a 'revolution', for it is crucial in establishing a perspective on the period that followed.

- Was the tsarist regime beginning to modernise politically, and harmonise with continuing social and economic change?
- Or was it essentially unchanged, and therefore blind to the dangers inherent in Russia's instability, an instability that wiped out autocracy in the cataclysm of 1917?

1905: a 'dress rehearsal' for 1917? Was 1905, in the words of Lenin, merely a 'dress rehearsal' for 1917 and not a revolution in its own right? Historians who broadly agree with **Leon Trotsky** stress the fact that the tsar retained most of his power and that, in the last twelve years of the monarchy, Nicholas strove hard and often successfully to recover that lost power. Where the 1905 revolution stands on the scale of modern revolutions, one point is clear: in 1905–6 Russia did not undergo the total political, social and economic meltdown it suffered in 1917–21. In 1917–21 Russia underwent a full-scale revolution in which politics, society and the economy were in free fall. Of modern revolutions, only the French Revolution of 1789–99 brought such profound turmoil. Many other dramatic political changes, such as the revolutions in France in 1830, or in Austria and Prussia in 1848–9 had, perhaps, less real impact than the Russian 'revolution' of 1905, yet they are still termed 'revolutions'.

CAUSES OF THE 1905 'REVOLUTION'

The causes of the 'revolution' are clear.

- Russia was in the throes of modernising the country's economy and industry was depressed after 1900. This made the urban workforce rebellious.
- The combination of a population explosion, backward farming techniques and poor policy making had made for a grave crisis in agriculture.

KEY PEOPLE

Leon Trotsky (1879–1940)
Perhaps the most gifted of his generation of Russian revolutionaries. Having taken up revolutionary politics at university Trotsky was arrested and exiled, becoming a convert to Marxism. His ability as a writer earned him the nickname 'The Pen' and he was spokesman for the St Petersburg Soviet in 1905. After 1905 he developed his idea of Permanent Revolution – interlocked class and national revolutions to bring the international proletariat to power. Trotsky played a crucial role in the Bolshevik revolution. His dramatic rise to leadership caused Stalin to dislike him, resulting in his exile in 1927 and assassination with an ice pick by one of Stalin's agents in 1940.

The dawn of modern Russia?

- The government faced political challenges from terrorists, students and from the westernised, non-revolutionary educated classes.
- The government went to war with Japan.

ENCOURAGEMENT FOR THE LIBERALS

In this volatile situation the government seemed to relax its anti-liberal stance. The conservative Minister of the Interior, von Plehve, was assassinated in April 1904. He was replaced by a liberal, Svyatopolk-Mirsky. The new Interior Minister's belief that a liberal approach was needed to steer the tsarist regime out of its crisis meant that his appointment triggered a wave of liberal enthusiasm among the educated classes. The journalist and writer Pyotr Struve (see page 86) pressed for major concessions. He set up a 'Union of Liberation', which aimed to give Russians the basic liberties, in politics and the press, that citizens of western European states enjoyed.

BACKDROP OF THE WAR

The Russo–Japanese war, which had already seen a number of serious setbacks for the Russian forces, was not an appropriate backdrop for political experiments. The war framed the revolution in its early phases. There is little doubt that had the war been victorious for Russia, the tsarist regime would have escaped some of the political pressure. In addition, it would have been to Russia's advantage to continue fighting in the summer of 1905 rather than make peace and unleash a chaotic demobilisation. As it turned out, the government suffered the worst of both worlds:

- it made itself unpopular by ending the war lamely, and
- by committing its armed forces to the Far East, it was temporarily deprived of reliable troops in the major cities.

1905: THE THREE TURNING POINTS

The 1905 'revolution' revolved around three turning points.

- Bloody Sunday, the massacre of January 1905.
- The October Manifesto, when Nicholas II (crowned tsar in 1894) made crucial concessions.
- The restoration of order, beginning in December 1905.

BLOODY SUNDAY, JANUARY 1905

On his appointment in April 1904, Svyatopolk-Mirsky partially freed the press. This gave momentum to the 'Union of Liberation' but also to direct attacks on the government, especially after the Russian surrender of Port Arthur on 6/19 December 1904.

Protest by the working classes. Protest then spread to the disgruntled working classes of the capital, St Petersburg. Their demands for freedom of speech, an eight-hour day and an elected assembly were incorporated into a petition to be presented to the tsar at the Winter Palace on 9/22 January 1905. The petitioners, from the working-class districts of the city, were led by a politically active priest, **Father Gapon**.

Marching to Palace Square. Gapon had formed a union, a development of one of Zubatov's police trade unions. This semi-official status may have encouraged its members to think that the regime could not possibly turn on them. However, the protest march grew out of control as 150,000 people headed for Palace Square to present their petition, the marchers ignorant of the fact that the tsar himself was not in the Winter Palace.

A massacre of the people. The ensuing tragedy revealed yet another inadequacy of the Russian government. A regime that had been accused of trying to build a police state had no policemen to hand. Instead, the regime had to rely on troops. This inadequacy was made all the worse by the deployment of infantry, rather than the more customary

KEY PERSON

Father Gapon Vain and simple – 'completely ignorant of political theory' (Figes, 1997) – Father Gapon worked up his followers 'into a hysterical religious fervour', swearing them 'to die'. When a few minutes later many of them did die, Gapon was astonished, declaring: 'There is no God any longer. There is no Tsar.' After the massacre Gapon went to Geneva (Switzerland), where he found himself out of his depth among the exiled Russian revolutionary intellectuals. He then moved to London to write his autobiography. When he returned to Russia as a celebrity in December 1905 he became a government supporter. He was mysteriously murdered by government agents in March 1906.

The dawn of modern Russia?

cavalry or Cossacks. The only weapons the troops had were rifles, so casualties were bound to be high if they were forced to fire. Sensing that Gapon's petitionary crowd was a revolutionary mob out of control and bent on mayhem, they fired. The result was a massacre. Over 200 people were killed and many more injured.

The impact of Bloody Sunday

The massacre became known as 'Bloody Sunday' and had the effect of giving coherence to the growing wave of uncoordinated protests. The inhumanity that the regime had shown gave workers, peasants and middle-class liberals a common sense of grievance and, in the key elements of Gapon's petition, a common programme.

The first general strike. On 17/30 January 1905 the first of Russia's general strikes took place in protest at the massacre. It failed to have a direct impact on government policy, the government preferring to buy time until Russia's fortunes in the war turned for the better.

The government's response. Delaying tactics simply helped the government's opponents to organise themselves more effectively. Svyatopolk-Mirsky made way for Alexander Bulygin, the new Minister of the Interior, on 22 January/4 February 1905. Not wishing to repeat the mistake of 9/22 January, he began to relax restrictions on universities and proposed a consultative assembly.

Open political meetings for students. By spring 1905 St Petersburg university was effectively free of police interference. Its lecture halls were used by students, professors and the general public for open political meetings to carry the torch of liberal and radical reform.

Formation of the Union of Unions. In May 1905, after the naval disaster at Tsu-shima (see page 90), the government lost control of the political situation completely. That month, Pavel Miliukov formed a Union of Unions – in other words, an assembly of leaders of professional and industrial workers as well as the leaders of the *zemstva*. The Union of Unions demanded a democratically elected Constituent Assembly.

FROM FATHER GAPON'S PETITION

Sovereign!

We, the workers and the inhabitants of various social strata of the city of St Petersburg, our wives, children, and helpless old parents, have come to you, Sovereign, to seek justice and protection. We are impoverished; our employers oppress us, overburden us with work, insult us, consider us inhuman, and treat us as slaves who must suffer a bitter fate in silence. Though we have suffered, they push us deeper and deeper into a gulf of misery, disfranchisement, and ignorance. Despotism and arbitrariness strangle us and we are gasping for breath. Sovereign, we have no strength left. We have reached the limit of endurance. We have reached that terrible moment when death is preferable to the continuance of unbearable sufferings.

1 Measures to eliminate the ignorance and disfranchisement of the Russian people.
a The immediate release and return (from exile) of all those who have suffered because of their political or religious beliefs, or because of strikes or peasant disturbances;
b An immediate declaration of freedom and inviolability of person, freedom of speech and press, freedom of assembly, and freedom of conscience;
c Universal and compulsory public education, financed by the state;
d Responsibility of Ministers before the people and a guarantee of a law abiding administration;
e Equality before the law for everyone, without exception.

2 Measures to eliminate the poverty of the people.
a Abolition of indirect taxes and the substitution of a direct progressive income tax;
b Abolition of redemption payments, (introduction of) low interest rates, and the gradual transfer of the land to the people;
c Placement of military and naval orders in Russia, not abroad;
d Termination of the war by the will of the people.

3 Measures to eliminate the oppression of labour by capital.
a Abolition of the institution of factory inspectors;
b Establishment at the factories and mills of permanent committees elected by the workers which, jointly with the management, would consider complaints of individual workers. The dismissal of a worker would not take place other than by the decision of this committee;
c Immediate freedom for consumer and trade unions;
d An eight-hour working day and standardisation of overtime work;
e Immediate freedom for the struggle between labour and capital;
f Immediate standardisation of a minimum wage;
g Immediate and continued participation of representatives of the working classes in the preparation of legislation for a state insurance for workers.

Source: B. Dmytryshin, 1967

First meeting of All-Russian Peasants' Union. In July 1905, the first ever All-Russian Peasants' Union met in Moscow. The key demands remained similar to Gapon's petition, although the peasant congress saw the land issue – that of land transfer from the nobility to the peasantry, with or without compensation – as equally important.

Growing problems for the government

Bulygin was in a difficult position.

- Defeat in the war was followed by a series of mutinies, the most famous of which happened in the Black Sea fleet on the Battleship *Potemkin* (see page 205).
- Bulygin's other major problem was the tsar. Nicholas II's ingrained conservatism was a major obstacle to defusing the crisis. Bulygin's consultative, rather than legislative (law-making), assembly was not adopted by Nicholas until August 1905, by which time the opposition was not in a mood to compromise.

In September 1905 the Union of Unions reaffirmed its original demands, which were:

- a **Constituent Assembly**, democratically elected, which had real power
- regulation of hours of work, and
- a measure of land redistribution, with compensation.

A railway strike 6\19 October 1905 escalated six days later into a general strike. The ability of the railway workers to paralyse the railway system and thus deny the tsar his most efficient means of control forced Nicholas to try something new. He sacked Bulygin and appointed his most famous reformer, Sergei Witte (see pages 70–2), as his new prime minister. Witte recognised the seriousness of the situation and realised that, in the short term, Nicholas could only retain control by making some concessions. Nicholas objected. He considered abdication and possibly suicide, rather than accept Witte's strategy, for the simple reason that he did not want to be seen to be failing in his duty, sworn on oath at his coronation, to maintain the autocracy.

> **KEY TERM**
>
> **Constituent Assembly** An assembly/parliament which was to be elected by the people. It would have led to the formation of a government which could claim it ruled according to the wishes of the people.

1905: KEY EVENTS (Julian calendar)

9 January Bloody Sunday.

January Wave of strikes.

February Grand Duke Sergei killed by SR assassin, Moscow.

Russian army defeated at Mukden.

Nicholas II offers consultative assembly.

Peasant disorders begin.

May Russian navy defeated at Tsu-shima.

Formation of Union of Unions, chaired by Miliukov.

June General strike and *Potemkin* mutiny in Odessa.

July *Zemstva* and Union of Unions launch Kadet party.

Peasants' Union formed.

August 'Bulygin' *duma* announced.

12 October General strike.

13 October St Petersburg Soviet founded.

17 October 'October Manifesto'.

26–31 October Mutinies in Baltic and Pacific fleets.

8 November Formation of the Union of the Russian People.

3 December Arrest of St Petersburg Soviet leaders.

10–15 December Moscow uprising.

THE OCTOBER MANIFESTO AND THE ST PETERSBURG SOVIET

Eventually, Witte's influence over the tsar prevailed. On 17 October 1905 Nicholas published the '**October Manifesto**'. In it, the tsar conceded:

- freedom of speech
- freedom of assembly
- freedom of the press, and
- a constitution that would be drawn up in 1906 to include a **bicameral** legislative (law-making) parliament.

In one sense at least, this was a 'revolution'. After centuries of autocracy Russia appeared to be on the way to becoming a constitutional monarchy along western lines. Witte's suggestion proved to be a shrewd move. Struve, Miliukov and their liberal followers accepted Nicholas's offer and reserved any criticism for when the constitution appeared, in case it should not live up to Nicholas's promises. Thus Witte had split the opposition and isolated the militant workers.

A challenge to the government

Nicholas was not satisfied. A concession of such magnitude should, he thought, have put an end to challenges to authority. Instead, the momentum, which had built up since January, produced a direct challenge to the government.

- To direct the general strike, St Petersburg workers set up a **soviet** in mid-October. It lasted until 3/16 December.
- A week later a bloody five-day workers' rising took place in Moscow. It was led by the Bolshevik faction of the Social Democratic Party.
- November and December also saw the year's most bloody and widespread peasant risings.

So alarming was the combination of the collapse of authority in the two principal cities and on the land that many thought that the tsarist regime would be swept away.

The dawn of modern Russia?

Non-Russian protests and disturbances

The russification (see pages 61–6) policies pursued by the government after 1881 ensured that there would be protests in many of the non-Russian parts of the empire during 1905.

Riga. The first serious conflict was in Riga in the Baltic Provinces in January when 22 workers were killed in a scaled-down repeat of 'Bloody Sunday'.

Łódź. In the same month a clash between security forces and textile workers in Łódź in Poland left 100 dead. Historian Geoffrey Hosking (1998) describes Poland in 1905 as being, 'at times … in a state of virtual civil war'.

Baku. In February inter-communal violence between Azeris and Armenians in Baku produced a bloodbath. Around 1500 people died – about 1000 of them Armenians.

Finland. In Finland the government headed off protests by rapidly restoring the constitution, suspended in 1899.

The Jews. The worst anti-Semitic violence came after the October Manifesto. In a series of pogroms from October 1905 to January 1906, some 3000 Jews were killed, 800 in Odessa alone. The emergence of the **Union of the Russian People** and its paramilitary arm, the **Black Hundreds**, gave anti-Semitic violence a degree of co-ordination. Moreover, rather than suppressing violence against Jews, police and troops often took part themselves.

THE RESTORATION OF ORDER

Three factors proved decisive in preserving the monarchy.

- Nicholas, having seen concessions apparently fail, was both adamant and consistent in his support for the use of force. He was encouraged to take a tough line by the formation in November 1905 of the Union of the Russian People.
- The tsar appointed Pavel Durnovo as Minister of the Interior. Durnovo was decisive, intelligent and forceful.

KEY TERMS

The October Manifesto A document published by Nicholas II, which stated the following.

We impose upon the government the duty to execute Our inflexible will:

1 To grant the population … freedom of conscience, speech, assemblies and associations.

2 To admit in the participation of the duma … all those classes of the population which presently are completely deprived of voting rights … .

3 To establish as an unbreakable rule that no law shall become effective without confirmation by the State duma … .

Bicameral Upper and lower house, on the British model.

Soviet The St Petersburg Soviet was a workers' council elected by the workers not only to represent their interests, but also to assume leadership of the revolution, following the example of the revolutionary Paris communes of 1792 and 1871. The Soviet's chairman was the 26 year-old Social Democrat, Leon Trotsky. The Soviet's aims – to spread and consolidate the revolution – and its very existence were a blatant affront to the tsarist regime.

> **KEY TERM**
>
> **The Union of the Russian People** In the literal sense, this was a reactionary movement. It was a reaction against the liberal, worker and peasant unions that had made the running for most of 1905. Founded by A.I. Dubrovin and V.M. Purishkevich (later involved in the assassination of Grigory Rasputin), the Union was, in Figes's words (1997), 'a movement to mobilise the masses against the forces of the left. It was an early Russian version of the Fascist movement. Anti-liberal, anti-socialist and, above all, anti-Semitic, it spoke of the restoration of the popular autocracy which it believed had existed before Russia was taken over by the Jews and intellectuals.' Within a year the Union had 1000 branches and 300,000 members, including the tsar himself. To enforce its will the union formed paramilitary groups called **Black Hundreds**, who were prominent in violence against Jews and socialists. The success of the union helps to explain the tsar's confidence in adopting a reactionary, right-wing political stance for much of the rest of his reign.

He restored morale in his ministry and order on the streets and in the villages.

- Educated opinion wanted to halt the revolutionary momentum. Liberals who had made common cause with revolutionary parties before the October Manifesto were quick to see how this progress could be undone if Russia were to slide into anarchy.

Retribution was not long in coming for the St Petersburg Soviet.

- On 3/16 December 1905 it was closed down by troops from the Far East.
- On 15/28 December the Moscow rising was bloodily suppressed. This, after Bloody Sunday and the October Manifesto, was the third and decisive turning point in the 1905 revolution. It showed that the tsarist regime was no longer on the run, that its powers of repression were recovering and that, therefore, it had regained the political initiative.

Witte's final months. Although the regime had survived, the tsar had lost confidence in Witte, simply because the economic guru had proved inconsistent as Russia's first prime minister. Having persuaded the tsar to grant concessions in October, the turbulence of the winter found Witte advocating the harshest repression. The hysteria of some of his outbursts led many to conclude that he had lost his nerve. Even so, the tsar kept him in office until April 1906, using his reputation as a master of finance to reassure the French during negotiations for another vital French loan to Russia of 850 million roubles. The loan was secured in May.

Stolypin replaces Witte. Witte was replaced by the agrarian reformer Pyotr Stolypin (see page 76). Stolypin set about restoring order in the countryside after another wave of peasant anarchy in 1905–6. He imposed martial law, with extensive use of the death penalty, on the worst-affected provinces – mainly those in the Volga region. The hanging noose was so frequently used that it earned the bitter nickname 'Stolypin's necktie'.

The dawn of modern Russia?

The constitutional monarchy

In this atmosphere it is hardly surprising that the **constitutional monarchy**, or **Fundamental Laws**, did not turn out to be as liberal as the October Manifesto had suggested. Nevertheless:

- For the first time in its history Russia was given a nationally elected assembly with legislative power and some control over the budget.
- The lower house, or State *duma* (see page 102), was popularly elected. The vote was given to the peasantry and most urban dwellers.
- The system of voting was indirect. The voters elected electoral colleges, which then elected the *duma*. This gave Stolypin and the tsar the opportunity to reduce the influence of the urban lower classes and bias the electoral system in favour of rural Russia. They hoped that the peasants, once order had been restored, would support the regime.

The role of the *duma*

The role of the *duma* in the constitution was similar to that of the contemporary German *Reichstag*. It was an indispensable part of the political process but it did not have any influence on the initiation of government policy or on governmental appointments. Like the *Reichstag* it was overseen by an unelected upper house, the Council of State. This was half nominated by the tsar himself, with the other half chosen from the tsarist administration. The balance of power was further tilted towards the tsar by specific articles of the Fundamental Laws. These gave him the power to:

- dissolve the *duma* and hold elections whenever he saw fit, and
- rule by decree in a period of emergency (Article 87).

The *duma* was also forbidden to discuss the military budget.

KEY TERM

Constitutional monarchy/Fundamental Laws A monarchy in which the power of the monarch and all other institutions is defined by a series of laws, often known as a constitution. It makes the rule of law supreme, rather than the head of state. Hence the description of the Russian monarch as an 'autocrat' in the Fundamental Laws of 1906 was not really appropriate for a true constitutional monarchy. The tsar and other Russian conservatives also wanted to avoid the term 'constitution' for the new governmental arrangements in Russia, as 'constitution' had strong democratic associations (for example, the US Constitution), hence the Russian term 'Fundamental Laws'.

A breakthrough in political development. Despite these important restrictions the fact that the *duma* existed in any form at all represented a fundamental breakthrough in Russia's political development. Nicholas II may still have carried the title of autocrat, but he was one in name only after 1905. In the Russian conception autocracy meant that the entire political process was the sole responsibility of the ruler: he was the entire political process. No alternative source of authority could exist, nor could there be any formal opposition. Therefore, from 1906, instead of being an autocracy, the Russian state was now a top-heavy constitutional monarchy.

THE CONSTITUTIONAL MONARCHY IN ACTION: 1906–7

This section takes a look at both the first and second *dumy*.

The first *duma*, 1906

The Fundamental Laws were issued in March 1906. Elections then took place and the first *duma* met in May. Its composition was not what Stolypin and the tsar had hoped it would be. By and large it was a vote for the opposition to the regime, both constitutional and revolutionary. The most successful parties were:

- the Kadets or Constitutional Democrats, who wanted proper parliamentary government and extensive land reform, and
- the **Trudoviki**, or Labourers' party.

> **KEY TERM**
>
> **Trudoviki** Those SRs who had disobeyed their party's official boycott of the election.

Another important feature of this first Russian parliamentary election was the substantial number of parties, or simply groups, representing national minorities, the largest of which was the Polish Circle, led by Roman Dmowski, with 55 seats. Parties on the right were still ill-defined, and the Octobrists, the more conservative liberal party who were content with the October Manifesto, fared less well. Such a parliament was hardly likely to prove congenial to the government, and so it proved.

The first *duma*, 1906

Nicholas showed his contempt for the *duma's* radicalism by making its first business in a new era of Russian politics a draft legislation concerning greenhouses. The *duma* responded by opening the land question and demanding further constitutional reform. After six weeks Nicholas and Stolypin had had enough. The *duma* was dissolved with new elections to be held in 1907. The most militant MPs, mainly Kadets and Trudoviki, responded angrily by decamping to the St Petersburg suburb of Vyborg and issuing the Vyborg Manifesto, demanding that the people should refuse to pay taxes or serve in the armed forces until the *duma* was restored. The Manifesto was largely ignored.

The second *duma*, 1907

With the countryside now brought to heel (the most dangerous revolutionary agitators in exile or in prison and the strike wave spent) the tsar and Stolypin hoped that a second *duma* would be more manageable. They were to be disappointed. The second *duma*, which met in April 1907, was even more radical than the first. The SRs had decided to participate fully this time. Their success and that of other radical groups tilted the *duma* to the left. Given the irreconcilable antagonisms and distrust that had built up between government and *duma* over the previous twelve months, a showdown was inevitable. After a few weeks of angry exchanges it came on 3 June 1907.

THE 3 JUNE REFORM

On 3 June 1907 Stolypin and the tsar dissolved the second *duma* and announced important changes to the electoral provisions of the Fundamental Laws. As historian Richard Pipes (1990) points out, this was not a *coup d'état* (an attack on the state) but a forcible, right-wing revision of the electoral provisions of the constitution. The experiment of giving the peasantry significant influence had proved to be a bad mistake from the government's point of view. The peasants had elected too many radicals. Under the new system the lower classes' influence was severely reduced.

DUMA ELECTIONS, 1906–14

	First *duma* 1906	Second *duma* 1907	Third *duma* 1908	Fourth *duma* 1912
CENTRE LEFT				
Kadets	170	98	54	59
Progressists	–	–	28	48
Non-Russian groups	63	94	11	15
CENTRE RIGHT				
Octobrists	13	54	154	98
Centre	–	–	–	32
RIGHT				
Moderate Right (Nationalists)	–	23	140	96
Extreme Right	–	10	35	51
Independents	105	59	15	7
LEFT				
Trudoviki	100	104	14	9
SRs	–	37	–	–
SDs	–	65	19	15
Popular Socialists	–	16	15	–

Notes to table

As this table shows, Russian political parties were barely formed and very unstable. The SRs boycotted the 1906, 1908 and 1912 elections, and the SDs boycotted the 1906 election. Three main features should be noted.

1 The left and centre left were dominant in the first two *dumy*.
2 After the June 1907 electoral reform the balance moved to the centre right. The third *duma* was much more co-operative with the government.
3 In the fourth *duma* the far-right (mostly pro-government) and left (anti-government) roughly balanced each other out, leaving the balance with the centre right. However, after 1912 the Octobrists opposed the government, making the fourth *duma* much more uncooperative than the third *duma*.

Source: Adapted from S. Pushkarev, 1963.

- The wealthiest 1 per cent of the electorate controlled 66 per cent of the seats in the new *duma*.
- Peasant and worker representation was cut by roughly 50 per cent.
- The mechanism of election was revised to slash non-Russian representation. (The number of Polish deputies

was reduced by 58 per cent, the number of deputies from Siberia and the Caucasus by 65 per cent, and Central Asia lost its representation altogether.)

Significance of 3 June reform
Anti-democratic though it may have been, the 3 June constitutional revision marked the end of the acute political instability in Russia that had begun in 1904. It is therefore of considerable importance. Two aspects of the 3 June reform are especially significant.

- It showed that the constitutional opposition to the tsarist regime, so threatening in 1905, had run out of steam. A repetition of the Vyborg tactics of 1906 came to nothing because political parties in Russia were so shallow-rooted and had little popular appeal except in a 1905-style crisis.
- It showed that there were limits to Stolypin's conservatism. The *coup* was not a return to autocracy. After all, the *duma* remained in existence with none of its constitutional powers reduced. Moreover, there was no indication that the government had the will or ability to influence elections directly by having 'government candidates' or a 'government party'.

Stolypin's *duma*
Although the tsar regarded the *duma* as a mark of his failure to be a true autocrat, there is evidence to suggest that Stolypin took it more seriously. He was prepared to work with the *duma* and within the constitution, allowing the *duma* to debate and pass his reforms. This *duma* was, in a sense, his *duma*, elected under the new 3 June provisions. It was, as intended, much more conservative than its predecessors and, therefore, much more capable of constructive political dialogue with the government. Although unattractive from a purist, democratic standpoint, the 3 June coup did make Russia's constitutional monarchy workable.

How Russia measured up to its contemporaries
Before concluding that the 3 June reform was a cynical return to Russia's undemocratic past, one must bear in

mind Russia's lack of social and political development in comparison to its great power contemporaries.

France. In France there was universal manhood suffrage (meaning all men were able to vote) and the parliament had a real grip of the government. However, at the time, no other European power fulfilled both of these democratic criteria.

Germany, Austria and Great Britain. In Germany and Austria (not Hungary), the only other great powers with universal manhood suffrage, the parliament's control of the government was seriously limited. Elsewhere the franchise (the right to vote), even in Great Britain with its deep-rooted parliamentary control of government, was restricted in some way or other.

Moreover, these countries were socially and economically more advanced than Russia (still 80 per cent peasant before the First World War) with a significant middle class. To expect Russia to move in one step to a genuinely popular government was quite unrealistic, especially as the 3 June system was not that dissimilar from the constitutional monarchies operating in much of the rest of Europe.

1905: A CONCLUSION

In conclusion, the 1905 revolution did not end the tsarist tradition of an immensely powerful monarchy. However, it did signify a major shift in Russia's political culture. Under the new arrangements Nicholas II no longer had unlimited power, either in politics or over the press. If this did not amount to a revolution, then it was the most important and potentially far-reaching change that the Russian political system had ever seen. The constitutional changes ushered in a short period of spectacular social and economic recovery for Russia, giving weight to the argument that Russia was moving on to a path of evolution rather than revolution.

STOLYPIN'S REFORMS: THEIR AIMS AND IMPACT

As prime minister, Stolypin is chiefly remembered for a series of agrarian reforms implemented in 1906 and 1907. The work that he had done on the agrarian question as a member of the 1903 Commission on Agriculture became the mainspring of government policy and had a profound effect, both in the short and long term.

Stolypin's aims

Stolypin's initiatives were essentially an exercise in social engineering with the aims of pacifying the peasantry, and breaking out of the vicious circle of backwardness and rural overpopulation.

His aim was to create a new class out of the richer peasants by encouraging them to set themselves up as independent small farmers.

Mirs. This made Stolypin's chief target the ancient peasant commune or *mir* (see page 30), wedded as it always had been to treating its members equally and to redistributing land periodically according to family size. These customs meant that no peasant family had much incentive to invest in the land it worked. The *mir* also reinforced primitive agricultural techniques. All key decisions in the *mir* were made by the village assembly, or **skhod**. The tradition of allocating land in strips to families led to inefficiencies. For example, peasants were allocated strips of land so narrow that they could only be ploughed one way, sometimes for a mile or more. This meant that ploughing took twice as long as it should have.

Decline of the nobility. Another factor prompting Stolypin's reforms was the relative decline of the nobility. Faced with two destructive outbursts of peasant violence in 1902 and 1905–6, there was a rush on the part of indebted nobles to sell up. This phenomenon was depicted in Anton Chekhov's play *The Cherry Orchard* (1904). Stolypin reacted to this trend and recognised that, although in southern Russia some of the best, most advanced, farms were run by the nobility, the nobles could not be relied on, collectively, to lead Russia out of its agrarian crisis. They

KEY TERM

Skhod Comprised all the elderly heads of village families within the *mir*. Most of these heads were illiterate and highly suspicious of change.

KEY PLAY

***The Cherry Orchard* (1904)** Anton Chekhov's last play. Chekhov understood the problems of Russian rural society as well as any of his contemporaries. He perceived a sense of hopelessness spreading among the rural property-owning classes, which created new opportunities for the more entrepreneurially minded peasants. The climax of his play is the forced sale of the orchard by its owner, Mrs Ranyevskaya, who is from an old gentry family. Yermolai Lopakhin, son of a peasant, has bought it and is exultant.

'Great God in heaven, the cherry orchard's mine! ... If my father and grandfather could only rise from their graves and see what happened, see how their Yermolai – Yermolai who was always being beaten, who could hardly write his name and who ran around barefoot in winter – how this same Yermolai bought this estate, the most beautiful place in the world. I've bought the estate where my father and grandfather were slaves, where they weren't even allowed inside the kitchen.'

needed the support of a new independent peasant farming class.

Russia's financial predicament. Stolypin's strategy was also influenced by Russia's financial predicament. Stretched to the limit in the early phases of industrialisation and having just lost a war, Russia's finances were unable to offer much of a stimulus to agriculture. Any practical reform would have to rely on 'natural' economic forces, on encouraging and exploiting any progressive tendencies in Russian agricultural society.

Stolypin and industrialisation

Implicit in Stolypin's reforms was the continuation of industrialisation along the path indicated by Witte. Making Russian agriculture more efficient and encouraging successful peasants to increase their landholdings was bound to reduce the number of peasant landowners and force large numbers to look for alternative employment. Industrialisation and urbanisation were the only ways to achieve this and avoid major social unrest, even though this would enlarge the much-feared 'landless proletariat' (see page 19). Stolypin's policies were therefore complementary to Witte's, and offered for the first time an integrated strategy for Russia's economic modernisation in which both agriculture and industry would play their part.

Stolypin's social engineering

Stolypin's policies had a progressive political dimension. In aiming to create a new class of capitalist peasant proprietors, he hoped to create a class that had both a stake in the developing economic and political system and would retain its basic traditional sympathy for the tsar. Stolypin envisaged a tsarist regime that, for the first time, would have active rather than passive public support from a substantial section of the populace. In this regard, he was not the first to note the ingrained conservatism and traditionalism of a prosperous, landowning peasantry such as could be found in nineteenth- and early twentieth-century France. But this process obviously needed time.

Stolypin's reforms: success or failure?

Stolypin's reforms consisted of three crucial measures:

The dawn of modern Russia?

- the annulment of redemption dues (1906)
- a law allowing peasant families to leave the commune (1907), and
- a law encouraging peasants to consolidate their holdings of land (1907).

The successes. These measures had an immediate impact. In the first two years some 15 per cent of the peasantry took up the new opportunities. By 1914, 25 per cent had left the communes and 10 per cent had consolidated their holdings. Given that Russia's peasant population was around 100 million in this period, this was a huge and rapid change.

The weaknesses. Stolypin's reforms were not an unqualified success. Two points are significant in this regard: the rate of applications to leave the communes and consolidate holdings was declining after an initial rush; and 'Stolypin' peasants (those who had taken advantage of his reforms) were mostly to be found in the more prosperous agricultural areas, notably the black earth regions of the South Russian and Ukrainian steppe.

The overall effectiveness. Stolypin predicted that the beginning of the transformation of the Russian peasantry would take a generation. It is therefore impossible to arrive at a simple judgement on the effectiveness of Stolypin's reforms as the First World War intervened to throw Russia's economy and society off course. 'Stolypin' peasants were the first victims of the inflation and internal trade crisis that hit Russia in 1916. In 1917 the rural anarchy that followed the March revolution had the effect of a black repartition (see page 74) – the egalitarian (making equal) redistribution of all the land that had been part of peasant folklore for ages. Stolypin peasants were victims again. As things turned out, there is insufficient evidence to make a real estimate of the Stolypin reforms.

Those banking on a peasant revolution to transform Russia were seriously worried that Stolypin's reforms were working. They were also worried that the revolutionary potential of the peasantry was being eroded in the years immediately preceding the First World War. Lenin, in particular, held this view in 1914. He saw Stolypin's reforms as a threat to his scheme of harnessing peasant protest to the workers' revolution. However, he also welcomed the growing stratification among peasants and believed it would lead to a class war between landed and landless peasants.

Stolypin's reforms – conclusion. The Stolypin reforms were the only serious attempt that the tsarist regime made to tackle peasant backwardness and the problem of rural overpopulation. Initially, at least, there was real hope that Stolypin might be achieving his twin aims of social stability and economic progress without having to make too many political concessions.

FOREIGN POLICY, MILITARISM AND INDUSTRIAL RECOVERY, 1908–14

Coping with the revolutionary disturbances of 1905, defeat by Japan and a new political system, Stolypin's government may have felt it deserved some respite in foreign affairs. It was to be disappointed. The unpredictable, aggressive German *Weltpolitik*, combined with momentous changes such as the **Young Turk Revolution** in the Ottoman Empire and an accelerated arms race produced international crises that Russia could not ignore.

Power status. European status had been a key consideration in Russian statecraft since Peter the Great. With the empire now weak and relatively vulnerable, the tsar's government made the maintenance of Russia's great power status its top priority. This was a huge task. A strong military establishment was vital to Russian diplomacy, yet the Russian military had just been beaten by the Japanese and, of all the major powers, Russia had the least developed heavy industry to restore its strength. Worse still, after 1905, a fast-moving arms race breeding a new generation of costly, technologically sophisticated weapons meant that, to retain its status, Russia had to do more than recover to its 1904 position. Matters were made worse by the after-effects of the world recession after 1900, a militant workforce, and financial instability caused by the war.

> **KEY TERM**
>
> **Weltpolitik** The name given to Germany's aggressive pursuit of a colonial empire from 1897 to 1918. *Weltpolitik* was at the root of several major international crises in this period and an important cause of the First World War.
>
> **Young Turk Revolution** The Young Turks were a group of army officers and Turkish intellectuals who forced the Sultan to westernise the Ottoman Empire and give up much of his power in 1908. The revolution marked an acceleration of the Ottoman Empire's decline. It triggered instability in the Balkans, leading to the Balkan wars and the First World War.

The dawn of modern Russia?

The government's response. The Minister of Finances, Kokovtsov, was in an unenviable position. However, both he and the Russian government as a whole achieved a remarkable turnaround. By 1914 Russia was so strong militarily and economically that Germany was prepared to launch a **preventive war** to arrest its development. This shows that Kokovtsov and his colleagues did a remarkable job and that the tsarist regime was by no means on its last legs.

Anglo–Russian co-operation

A new diplomatic strategy was essential to rebuilding Russia's position in Europe. The threat to Russia's great power status was made obvious in 1905 when Germany's demands in Morocco almost triggered a Franco–German war, in which Russia (extricating itself from the war with Japan) would have been little help. This pushed Russia towards an *entente* with Great Britain in 1907, which settled formerly disputed spheres of interest in Persia, Afghanistan and Tibet.

THE BOSNIAN CRISIS, 1908–9

The Young Turk Revolution offered an opportunity and an incentive for Turkey's rivals in south-eastern Europe to stake their territorial claims. The first to do so was Austria-Hungary.

Austria-Hungary

Austria-Hungary had been granted a right to occupy the province of Bosnia-Herzegovina by the Treaty of Berlin (1878). It had also struck agreements to build railways linking Austrian territory with Sarajevo, the Bosnian capital. In the wake of the Young Turk Revolution, Austria moved to annex Bosnia-Herzegovina outright. Count Alexis von Aerenthal, the Austrian Foreign Minister, authorised this policy lest the province fall into the hands of **Serbia**.

The importance of the Bosnian Crisis
- The crisis showed that Russia had to restore its military if it were to retain its established great power status.

KEY TERMS

Preventive war A war launched to prevent a military advantage being lost in the future. From 1912 German generals feared that, unless Russia was engaged soon (1914), it would become too strong (1917) for the German army.

Entente In diplomacy, an agreement between two states to co-operate in certain defined areas. It is, therefore, a more limited agreement than a treaty or an alliance. The Anglo–Russian *entente* had a hidden military agenda in the form of naval co-operation. In 1907 the Russian admiralty placed an order for an armoured cruiser, *Rurik*, with the British yard Vickers. Over the next seven years Vickers was to play a major role in rebuilding the Russian navy through shared technology and manufacturing, some of it on Russian soil.

KEY EVENT

Serbia Since a palace coup in 1903, the Serbs had been pursuing an aggressive foreign policy to create Greater Serbia of which Bosnia-Herzegovina, with its substantial Serb population, was a key objective. Russia had co-operated with Austria-Hungary in the Balkans as late as 1906, but the arrogance of the Austrian annexation of 1908 was taken as an insult in St Petersburg. It was felt that Austria was taking advantage of Russia's post-war weakness and deliberately ignoring Russia's Pan-Slav instincts. The Russian Foreign Minister, Alexander Izvolsky, played on Russian national feeling to try to force the Austrians to climb down by demanding a conference to discuss Bosnia-Herzegovina. When, later in 1908, this was rejected by the Austrians and their allies, the Germans, Izvolsky had a problem. Attempts to pursue the matter further in January 1909 led to a curt note from the Germans, appearing to threaten military action. Russia, suffering the effects of recent defeat and political unrest had to back down, humiliated. This episode hurt the Russian government, and was a key determinant of foreign, military and industrial policy up to 1914.

KEY CONCEPT

Basic provisioning and organisation Before 1905 Russian soldiers were expected to make their own uniforms and footwear from raw materials supplied by the state. This proved disastrous in the war against Japan when footwear disintegrated after a few weeks in some units, crippling their fighting capacity. It also tended to produce an army of tailors and cobblers rather than an army of modern soldiers.

- It also showed that France's enemy Germany was Russia's enemy too, especially as, after 1909, the Germans were quick to offer military assistance to the infant Young Turk government.

THE RUSSIAN ARMY

Although the tsar laid particular stress on the strategic importance of rebuilding the navy after the Japanese debacle, the Russian army was also in a difficult state.

The army before 1905

Despite the reforms of Nikolai Miliutin (see page 27) in the aftermath of the emancipation of the serfs, Russia's army struggled to keep pace with modern developments. Nowhere was this more true than in **basic provisioning and organisation**.

The reforms of 1908

The reforms of 1908 addressed these problems head on.

- Provisioning of uniforms was passed to outside contractors.
- The regimental structure of the army was overhauled.
- New regulations were introduced to improve the quality of education offered to new recruits.

Harsh lessons learned about the inadequacy of equipment in the Russo–Japanese war were put to good effect. The main priorities were standardisation of artillery, the provision of more mobile artillery and machine guns, and the re-equipment of the key fortresses defending Russian Poland.

Russian rearmament

Russia's army and navy faced the same basic problem. How could the state meet its strategic commitments with such a limited budget? How could it order its priorities? The navy had to decide on the relative priorities of the Baltic and Black Sea fleets. The army had to resolve a similar dilemma, pursuing:

The dawn of modern Russia?

- either a defensive strategy in the West by strengthening the Polish fortresses and building strategic railways
- or building an army with a greater offensive capability.

Not surprisingly, the French made their views known. Faced with the prospect of a German onslaught in the West, the French general staff feared that the Germans would be given too free a hand if Russia adopted a defensive strategy in the East. As a consequence, the French pressed the Russians towards creating an offensive strike force to attack Germany on Russia's western border.

THE ARMS RACE, 1912–14

Attacks on an ailing Turkey by Italy in 1911 and the Balkan league (Serbia, Greece, Bulgaria and Montenegro) in 1912 created further tension in the Balkans. This in turn fuelled the rivalries of the great powers.

- The success of the Balkan league and the subsequent victory of Serbia, Greece and Montenegro in the second Balkan war of 1913 saw Serbia, furnished with Russian military advisers, double in size. Austria, and its ally Germany, were most concerned.
- The Germans raised the stakes by reallocating resources from the navy to the army in their 1912 Army Bill, which increased German peacetime strength by 112,000. Russia responded.
- In 1913 the Minister of War, **Vladimir Sukhomlinov**, announced the **'Grand Plan'**.
- This plan was exactly what the French wanted. It also had the predictable effect of making the Germans nervous and anxious to engage Russia sooner rather than later.
- In December 1912 the German Chief of Staff, General Helmuth von Moltke, had declared at a meeting of the German War Cabinet 'war the sooner the better' mainly because the increasing Russian threat prejudiced the success of Germany's **Schlieffen Plan**. This required Russia to be slow to mobilise so that Germany could have a free hand in the first few weeks of war to crush the French and avoid fighting a war on two fronts.

KEY PERSON

Vladimir Sukhomlinov Minister of War 1909–15, Sukhomlinov became the scapegoat for Russia's defeats early in the war. He was also fond of intrigue and internal espionage. However, he was a determined military moderniser and can be credited with the progress that Russia made in military preparedness before 1914.

KEY TERMS

The Grand Plan Over five years, this plan would add 500,000 troops to Russia's peacetime strength and would give Russia a formidable system of strategic railways to support an army in Russian Poland.

Schlieffen Plan Drawn up in 1906 by the German Chief of the General Staff, Count Alfred von Schlieffen, as the Military's response to the possibility of a war on two fronts. Schlieffen planned for a quick war in the west against France to be followed by war against Russia.

Vladimir Sukhomlinov, Russian Minister of War, 1909–15.

It is not surprising, therefore, that Russian militarism has been considered an important cause of the First World War. Ironically, it was perhaps Russia's success in recovering from 1905 that made its diplomatic position so difficult in 1912–14.

Industrialisation and rearmament, 1908–14

Russia's second industrial spurt from 1908 to 1914 could not be directly attributed to Witte. Clearly, however, it was a continuation of his economic strategy, to 'save Russia by rapid and forceful industrialisation'.

The dawn of modern Russia?

- Whereas Witte had concentrated heavily on railway building in the 1890–1900 phase, in the second phase (1908–14) the focal point was rearmament. Russia's rearmament in this period was striking and it had an equivalent impact on the economy.
- The Witte legacy can also be seen in the degree of state intervention in the expansion of the economy, which often revealed disdain for private enterprise among high-ranking tsarist officials and members of the *duma*. This was characteristic of their approach to rearmament and was reinforced by fears that too much private and foreign involvement in Russia's arms industry would compromise its security.

Russia's industrial progress, 1908–14

In the wake of Russia's massive rearmament, how much further had Russia industrialised in the 1908–14 period? Russia's growth rate of 8.8 per cent per annum was certainly impressive. But it is difficult to know whether Russia was making progress relative to its competitors.

- In 1913 industry only contributed around 20 per cent of national income and employed only 5 per cent of the labour force.
- On the other hand, Russia was huge and the population was expanding at a phenomenal rate of 1.6 per cent every year from the 1880s to 1913, so absolute progress was impressive.
- The cancellation of redemption payments from 1907 coupled with a rise in cereal prices after 1900 meant that, in Peter Gatrell's words, 'by 1914 the agrarian crisis, like the peasant revolution seemed like a bad dream' (Gatrell, 1986).
- Moreover, Russia was financially stable after another French loan in 1909, gold reserves were rising and the proportion of foreign investment was beginning to fall as domestic financial institutions expanded to provide loans and credit.

Legacy of the Witte boom. The main statistical problem in trying to assess Russia's relative progress is that its competitors' economies were also growing very quickly at this time and they were not suffering a population

Major industrial regions of Russia, 1900–14.

explosion. Hence, the fact that per capita income in Russia, which had been one-half of the western average in 1860, was one-third in 1914 is somewhat misleading. More significant is the one-third rise in the purchasing power of the agricultural sector, which indicates a domestic market was beginning to develop. In particular, the textiles industry matched heavy industry for growth. Russian exports also grew rapidly, indicating a greater degree of competitiveness with western economies. This was all possible because of the infrastructure and heavy industrial capacity established by the Witte boom in the 1890s.

Gigantism. Another feature of the second boom in tsarist industrialisation was **gigantism** (see the table on page 121). Regional concentration continued. Whether Russia had reached the point for a sustained industrial revolution is a technical abstraction. The facts are:

- Russia was industrialising quickly and would continue to do so in normal peacetime conditions
- if it had not already reached the point for a sustained industrial revolution it would soon, and
- there was little chance of industrialisation going into reverse.

As for Russia's future industrial-military prospects as seen in 1914, the German general staff were certainly convinced that they were worth the risk of a major war.

Opposition, 1908–14

Opposition had been transformed by the events of 1905–6. For Russia's liberals, the outcome had been a triumph. Russia had been given a new political culture, and the 3/16 June coup (1907) illustrated this better than anything. It showed that even Russian conservatism had to accept the new political context. There was no serious possibility of returning to a pure autocracy. Therefore, it is possible to speak of Russia's liberals after 1907 as a constitutional, non-revolutionary opposition, a definition proved by the mainly constructive role that the liberal parties – Octobrists, Kadets and Progressists – played in the new system. Moreover, moderate SRs were also prepared to play a parliamentary role, albeit one of permanent opposition to the government on most issues. Hence opposition to the tsarist government after 1907 was more deeply divided than it had been previously.

Non-revolutionary opposition

The non-revolutionary opposition in the *duma* was obviously prepared to co-operate with the regime and to

KEY TERM

Gigantism Building huge factories and other industrial plants. It achieved two goals: economies of scale (costs were reduced by improved productivity and efficiency) and the full application of modern industrial technology for mass production on the US model. By building in large, modern units Russian industrialists hoped to overtake foreign competitors and make up for Russia's relative industrial backwardness. The downside to gigantism was that huge factories created a mass, undifferentiated workforce, the classic class-conscious proletariat that Marx had anticipated.

> **KEY EVENTS**
>
> **Naval Staffs crisis** During this crisis in 1908–9 the State Council threw out a *duma* bill to set up a modern naval general staff (military planning office) on the grounds that the *duma* was exceeding its powers by interfering in military affairs. In 1909, after much pressure from Stolypin, the State Council gave in.
>
> **Stolypin's Western *Zemstvo* Bill** The State Council's opportunity for revenge came in 1911 with Stolypin's Western *Zemstvo* Bill, a proposal to extend *zemstva* (see pages 33–5) to Russia's western provinces, areas of mixed population situated between Russia itself and its Polish provinces. To give the new *zemstva* secure foundations, Stolypin devised an electoral system which would prevent them being dominated by Polish landowners. When the State Council threw out the bill, Stolypin resorted to Article 87 of the Fundamental Laws to make the bill law. In doing so, he infuriated his Octobrist supporters in the *duma*, who accused him of acting against the spirit of the constitution. The Octobrist group split, seriously weakening Stolypin's position.

encourage it to take the path of further constitutional reform, more insistently in the case of the Kadets and Progressists than in the case of the Octobrists. However, although Stolypin appeared to have solid support from the centre-right grouping in the *duma*, two crises between the *duma* and the upper house, the State Council, seriously undermined the beginnings of parliamentary government in Russia. These crises were the **Naval Staffs crisis**, and **Stolypin's Western *Zemstvo* Bill**.

On 1/14 September 1911 Stolypin was assassinated in Kiev by a revolutionary double agent who had also worked for the secret police. His death simply accelerated the drift to the right in Russian politics, seen in:

- the violent treatment of the Lena Goldfields workers in 1912 (see page 123), and
- the appointment of Minister of Interior Maklakov in 1913
- the notorious **Beilis affair**.

The liberals had to play a long game, at least until the defeats in the First World War. One good reason for patience was the liberal parties' shallow roots. In 1912, the Kadet party only had nine provincial branches, the Progressists had none, and the Octobrists were splintered into different factions.

Revolutionary opposition

Revolutionary opposition was also seriously affected by the events of 1905–7.

GIGANTISM

Overall % of workers in each size of factory/plant

Size of factory/plant	1901	1914
Less than 100 workers	24.4	17.8
101–500 workers	28.9	25.7
501–1000 workers	15.8	15.1
More than 1000 workers	30.9	41.4

Source: D. Christian, 1997

The dawn of modern Russia?

- It suffered a rapid decline in membership as its utopian dreams of a revolutionary transformation of Russia turned to ashes in 1906. SD (see pages 81–3) membership declined from 150,000 to 10,000, 1907–10 and SR (see pages 83–4) membership was similarly reduced, especially after it was discovered that the head of the Combat Detachment, Evno Azev, was actually working for the *okhrana* (secret police).
- The differing reactions to the 'failure' of 1905 caused a realignment of the revolutionary opposition that was at the root of their divisions in 1917.

The SRs and the SDs. Broadly, the SRs and the Menshevik wing of the SDs accepted the obvious fact that the revolution in 1905 had failed to deliver socialism because it had been premature. Thus both groups were prepared to work with the liberals, providing the latter continued to push the tsarist regime towards greater democracy and parliamentary power.

Chernov and Martov. The SR leader Victor Chernov and the Menshevik leader Martov were both disappointed by the role the peasants had played in 1905, and were forced to downgrade their expectations of the role the peasantry might play in any future upheaval. Julius Martov, in an orthodox Marxist vein, suggested that the peasantry needed to learn from 'the school of the capitalist **bourgeoisie**' in order to become more effectively revolutionary.

Like the liberals, therefore, both SRs and Mensheviks were prepared to play a long waiting game, although both believed that a 'proper' revolution was inevitable and mainly a matter of time.

Lenin and his followers. Lenin and his Bolshevik followers took a quite different line. Lenin agreed that 1905 had been, at best, only a partially successful bourgeois (middle-class, liberal) revolution. However, rather than seeing Russian society as simply too backward to carry off a successful revolution, Lenin saw real potential in the common protests and common interests of the workers and peasants in 1905.

KEY EVENT

The Beilis Affair (1913)
An affair that scandalised Russian politics. A Jewish clerk, Mendel Beilis, after a hysterically anti-Semitic press campaign, was accused of the brutal murder of a thirteen year-old schoolboy in Kiev in 1911. Beilis was then arrested and held in prison while evidence was concocted against him by those, including the Ministers of Justice and of the Interior, who were convinced of the ritual murder theory. In the meantime, two junior policemen had discovered the real circumstances of the murder. It had been carried out by a criminal gang. When the trial began in 1913, the liberal press had already disclosed the identity of the real murderers and Maxim Gorky mobilised a number of prominent European intellectuals to appeal against the 'Jewish witch hunt'. Despite this, the authorities were not deterred. Nicholas II himself was personally involved, promising the presiding judge promotion if there were a 'government victory'. However, the prosecution case was shambolic and Beilis was acquitted.

KEY TERM

Bourgeoisie The middle classes, above workers and peasants but below the nobility.

KEY PERSON

Josef Stalin (1879–1953)
(from the Russian for 'steel') The final adopted name of the Georgian SD revolutionary Josef Djugashvili. In the 1906–14 period he usually operated under the nickname 'Koba'. Stalin joined the SDs in 1906, becoming a loyal Lenin supporter. Lenin appreciated Stalin's zeal (he was imprisoned five times) and energy. Stalin succeeded Lenin as leader of the Soviet Union following Lenin's death in 1924.

KEY EVENT

Lena Goldfields Massacre
The goldfields on the river Lena (the origin of the pseudonym Lenin) in Eastern Siberia were the scene of a massacre in April 1912 of workers petitioning for better conditions of employment. A strike led to troops firing on a crowd of 5000 people, killing 270 and wounding some 200 more. The troops' conduct was defended by the Minister of the Interior, Nikolai Makarov. Like 'Bloody Sunday' in 1905, the massacre provoked sympathy and outrage among fellow workers and left-of-centre politicians.

The strength of peasant activity. To Lenin, the peasant activity in 1905 did not represent a weakness, but a strength. Moreover, Lenin had little faith in the Russian bourgeoisie, which he thought was too small and therefore too inclined to throw in its lot with tsarism. The result was Lenin's derailment of the entire Marxist scheme of revolutions. A non-revolutionary bourgeoisie would make a bourgeois revolution impossible. Therefore, according to Lenin, the workers with the support of the peasants, would have to be prepared to seize power as soon as possible to keep Russia's revolutionary future on track.

The contradictions of the worker–peasant alliance would, Lenin felt sure, be resolved by the European-wide revolution that would be sparked off by a successful revolution in Russia.

Lenin's faith in revolution. This departure from Marxist convention illustrated Lenin's absolute faith in revolution, any revolution, as the best means of political education and political progress for workers and peasants. It is also the key to the tactical flexibility that gave him such an advantage over his political rivals in the chaos of 1917.

This change of revolutionary philosophy among the Bolsheviks deepened the divide between the two wings of the SDs. In 1912 the Bolsheviks set up their own newspaper *Pravda* ('The Truth') and established a degree of financial independence from the Mensheviks, not least by bank raids led by one of Lenin's more resourceful converts, the Georgian Josef Djugashvili/Koba/**Stalin** (false names were, by now, standard practice for dedicated revolutionaries).

As a new wave of industrial unrest hit Russia in 1912–14 the revolutionary parties tried to take advantage. The most notorious incident was the **Lena Goldfields Massacre** in April 1912.

Two years of protest. This insensitivity on the part of the government sparked off a wave of protest over the next two years, beginning with a May Day strike in 1912 involving

The dawn of modern Russia?

Victims of the Lena Goldfields Massacre, April 1912.

500,000 workers, and culminating in a general strike in St Petersburg in July 1914. However, there is mixed evidence about the revolutionary parties' ability to direct working-class protest, despite the efforts of official Soviet historians like Yakushkin trying to prove that the general strike in 1914 was directed by Bolshevik agitators. Much more significant, and an indicator of the revolutionary parties' weakness, was the surge of patriotism and loyalty to the tsar that swept Russia in the crisis leading to the outbreak of the First World War. Fierce patriotism was a strong characteristic of all the Russian liberal parties.

The real danger for the tsarist regime. In conclusion, opposition to the tsarist regime was much less dangerous in 1914 than it had been in 1905–6, mainly for the simple reason that Witte's tactic of making substantial liberal concessions to split the opposition had worked. The liberals were no longer truly revolutionary. The hard-line revolutionary opposition was badly divided, the non-revolutionary opposition less seriously so. Perhaps therein lay the real danger for the tsarist regime – that it was too easy to underestimate the risk of the opposition regaining its strength should a return to autocracy be attempted. This is roughly what happened in the First World War.

CONCLUSION: WAS RUSSIA TAKING AN EVOLUTIONARY OR REVOLUTIONARY PATH FROM 1905–14?

Russia in 1914 was in a state of flux. Economic and social modernisation was gathering momentum. In 1905–6 this had, for the first time, produced major political change in the form of the constitutional monarchy.

Stolypin's assault on peasant agriculture, although not as far-reaching as it might have been, offered real hope of alleviating Russia's major social and economic problem – rural overpopulation and agricultural backwardness.

In industry progress was impressive – Russia was showing the potential to become an industrial giant.

Overview

An overview of the period 1861–1914 would indicate that Russia was evolving into a modern European-style state with an increasingly 'civil' society. However, three difficulties remained, all of them peculiarly Russian.

- The tsarist regime had an unquenchable desire to play a world historical role, especially in south-eastern Europe. This, combined with its militarist tendencies and fuelled by the general climate of militarism in Europe before 1914, pitched it into a war against stronger, more advanced enemies in the form of Germany and Austria-Hungary. Such a war, if it went badly, would have worse consequences than the war against Japan.
- Russian society in 1914 was deeply divided. These social divisions and inequalities, which risked revolutionary upheaval, were principally caused by the slow development of the Russian middle class. The elections of 1906 and 1907 (before the electoral system was heavily biased in favour of the wealthy) reflected the deep social divide between middle- and upper-class élites on the one hand, and the mass of peasants and workers on the other. The parties that could most easily appeal to these workers and peasants (the SRs and SDs) remained fiercely committed to revolution. This reflected another tradition – the radical intelligentsia's

Tsar Nicholas II and his family in 1903.

deep antagonism towards the tsarist regime, dating back to the Populists in the 1860s. For continuing political evolution to be reasonably smooth the middle class would need to grow and antagonistic politics would have to be moderated. This would take time.

- The third difficulty was the traditional view of the Russian monarchy held by Tsar Nicholas II. His coronation oath to uphold the autocracy was reinforced by a peculiarly backward-looking, Slavophil attitude to Russian monarchy, exemplified by the lavish celebrations of the 300th anniversary of the founding of the Romanov dynasty in 1913. His reluctance to work with the *duma* and assist the evolutionary process in politics became all too apparent during the First World War.

On balance, tsarist Russia had recovered remarkably well from the traumatic events of 1905. Its prospects of stable evolutionary development in 1914 were good until foreign affairs intervened and Russia went to war.

SUMMARY QUESTIONS

1 Why was unrest so widespread in Russia in 1905–6?

2 What was the significance of the October Manifesto?

3 How effective was the '*duma* monarchy', 1906–14?

4 How effective were Stolypin's agrarian reforms?

5 How significant was Russia's economic progress, 1906–14?

6 What problems did Russia face in foreign policy, 1906–14?

7 How stable was the Russian Empire on the eve of the First World War?

CHAPTER 5

The collapse of imperial Russia, August 1914 to March 1917

Why did the tsarist regime collapse in March 1917? If Russia's prospects were healthy in early 1914, it is important to explain precisely how tsarist Russia was undone so quickly and so completely in the First World War. This section will consider five interlinked aspects of the problem:

- the decision to go to war
- strategic considerations
- the direction of the Russian war effort, 1914–17
- economic and social factors, and
- political developments.

THE DECISION TO GO TO WAR

Why did the Russian Empire collapse so quickly? The answer lies in the changing nature of warfare after 1914, and the social and economic strains imposed by war on such a vast scale. However, it is not enough merely to state that this war was too big and too demanding for the tsarist regime to have any chance of survival. This implies that the decision to go to war in 1914 was wrong. In fact, Nicholas II and his ministers had good reason to risk war in 1914.

- The combined resources of Great Britain, France and Russia far outweighed those of Germany and Austria-Hungary.
- Russia had at least two good opportunities to win the war – one in its initial attack in August 1914, and one in June–July 1916.

That said, Russia, which had been slow to modernise in the age of industrialisation, would have to change much more quickly to keep up with the social and economic change unleashed by a long war. Its opportunities to win were real, but fleeting. Once missed, Russia was plunged into a struggle for survival against the threats of a resourceful external enemy (principally Germany), and internal economic, social and political disintegration.

STRATEGIC CONSIDERATIONS

Perhaps the key strategic consideration is that the war that Russia was fighting in 1915–17 had changed out of recognition from the war which it entered in 1914. Within a few months, Russia's early hopes were dashed, a new kind of war had developed and economic weaknesses began to show.

Defeats instead of victories

Arguably Russia's best opportunity of victory came at the very beginning of the war when the bulk of the German army was invading Belgium and France. But instead of an expected victory, Russia's generals blundered to a calamitous defeat.

Tannenberg and Masurian Lakes. At Tannenberg and Masurian Lakes (August to September 1914) Russia's chances of a swift victory over Germany and Austria-Hungary were destroyed. It took Russia a year to recover from the side-effects of this catastrophe, side-effects that took the form of a series of further defeats in 1915.

A new kind of war

In strategic terms, Tannenberg and Masurian Lakes helped to equalise the forces of the two coalitions fighting the First World War and, therefore, greatly increased the chances of the war being a long struggle, a war of organisation and production, and a test of a state's ability to improvise. Such qualities were precisely the weaknesses of imperial Russia.

In purely military terms, the First World War was the first European war to be dominated by new technology and new ways of fighting to exploit this technology. In these crucial respects, the Germans were the masters.

The success of the German army. Historian Niall Ferguson (1998) concludes that the German army had, man for man, a much higher killing/wounding rate than its opponents on the western front and an even greater advantage on the eastern front. Ferguson concludes that the Germans understood best of all that trench warfare was best conducted without grand plans or mass movements but on a local scale with small units fighting in an improvised, independent way.

The German strategy put great reliance on the quality of junior officers and, particularly, **NCOs**. The lack of good junior officers and NCOs was the Russian army's most glaring structural weakness after 1915. This, in turn, reflected the social backwardness of imperial Russia with its small lower middle and upper working classes.

Economic weaknesses

In November 1914 Turkey joined the Central Powers (Germany and Austria-Hungary), having previously been neutral. This was a second disaster for Russia. Although Turkey itself did not pose a critical military threat, its entry into the war put a stranglehold on the Russian economy because it was easily able to sever Russia's main trade artery, from the Black Sea through the straits (the Bosphorus and Dardenelles) to the Mediterranean. During 1915 this did not have a critical effect. However, by 1916–17 the fact that Russia was largely cut off from its economically powerful allies, and had lost 90 per cent of its pre-war imports and exports, helped to guarantee economic strife.

THE DIRECTION OF THE RUSSIAN WAR EFFORT, 1914–17

The Russian war effort followed a switchback course all of its own. It was punctuated by a number of key turning points and developments.

- The Tannenberg disaster, 1914.
- Confusion and the shell shortage, 1914–15.

KEY TERM

NCOs, or Non-Commissioned Officers Common soldiers promoted to a maximum rank of Sergeant-Major. They perform a vital military role. More in touch with the men who do most of the actual fighting than commissioned officers, NCOs at their best give their men a sense of purpose and practical advice in combat. In the chaos of First World War battles, the ability to fight independently in small units was essential and put NCO leadership at a premium. NCOs usually came from the upper reaches of the working class and had some education. Hence they came from a social group that, in the West, was relatively more numerous and more integrated into society as a whole than it was in Russia. In 1917, after the Russian army had suffered huge losses and turnover of manpower, NCO class proved highly susceptible to revolutionary politics, and in several instances led the mutinies and popular revolution that overthrew the tsar.

- The Myasoyedov scandal and the change of command, 1915.
- Cause for renewed Russian optimism, 1915–16.
- The impact of Brusilov, 1916.
- Stagnation on the northern front, 1916.
- The Romanian entry into the war, 1916–17.

The Tannenberg disaster, 1914

Russia's military leadership during the war emerges time and again as a decisive factor. The disaster at Tannenberg in September 1914 was caused by bad planning, poor co-ordination between the armies of General Alexander Samsonov and General Pavel Rennenkampf, and skilful improvisation by General Erich von Ludendorff, the recently appointed commander of the German armies in the east and his subordinate, General von François.

Samsonov shot himself after his army was surrounded. However, Rennenkampf executed a skilful retreat at Masurian Lakes so that his First Army avoided the fate of Samsonov's Second Army. Total Russian losses from these two battles were 230,000, roughly twice that of the Germans.

At this point the planners were thrown into confusion. They were not helped by the fact that the Russian First

The Russian II Army captured after the battle at Tannenberg, September 1914.

and Tenth armies had commanders with chiefs of staff to whom they would not speak as a result of Vladimir Sukhomlinov's intrigues.

Essentially, the northern Russian armies had been defeated and thrown into retreat by the Germans while the south-western armies had the Austro-Hungarians on the run. Although this situation was not always the case, it set the pattern for the rest of the war. Should the Russians concentrate on the southern front against the weaker enemy, or the northern front against the stronger enemy?

Confusion and the shell shortage, 1914–15

The result of the indecision about which front to concentrate on was confusion. In November 1914, after four sets of contradictory instructions, the commander of the south-western front, General Nikolai Ivanov, confessed that 'it is impossible to detect in *Stavka*'s instructions either an exact task or a fixed objective' (Stone, 1998).

Stavka did not set up an artillery section until early 1916. Until this was done *Stavka* often did not even know how many shells the Russian army possessed. This helps to explain why, in May and June 1915, with the south-western front in headlong retreat after the German Gorlice-Tarnow offensive, *Stavka* was quick to blame Russia's problems on a 'shell shortage'. Certainly, Russian

> **KEY TERM**
>
> ***Stavka*** The name given to the command centre of the Russian army, first at Baranovichi, then Mogilev (derived from the Russian word for 'grave'). *Stavka* acquired an unenviable reputation for extravagance and inefficiency before the change of command to the tsar and Alexeyev in September 1915.

A Russian cartoon of a peasant spearing a soldier. The original caption, translated from Russian, reads 'This Austrian was full of talk, till granny got him with her fork'.

artillery was less well provided for than the Germans'. But inefficiency of supply – having shell stockpiled in fortresses that surrendered easily – was more of a problem than outright shortage. What the 'shell shortage' did, however, was give *Stavka* an excuse to avoid a review of the inadequacy of its strategic planning and control.

The Myasoyedov scandal and the change of command, 1915

The Russian press and public looked for scapegoats for Russia's poor performance, causing further instability in the command structure.

- In February 1915, one of Sukhomlinov's internal spies before 1914, Colonel Sergei Myasoyedov, was put on trial by *Stavka* for spying for the Germans.
- In March, Myasoyedov was executed on dubious evidence with full publicity.
- In June, the tsar caved in to pressure from the allies and major Russian industrialists to dismiss Sukhomlinov.
- Sukhomlinov remained in prison until October 1917.
- Alexander Polivanov, an ally of leading *duma* politicians including Guchkov from the Octobrist party, was Sukhomlinov's replacement.

The Great Retreat. In August 1915 when the defeats on the south-western front had become the Great Retreat (a result of the 'shell shortage', according to *Stavka*), the tsar was forced to dismiss his uncle, Grand Duke Nikolai. The tsar took the figurehead role himself, but in practice the new commander-in-chief became the tsar's chief of staff, **General Alexeyev**.

Problems of the retreat. Alexeyev, very much the professional soldier, saw that the greatest problem revealed by the retreat was not the shell shortage but the quality of the commanders. He wrote that, according to his son, also a serving officer, 'there is hardly a single general you can name who has become popular with the men' (Stone, 1998).

Losses caused by the retreat. The Great Retreat had inflicted huge losses on the Russian army, some 1.5 million men and a string of expensive (but ineffective)

> **KEY PERSON**
>
> **General Alexeyev** A pivotal figure in Russia's fortunes in the First World War, the tsar's prestige as Commander-in-Chief depended on Alexeyev's success. Unquestionably, Alexeyev was a major improvement on his predecessor, Yanushkevich. However, he suffered from the obsession with logistics common among First World War generals and was not prepared to take strategic risks in pursuit of a quick victory in 1916. Russia's political collapse in March 1917 came too soon for Alexeyev, although, at this point, he was quick to realise that the tsar was a liability. Alexeyev's recommendation that Nicholas abdicate was perhaps the decisive influence on the tsar on 2 March 1917. Alexeyev was a co-founder of the White, anti-Bolshevik army in the civil war. He died in October 1918.

fortresses, railway lines and important cities. It culminated in the German capture of Vilna on 5/18 September, the lowest point of the war for Russia before the revolution. However, the emergence of Polivanov and Alexeyev offered hope of greater co-ordination and less in-fighting in the Russian high command. Sadly, Nicholas II's decision to remove himself from Petrograd had the reverse effect on domestic politics, as we shall see.

The spread of war in 1915. The year 1915 had also seen the war spread.

- Italy had entered on the *entente* powers' side and had opened a new front against Austria-Hungary with obvious strategic implications for Russia. But in practice the Italian front was relatively easily contained by the Austro-Hungarians.
- The Balkan origins of the First World War played themselves out further in 1915 as Bulgaria decided to join the central powers in their campaign against Serbia.
- Romania, a long-standing enemy of Hungary because of the repressed Romanian minority living there, waited on events. Romania's strategic position was very important as it determined the southern boundary of the eastern front and controlled the relatively accessible route into Russia around the north-western coast of the Black Sea.

Cause for renewed Russian optimism, 1915–16

The Germans had run out of steam in September 1915. Ludendorff decided to dig in on 13/26 September after successful minor counter-attacks by the Russians. The Germans' problem was that the Russian retreat made strategic sense for the Russian army because it shortened the front by approximately 400 kilometres, or 25 per cent.

- Despite the Russian losses, this made Russia's ultimate manpower superiority more of a threat.
- Moreover, the Russian retreat, in its later stages, had been orderly. The Germans had captured very few guns in the thrust to Vilna, and the troops they had captured were often lower quality units, whom the Russian artillery simply abandoned.

- Finally, the Germans had been led into an infertile, marshy area (the Pripyat marshes). Further progress, some 125 kilometres from their main railheads, became extremely difficult.

In 1916 Russia's prospects were much better.

- Despite its backwardness, remarkable progress had been made in shell production and transport.
- Alexeyev had a bigger, better equipped army than his predecessors with a front-line strength of 1.7 million.
- The Germans, having failed to break Russia in 1915, launched their assault on Verdun in February 1916 in the hope of breaking France, thus reducing their offensive capability in the east.

However, the losses of 1915 meant that the 1916 call-up was the last Russia could make before it had to recruit mainly from its vast, unreliable territorial reserve. Alexeyev was therefore under great pressure to win the war in a year. His first attacking moves were in eastern Galicia in late-December 1915, and around Lake Naroch in the centre of the northern sector of the front in March 1916.

Both were failures, mainly because the commanders (Alexei Evert and Alexei Kuropatkin) now felt that with sufficient supplies of shell they could win by bombardment alone.

- The Germans knew of the Lake Naroch attack two weeks in advance.
- The bombardment was indiscriminate due to insufficient reconnaissance, command and communication.
- Losses, twice those of the eastern Galician offensive, were at 100,000.
- In both cases, gains were negligible.

All that could be said in Alexeyev's and his commanders' defence was that they had been forced into the Lake Naroch offensive by German pressure on Verdun.

The impact of Brusilov, 1916
Alexeyev was now at a loss as his northern commanders

had nothing to offer. But on the south-western front, a change of command in March, from Ivanov to **General Alexei Brusilov**, led to a remarkable change of fortune.

- Brusilov realised that the slow preparations for artillery-led offensives sacrificed surprise and played into the defenders' hands.
- Therefore, he proposed a carefully prepared infantry assault with minimal preparatory bombardment.
- Most importantly, he wanted his troops to attack at several points, thus confusing the enemy's deployment of reserves.

Brusilov's staff went to great lengths to map and detail the enemy's positions, then dug their own front line forwards, close to enemy lines, with huge dugouts to conceal the Russian reserves. When they attacked, the results were spectacular.

- The Austro-Hungarian armies were caught by surprise by four simultaneous attacks on 22 May/4 June.
- After eight days the Austrians were in headlong retreat.
- Two whole Austro-Hungarian armies had fallen apart with the loss of nearly 200,000 men and much of their equipment.

It was the greatest single victory of the entire war so far and threatened to achieve outright victory.

Stagnation on the northern front, 1916

For Brusilov's success to be fully exploited, he needed an attack in the north to occupy the Germans. General Evert, commander of the northern sector, failed to deliver, delaying for a month. When he did attack, in July 1916, the result was another artillery/trench **attrition battle** around Kowel. Despite the pressure of the British attack on the Somme from 1 July, the Germans were able to cope mainly because the marsh terrain made advances so difficult.

Romanian entry into the war, 1916–17

Brusilov's success was further compromised by the entry of Romania into the war on Russia's side in August 1916, partly as a result of Russian success. This decision was a supreme act of folly.

KEY PERSON

General Alexei Brusilov Russia's outstanding commander of the First World War. He was distinguished by two key qualities: concern for his men and their conditions of service, and a willingness to learn and improvise, tactically and strategically. The latter quality explains his success on the south-western front in 1914 and, more spectacularly, in 1916. In the backbiting world of wartime tsarist politics, Brusilov's early successes caused concern. They were played down, in case he should become a focus of public opposition to the court's command of the armed forces. Brusilov was a sincere patriot. He joined the Reds in the Russian Civil War in 1920 after the Poles had invaded Ukraine and taken its capital Kiev. Brusilov died in 1926.

KEY TERM

Attrition battle A method of fighting where the two sides try to wear down their enemy using constant bombardments and attacks.

- The Romanian army was inadequate in almost every respect. It was crushed by a combined German/Austrian/Bulgarian offensive under General Erich von Falkenhayn.
- Bucharest fell on 24 November/7 December and the Romanians were forced out of the war.
- Recognising the weakness of their position, Alexeyev had offered only limited Russian support. With Romania's swift collapse, he was left with an even longer, more complex front to defend.

The disparity between the success of Brusilov and the failures of his northern compatriots does not reflect well on the quality of leadership of the Russian army. Alexeyev was a more successful commander than his predecessors, but he still failed to exert the influence that might have capitalised on Brusilov's successes. Worst of all, he and the tsar failed to get rid of negligent and incompetent commanders like Evert and Kuropatkin.

Alexeyev had failed to win the war in 1916, although Russia's war effort had improved in most respects. For 1917 he was planning a spring offensive with an army better supplied than ever. Unfortunately for him, Russia's failure to win by the winter of 1916–17 had exposed the country's relatively fragile economic, administrative and political systems. These broke down in February/March 1917 before Alexeyev was able to launch his offensive. After this the war effort was seriously compromised by the politics of revolution and Russia's chances of victory on the Eastern front evaporated.

ECONOMIC AND SOCIAL FACTORS

As the First World War dragged on into 1915 and swift resolution became more remote, so economic and social considerations assumed ever greater importance.

- First came the challenge of supplying mass armies, a test of the adaptability of an economy.
- Second came finance, finding a way of bearing the enormous costs of war without undermining the domestic economy.

Of the major powers, Britain was in the best position on both counts and Russia in the worst.

The position of Britain
- Britain had a highly developed industrial base that enabled it to supply a full-size conscript army by 1916.
- Britain had control of maritime trade. It could thus exploit its imperial resource base and sustain its domestic economy more easily than its allies and rivals.
- Britain had the greatest financial staying power of the main participants.

The position of Russia
- Russia's recent industrialisation left little spare capacity when the losses of the war began to bite.
- Russia was hard pressed in key areas of munitions production.
- Russia's industry was unhealthily concentrated in the vulnerable western provinces. Significant industrial centres such as Warsaw and Bialystok were lost in the Great Retreat of 1915.

Military production
Most historians agree that in terms of munitions production, Russia responded remarkably well to the setbacks of 1914 and 1915. Although Alexeyev's armies of 1916 may have lacked training, they were as well supplied as their Austro-German counterparts.

- Russian shell production quadrupled between 1914–16.
- By July 1916, some 30,000 motorised vehicles had been procured (there had been 710 at the outbreak of war).

The concentration on military production acted as an accelerator on the growth of the economy as a whole. Sidorov's estimate of growth is shown in the table below.

SIDOROV'S ESTIMATE OF GROWTH OF MILITARY PRODUCTION

(1913 = 100)	1914	1915	1916	1917
	101.2	113.7	121.5	77.3

Source: N. Stone, 1998.

Industrial economy

The idea that the Russian economy simply buckled under the demands of war is misleading. In fact, the industrial economy made remarkable progress during the first two years of war.

- Russia was experiencing rapid growth and was becoming more industrially self-sufficient.
- Chemical industry output doubled.
- Output of machinery by value trebled.

By 1917 roughly 80 per cent of Russia's light calibre artillery and 100 per cent of heavy artillery was of Russian manufacture. Ironically, the main beneficiaries of this huge munitions stockpile proved to be the Bolsheviks in the Russian Civil War. In terms of military supply the Russian economy adapted quite well. However, this success was bought at a very high price in terms of the civilian economy and finance.

WHY DID ECONOMIC PROGRESS BREAK DOWN?

The wartime economic problems that were to bring the tsarist regime to its knees only became fully apparent in autumn 1916. The Russian economy adapted quite well to the immediate demands of the new warfare, but was unable to maintain this progress for a third year of all-out war, due to a number of weaknesses, including financial weakness and inflation, social strains, profiteering, agriculture and strain on the internal market.

Financial weakness and inflation

The first problem was finance. Russia's currency was vulnerable as the country came off the gold standard in 1914. Russia may have been capable of a home-grown industrial revolution during the war but was unable to finance this revolution itself.

A reduction in tax revenue. The government's first move, in August 1914, was to ban the production and sale of alcohol for the duration of the war. This was Nicholas II's personal decision and defied fiscal logic, whatever it might do for public morals. As the government liquor monopoly made up 30 per cent of taxation revenue this was further evidence that the tsar thought the war would be short. In 1916 the Minister of Finances confessed it had taken two years to recover from **prohibition**.

The cost of war. The cost of the war meant a new financial strategy. By 1916 'the war alone cost 4.7 times total government expenditure in the last peacetime year' (Christian, 1997).

Increase in national debt. The only realistic solution to such extreme demands was to borrow and increase the money supply (that is, print money and encourage inflation). In two and a half years of war to early 1917 inflation was running at 400 per cent (the same currency devaluation that Germany suffered in four years to 1918). Between 1914 and 1917 the tsarist government offered six issues of war bonds and introduced a new excess profits and income tax in 1916. However, these efforts failed to have much impact on the national debt, which quadrupled between 1914 and 1917 (Figes, 1997).

The international perspective. Such figures can be misleading. All the participants in the First World War ran up huge debts (in Britain the pre-war debt increased by a factor of eleven to 1919), risked inflation and were short of revenue. Russia's turmoil in 1917 cannot be explained solely by these statistics. It was the impact of such changes on the peculiar Russian social and political system that proved explosive.

Social strains

The first peculiarity was the dramatic social impact of an industrial revolution accelerated by the war economy. The industrial workforce expanded too quickly for costs to be controlled or for living standards to be maintained.

> **KEY TERM**
>
> **Prohibition** The banning of the production, sale and consumption of alcohol.

THE COST OF WAR (billion roubles)

1914	1915	1916	January to August 1917
1.7	8.8	14.6	13.6

Source: Figes, 1997

- Between 1914 and January 1917 Petrograd's population grew from 2.1 million to 2.7 million, and Moscow's from 1.6 million to 2.0 million (Christian, 1997).
- The workforce in metal-working industries alone increased by over 44 per cent (Stone, 1998).

The combination of such dramatic population shifts with inflation was bound to lead to a decline in living standards as wages increased at roughly half the rate of prices. In such a situation it was only natural to expect labour unrest. In October 1916, there was a wave of strikes in the capital more severe than anything seen since the abortive general strike of July 1914.

Profiteering

Excessive profiteering was and still is a common and justified criticism of the Russian war economy. Russia's newly established manufacturing industries could not perhaps compete on price with the latest US industries. But the fact that US factories could supply locomotives to Russian railways at two-thirds the cost of Russian factories *and* meet shorter deadlines is noteworthy (Stone, 1998).

The pre-war syndicates that dominated raw materials and heavy industrial production in Russia were both efficient producers and efficient price-fixers. The Ministry of Finance calculated that profit rates as a percentage of basic capital had shot up from around 10 per cent in 1914 to 77 per cent in 1916 (Stone, 1998). However, in generating profits, Russian industry did provide a rich seam of investment.

Agriculture and strain on the internal market

Perhaps the most difficult problem facing the tsarist war economy was agriculture. As we have seen, Stolypin and Krivoshein had made real progress in stabilising and modernising Russia's agriculture. However, they were nowhere near completing the process of creating a strong, economically efficient class of individual proprietors.

The development in agriculture after 1907 had been tied to three things – the rapid expansion of Russian industry, the development of consumer goods, and stable terms of trade.

This delicate, favourable climate was undermined by the war economy. Productivity was not seriously affected (in 1915 and 1916 the harvests were normal) but a crisis developed in the marketing of grain. This crisis was caused by two interlinked problems.

- Inflation hit agriculture severely. Peasant and non-peasant agriculture faced a steady erosion of its purchasing power as it was not sufficiently co-ordinated to fix prices like the industrial cartels.
- The diversion of manufacturing industry into the war effort made for a consumer goods famine and even higher prices.

Irregular supplies resulted in exceptional price fluctuations. For instance, the price of horse-shoe nails in Ivanovo-Voznesensk rose by a factor of eleven from 1914–16. Unable to fix the price of their own produce, agricultural producers began to withdraw from the market, using more grain for domestic consumption and animal feed.

- The proportion of the total harvest marketed dropped from 25 per cent in 1913–14 to 10 per cent in 1916–17.
- The quantities marketed dropped from 95 million tonnes in 1914 to 77.3 million tonnes in 1915 and finally to 62.8 million tonnes in 1916.

The result was a grain shortage in the cities. This was most acute in Petrograd and Moscow with their mushrooming populations. In January 1917 Petrograd received only 48 per cent of its grain requirements. Moscow and the Central Provinces received just 33 per cent. Even the army had to halve its lavish 4000 calories per day food ration in November 1916 (Stone, 1998). Combined with a rise in labour militancy, such shortages and consequent price rises were bound to make Petrograd and Moscow volatile in early 1917.

POLITICAL DEVELOPMENTS

The Russian autocracy should have been well-suited to wartime politics. Its authoritarianism, centralised power, distrust of representative systems and fondness for controlling the media were features of the administrations of all the participants in the First World War. By the Defence of the Realm Act (1915) with widespread control of the press and economy, and the formation of a coalition government to avoid an election in the same year, even Great Britain resorted to a form of military autocracy. However, the context of tsarist politics was entirely different from the underlying characteristics of the British system.

- First, representative government was barely established in Russia. So the struggle for power between the tsar and the *duma* was very much a live issue.
- Second, the degree of public awareness of, and participation in, the political process was entirely different. In Britain there was no hidden agenda in curtailing civil liberties. The issue was simply national efficiency in war. In Russia, Nicholas II saw the war as an obvious opportunity to reclaim the ground the autocracy had lost after 1905 and to assert his anachronistic (from another time) view of the autocracy as a mystical personal union between tsar and Russian people.

WAS NICHOLAS ON THE RIGHT TRACK?

In the public euphoria of August 1914 Nicholas could be forgiven for thinking he was on the right track.

- There was a rash of patriotic public meetings all over the country.
- These were underscored by the *duma's* virtually unanimous endorsement of the war effort.

Such a mood was based on the frequently-held view that the war would be short. When, in early 1915, it became clear it wouldn't, and that Russia wasn't doing particularly well, euphoria rapidly evaporated and scapegoats had to be found. Following this, the Germans defeated the Russians heavily in the Gorlice-Tarnow offensive, setting off the Russian army's Great Retreat.

The Progressive Bloc

The Sukhomlinov affair illustrated Nicholas's weakness and marked the beginning of a sharp political crisis in the summer of 1915. The crisis centred on the recall of the *duma*, which met from 19 July/1 August to 3/16 September 1915. This coincided with the worst part of the Great Retreat, with a succession of military reverses putting pressure on the government. Within the *duma* a new liberal coalition of Kadets, Octobrists and Progressists emerged. It had a majority and called itself the Progressive Bloc.

The aim of the Bloc. The primary aim was to encourage the tsar to form what it called a Ministry of Public Confidence, which would include some of its leaders.

The demands of the Bloc. From its own perspective the Bloc's demands were sensible. It would give the tsarist regime the broader base of public support it needed to fight a difficult, costly war. However, from the tsar's point of view it looked like another attempt to reduce the autocracy's power, or worse, an extension of the *duma's* vendetta against ministers it did not like, such as the now-disgraced Sukhomlinov.

Nicholas and the Bloc. Nicholas took two courses of action. First, he compromised with the Bloc by appointing a clutch of liberal ministers. Then he dismissed them and appointed himself figurehead commander-in-chief – a move that the liberals had tried to dissuade him from taking. The *duma* was then closed down temporarily and forced to witness the civilian government falling under the influence of the tsarina, Alexandra, and her spiritual adviser **Grigory Efimovich Rasputin**.

Tsarina Alexandra

As tsarina, Alexandra cut an awkward figure. Her chief characteristics were her literally Victorian insistence on 'good works' and her religiosity. She was an Anglo-German

KEY PERSON

Grigory Efimovich Rasputin Born in Pokrovskoe in Western Siberia around 1869, he became a *starets*, or travelling pilgrim/holy man. His blend of coarseness and spirituality gave him a strong appeal to high society in St Petersburg before 1914. His close association with the royal family and high politics, and the scandals that ensued, led to his assassination by Prince Felix Yusupov and V.M. Purishkevich of the Union of the Russian People in December 1916.

princess who was Queen Victoria of Britain's granddaughter and had been schooled according to the strict, self-denying values of her grandmother. Her attempt to introduce sewing circles among the ladies of the Russian high aristocracy underlined her eccentricity.

Alexandra balanced her alien characteristics with a mania for the Russian Orthodox Church. She had the enthusiasm of the convert (in her case from Protestantism).

Alexandra's further tendency to mysticism and spiritualism was not unusual for the time. In the early years of the twentieth century, St Petersburg was a magnet for religious cranks and faith healers, some of whom were 'taken in' by high society.

Alexandra and Rasputin

One such faith healer was Rasputin, who followed the practices of the marginal **khlyst sects** of the Orthodox Church. Alexandra's other-worldliness was bound to be vulnerable to someone like Rasputin. When this common trait was bolstered by Rasputin's faith healing of Tsarevich Alexis's (Alexandra's son) haemophilia the bond between the two of them became unbreakable, although there is no proof of any sexual relationship. What is certain is that they compared visions.

Nicholas's culpability

To expose Alexandra and Rasputin to public accountability in the greatest military and economic crisis that Russia had ever experienced was a foolish mistake by Nicholas. What is worse, he made no serious and effective attempt to remove them from the limelight until Rasputin was murdered in December 1916. For the monarchy this was a catastrophic failure of public relations.

The impact of Alexandra and Rasputin on the government

Such was Rasputin's power and friendship with the tsarina that he was often able to influence her in her choice of ministers and appointments. The tsarina and her adviser made neutral appointments that would avoid them having to alienate the *duma* too openly. Hence the succession of

> **KEY TERMS**
>
> **Khlysts** These monks practised redemption through sin and, therefore, tended to live lives of sexual and alcoholic indulgence – the opposite of conventional monks. This explains the scandalous aura that surrounded Rasputin when he was at the centre of politics in 1915–16.
>
> **Sects** The Russian Orthodox Church spawned several breakaway sects. Many were persecuted and driven underground or into remote areas of Siberia and the north including the most numerous of the sects – the Old Believers. The most extreme sects put the idea of Christ's second coming into practice, with the result that the appearance of 'Christs' was a regular occurrence in Siberia.

The collapse of imperial Russia, August 1914 to March 1917

An undated drawing of Tsarevich Alexis, Rasputin, Tsarina Alexandra and one of her daughters.

elderly gentlemen in the key position of Chairman of the Council of Ministers.

- **Ivan Goremykin**, aged 76, retired in January 1916.
- He was succeeded by the 68 year-old Boris Stürmer.
- Stürmer was succeeded by Trepov for just a month.
- In December 1916, 66 year-old Golitsyn took the post.

Another poor appointment was Minister of Internal Affairs, Alexander Protopopov, who proved quite out of his depth in his new role. The fact that, in December 1916, Alexandra had successfully pleaded for his retention after criticism from several quarters illustrates her influence over Nicholas. Protopopov's colleague Peter Bark (Minister of Finance) commented acidly that: 'His [Protopopov's] explanations and judgements were unusually superficial, he enjoyed no authority and seemed a pitiful figure because of his lack of competence or knowledge.'

Perhaps the most damaging dismissal was that of Alexei Polivanov, the Minister of War, in March 1916. Described by the British military attaché as 'undoubtedly the ablest military organiser in Russia', Alexandra recommended his dismissal on the grounds that his contacts with public organisations made him 'simply a revolutionist' (Figes, 1997).

KEY PERSON

Ivan Goremykin Chairman of the Council of Ministers from January 1914 to January 1916. He stuck by the tsar in the ministerial crisis of 1915 when the tsar decided to make himself Commander-in-Chief. A long-standing conservative, 'ancient, shrewd and loyal' (Lieven, 1994), Goremykin's growing exhaustion told against him in his last months in office. With the tsar at *Stavka*, the choice of Goremykin's replacement was especially critical. Alexandra's decision to appoint Boris Stürmer was less than inspired.

Were Alexandra and Rasputin really to blame?

It is convenient but wrong to blame Alexandra and Rasputin for these mistakes and to absolve the tsar. In reality, Nicholas made all the crucial decisions, influenced though he was by his wife and Rasputin. The string of dubious appointments came as a result of Nicholas having turned his back on a Ministry of Public Confidence in 1915. Younger and more able ministers, such as Maklakov (Minister of Internal Affairs to June 1915) were dismissed to appease public and *duma* opinion, or they resigned because Nicholas would not make concessions (for example, Krivoshein, Minister of Agriculture to October 1915). Whatever the precise responsibility for appointments, what made the charges against Alexandra and Rasputin so damaging to public confidence in the government were:

- Alexandra's German origins, conveniently ignoring her passionate devotion to Russia and its dynasty
- Alexandra's limited intellect; according to Paul Benckendorff she had, 'a will of iron, linked to not much brain and no knowledge' (Lieven, 1994), and
- Rasputin's notoriety and boasts about his own power.

Rasputin's murder

One cannot doubt that Rasputin's influence was taken very seriously at the time. His murder in December 1916 by **Felix Yusupov** had already been preceded by at least one attempt on the monk's life, in March, in which a government minister, Khvostov, had been involved. Certainly the political fortunes of the regime were at a low ebb in the autumn and winter, 1916–17. In November 1916 the *duma* reconvened to flay unpopular ministers. The Kadet leader Pavel Miliukov's attack on the government included the rhetorical question: 'Is this stupidity, or is it treason?' This was not intended to be a rallying cry for opponents of the regime, but the press reported it as such in a Petrograd darkened by right-wing plots against Rasputin and the monarchy.

The effect on Nicholas

Nicholas himself was exhausted and confused. He put all his faith in the 1917 campaign now that he knew

> **KEY PERSON**
>
> **Prince Felix Yusupov** A member of one of Russia's leading, and richest, aristocratic families. He had been converted to the idea that Rasputin had to be eliminated to save Russia by right-wing politicians like Purishkevich. The murder of Rasputin took place in the Yusupov Palace in central St Petersburg.

Russia's armies were well supplied. Speaking in February 1917 the tsar said: 'I know the situation is very alarming ... [but] ... Soon, in the spring will come the offensive and I believe that God will give us victory, and then moods will change' (Lieven, 1994).

THE COLLAPSE OF THE TSARIST REGIME

The process of revolution as it occurred in February 1917 is relatively straightforward.

- A break in very cold weather brought people onto the streets of **Petrograd** in protest at miserable economic conditions.
- When Cossacks failed to intervene effectively on 23 February/8 March the protests gained momentum.
- On Nicholas's orders two days later, troops eventually fired on the protesters.
- The capital slid out of control and key units mutinied.

An attempt at restoring order

The only way to restore order was to sanction a major military operation using front-line troops. However, the generals were convinced by the *duma* leaders that 'they [the *duma* leaders] were in control of events and that military intervention would lead to civil war' (Lieven, 1994). On either count, this was hardly the case. The political momentum of the revolution on the streets had already produced the socialist Petrograd Soviet. Had this been fully appreciated by the generals, they might well have intervened with 'a real chance that it would have been successful' (Lieven, 1994). But, for the few days during which Nicholas made his attempted return to the capital from 28 February/13 March, the die was cast against any such operation.

The abdication of Nicholas

After years of frustration with Nicholas, the *duma* leaders (including their chairman Rodzianko), saw the opportunity to turn the tables. General Nikolai Ruzsky, commander of the northern front, made his way to the royal train in Pskov to join the tsar and Alexeyev. They helped to

> **KEY PLACE**
>
> **Petrograd** The name given to St Petersburg 1914–24. The city was then renamed Leningrad 1924–91. In 1991 the name St Petersburg was restored.

persuade Nicholas that it was in the interest of Russia's war effort that he should abdicate, which he did on 2/15 March. However, what people did not anticipate was that Nicholas would also abdicate on behalf of his son, Alexis.

The failure of compromise

The consensus view among Russia's leadership was that it would be desirable to lose Nicholas and Alexandra, but not the monarchy. To lose the monarchy would risk anarchy in the increasing instability of 1917. The proposed compromise among leading politicians was to retain Alexis as monarch with a regent who could act with the *duma*. Once Nicholas's double abdication had ruled this out, it was hardly likely, given the worsening situation in Petrograd, that Nicholas's brother Mikhail would accept the role of tsar. With Mikhail's abdication the Russian monarchy came to an end on 3/16 March 1917.

An eventual loss of order

As the *Duma* leaders had feared, after the abdication the situation in the cities spiralled out of control. To arrest Russia's social, economic and political disintegration in the middle of a war would be a huge task.

THE LEGACY OF NICHOLAS II'S ABDICATION

- The collapse of tsarist government was achieved on a wave of anarchic popular protest and violence in Petrograd and Moscow. At least 1500 people died in the capital.
- What followed was a rising tide of anarchy, spreading from revolutionary soviets in cities to the army and eventually to the peasants who began to seize land in late summer. The revolution had become a revolution against authority, then against private property.
- The *Duma* Committee had proclaimed itself a Provisional Government in March 1917 but had little chance of governing in a situation in which it had to abolish all police forces, open prisons and endorse all the freedoms or be overthrown by street protests.
- The Provisional Government, which was largely liberal, had to compete for power with the socialist Petrograd

Soviet. Even worse, the Provisional Government still had to keep the Germans at bay in the war.

A Socialist Revolutionary-based socialist coalition government looked the likeliest outcome. However, that was pre-empted by the brilliant opportunism and political manipulation of Lenin and Trotsky who, in the name of the soviets and an implied socialist coalition, seized power in October/November 1917. In reality, they set up a Bolshevik-dominated dictatorship. The intolerance and violence they meted out to their political opponents guaranteed a civil war.

Nicholas II and his family, trapped at Ekaterinburg on the Trans-Siberian Railway, were put to death on Bolshevik orders in July 1918 to prevent any of them acting as figureheads for the anti-Bolshevik White armies. The collapse of Russia in 1917 and the subsequent turmoil of the revolution had tragic consequences, not just for the Romanovs, but for the entire Russian people.

SUMMARY QUESTIONS

1 What strategic problems did the Russian Empire face in the First World War?

2 What were Russia's military strengths and weaknesses in the First World War?

3 What impact did the First World War have on the Russian economy and on Russian society, 1914 to March 1917?

4 What impact did the First World War have on Russian politics, 1914 to March 1917?

5 Why was the tsarist government overthrown in February/March 1917?

AS ASSESSMENT

This section offers examples of the main types of source-based and essay questions used by examiners at AS level and guidance on how best to answer them.

SOURCE-BASED QUESTIONS

Comprehension of sources

When considering historical sources it is necessary to bear in mind four key questions.

1 **Who?** Who is the author of the source? Is it a historian (and from which school of thought), a politician, a factory owner, a nobleman, a member of the intelligentsia, a worker or a peasant? The background of the author may affect the style and content of the source. It is important to consider the values and attitudes of the author as these may be reflected in the source.

2 **What?** What does the source tell us? What is the content of the source? Does it ignore or neglect certain aspects? What it does not say can also be important. It is always worth thinking about the overall message. The rest of the content may well be the development of one basic point. It is also useful to consider the style, language and tone of the source, as this often helps you to 'read between the lines' of what is being stated.

3 **When?** When was the source produced? Accounts produced at the time of the event have the advantage of immediacy; accounts written later have the advantage of hindsight. The fact that the author was an eyewitness can give the source considerable value.

4 **Why?** Why was the source produced? What is its purpose? Is it propaganda? What is the motive of the author?

By considering these four basic questions you will be able to address wider issues about the usefulness, reliability and value of the sources you are studying. This will enable you to comprehend the source in full.

Many questions involving sources will revolve around these considerations. Some questions may test your skills of comprehension by asking you to explain words or phrases in the context of the source. Other questions could ask you to explain the content and message of the source in a more developed manner; this type of question will require close reference to the source(s). This technique usually involves direct quotation of short phrases to support points you make.

Remember that source-based questions are designed to test your skills as a historian in understanding and using sources and that this is what you need to show in your answer.

SOURCES EXERCISES IN THE STYLE OF AQA

Although there are slight differences in 'house style' between the most popular exam boards (AQA, Edexcel and OCR), mainly in the number and/or length of sources each board uses, the types of question that all three set are very similar.

NICHOLAS II AND POLITICAL REFORM

Study the following source material, then answer the questions that follow.

These questions invite you to consider Nicholas II and his policies in the context of other factors – economic tensions, social backwardness, radical opposition – which contributed to Russia's halting political modernisation during his reign. Better answers will appreciate the importance of the two wars in 1904–5 and 1914–18 in exacerbating political instability.

Source A
I know that recently, in *zemstvo* assemblies, voices have been heard, carried away by senseless dreams about the participation of *zemstvo* representatives in government affairs. Let everyone know that, devoting all my strength to the good of my people, I will preserve the principles of autocracy as firmly and undeviatingly as did my unforgettable late father.

Adapted from Nicholas II's speech to *duma* representatives, January 1895.

Source B
We impose upon the government the duty to execute Our inflexible will:

1 To grant the population freedom of conscience, speech, assemblies and associations.

2 To admit in the participation of the *duma* all those classes of the population which presently are completely deprived of voting rights.

3 To establish as an unbreakable rule that no law shall become effective without the confirmation by the State *Duma*, and that the elected representatives of the people shall be guaranteed an opportunity of real participation in the supervision of the legality of the acts by Our government.

Adapted from the October Manifesto, October 1905.

Source C

'Criticism will come from the so-called educated element, from the workers and the middle classes. But I am convinced that 80 per cent of the Russian people will be with me' (Nicholas II, April 1906).

The Emperor's faith that 80 per cent of the population was on his side reflected his faith that Russian peasants were monarchists at heart and were uninterested in political democracy or constitutions … And he was not wrong in thinking that elements of traditional Russian political thinking were still deeply embedded in the Russian people's mentality.

Adapted from *Nicholas II*, by D. Lieven, 1994.

Questions

1 Study Source A. Using your own knowledge, explain briefly what was meant by the term '*zemstvo* assemblies'. (3)

2 Study Sources A and B and use your own knowledge. With reference to your own knowledge, explain why Nicholas II's views on public participation in government in Source B had changed from those he had expressed in Source A. (7)

How to answer this question. Candidates need to emphasise the dramatically different contexts of the two sources: the relative calm of Russia in 1894–5 as opposed to the violent upheavals of 1905. Nicholas's own political convictions are also relevant here.

3 Study Sources A, B and C and use your own knowledge. 'Nicholas II's political convictions were a major obstacle to Russia's political modernisation, 1894–March 1917.' Explain why you agree or disagree with this statement. (15)

How to answer this question. This question carries the greatest number of marks. Again, a balanced approach is essential. As well as revisiting and perhaps expanding on points from the sources that have already been made, candidates have the opportunity to consider the sources as a set, as well as individually. It is important that own knowledge should be used to complement the sources, so that source analysis remains the primary focal point of the answer. Candidates should also strive to structure their answers and provide a considered judgement as a conclusion.

THE PEASANTRY, 1848–1906

Study the following source material, then answer the questions that follow.

These questions invite you to consider the debate on the peasantry. Did the peasants pose a major threat to the regime or not? How dangerous to the regime were the peasants before and after emancipation? Did the autocracy need the peasants to remain uneducated in order for it to survive? What was the impact of the rural population explosion after emancipation? The questions give much scope for argument with sources that can be used to support a wide spectrum of interpretations.

Source A

For almost two hundred years his [the peasant's] whole life has been one dumb, long, passive opposition to the existing order of things: he has endured oppression, he has groaned under it: but he has never accepted anything that goes on outside the life of the rural commune.

The idea of the Tsar still enjoys some considerable prestige in the mind of the peasant. But it is not the actual Tsar Nicholas whom he adores, it is rather an abstract idea, a myth, a kind of Providence, an Avenger of evils, an embodiment of justice in the popular imagination.

Adapted from *The Russian People and Socialism*, by A. Herzen, 1851.

Source B

Some dog-like desire to please the strong ones in the village took possession of them, and then it disgusted me to look at them. They would howl wildly at each other, ready for a fight – and they would fight, over any trifle. At these moments they were terrifying and they seemed capable of destroying the very church where only the previous evening they had gathered humbly and submissively, like sheep in a fold.

From *My Universities*, by M. Gorky, 1908.

Source C

I went from village to village, nobody interfering with me. I went into their huts, I talked to them and felt at my ease among them. There were hardships and I saw penury too, of a kind I had never imagined to exist but there was also kindness, magnanimity and an unbreakable faith in God. As I saw it, those peasants were rich for all their poverty, and I had a sense of being a genuine human being when I was amongst them.

Nicholas II's sister, the Grand Duchess Olga visiting peasants on her husband's estate, quoted in *Nicholas II*, by D. Lieven, 1994.

Questions

1 Study Source A. Using your own knowledge, explain briefly what was meant by the term 'tsar'. (3)

How to answer this question. This question is testing your understanding of a specific term. Examiners would be looking for a clear definition of 'tsar', ideally to show the importance of the term in the context of the source.

2 Study Sources A and B and use your own knowledge. Explain the impact of the emancipation of the serfs (1861) on the life of the peasantry. (7)

How to answer this question. This question is asking you to draw from two sources and your own supporting knowledge in analysing an historical development. Answers would be expected to make explicit reference to both sources and to balance this with appropriate, carefully selected, own knowledge. It is important that you do not neglect the sources, using the question merely as a prompt for the deployment of extensive own knowledge. A balanced approach is the key to success. Although not always explicit in the question, an element of comparison between the sources, briefly pointing out their similarities and differences, can be helpful. The two sources focus on the peasantry's collective outlook and behaviour before and after emancipation, offering scope for different interpretations, even that the emancipation had, in some respects, little impact on the peasants. Your own knowledge should highlight the economic and social impact of emancipation, notably the land redistribution arrangements.

3 Study Sources A, B and C and use your own knowledge. 'The Russian peasantry was a source of stability, not instability for the tsarist government, 1848–1906.' Explain why you agree or disagree with this statement. (15)

ESSAY QUESTIONS

As a history student you are required to produce extended answers in the form of essays. At AS level these will be structured essays, often broken down into two parts. These questions are designed to test your ability to understand historical issues and use information to support your views in the form of an argument.

When you are asked to write an essay, it is worth remembering that this is the standard way of getting you to show your historical understanding and ability to present an argument. Essay-writing is rather like producing a report in that it is essential to organise material in a logical sequence. In order to ensure that this is done effectively, it is important to be aware of the demands of the question. You ignore the question at your peril!

If you spend some time thinking about the question and planning your answer you will save time later. This will also ensure that time is not wasted writing an inappropriate and irrelevant essay. Deconstructing questions is a good starting point for planning. The rest of your planning should indicate the direction your answer should take, breaking your answer into paragraphs to ensure clarity of organisation and coming to a conclusion that directly answers the question set. At AS level time for essays, and therefore essay planning, is necessarily short, so your plan may only consist of a few key words, pointing to the subject matter and the order of your paragraphs.

One of the most common reasons for underperforming in exams is the failure to

---

How to deconstruct a question

Break the question down into its constituent parts. Look for the following.

- The **instruction** (I) – for example, 'examine', 'assess'.
- The **topic** (T) – for example, the emancipation of the serfs, the 1905 revolution.
- **Keywords** (KW), which need to be focused on your answer.

Example question
What impact did the assassination of Alexander II have on Russian politics, 1881–1905?

I	=	'What'
T	=	Russian politics, 1881–1905
KW	=	'impact', 'assassination of Alexander II'

produce a relevant answer. By using this process you will be able to plan your essays to ensure that the specific question asked is directly addressed.

Types of structured essay questions in the style of OCR

Essay questions can be divided into various categories depending on the instruction given. It is useful to think about the demands of each type of question.

1 Cause/effect questions. These questions usually start with 'why' or 'what' – for example, 'Why was there a revolution in Russia in 1905?' For this type of question, a list of factors provides a useful starting point but there is the danger that each factor is described rather than assessed. Think about dividing the factors into those that are short-term (the conflicts in the universities, the strikes, peasant unrest and Russo–Japanese war) and those that are more fundamental (the conflict between maintaining the autocracy and modernising the economy) which lie behind the short-term factors. It is also essential to assess the relative importance of each factor. This will help you to develop an argument rather than just produce a list of relevant factors.

2 Discussion questions. These often appear as a statement followed by the word 'discuss' or the phrase 'Do you agree?' – for example, ' "The tsarist regime emerged from 1905 healthy and strong enough" (Trotsky). How far do you agree with this assessment of the tsarist regime in the period 1906–14?' To deal with this question effectively, you need to consider the evidence both for and against the statement. You also need to address the hidden question 'healthy and strong enough for what?' Was the regime strong enough to survive only in the short term without fundamental change or did it have the strength to reform so that another 1905 would be impossible?

3 Significance/importance questions. These questions often start with phrases such as 'assess', 'how far' or 'to what extent' – instructions that require you to weigh up the significance/importance of a given factor. Here's an example: 'Assess the contribution of Witte to the modernisation of Russia from 1861 to 1905.' These questions often look more specific than they actually are. So in order to assess the importance of Witte to the modernisation of Russia in this period, his contribution has to be compared with other individuals/factors – for example, the reforms of Alexander II and the economic reforms of Witte's predecessors, 1861–91.

4 Compare/contrast questions. These questions need to be approached with particular care. The key point is to ensure that the comparison/contrast runs right through the essay. For instance, if asked to compare and contrast Nicholas I and Alexander II as Russian rulers it is common for students to describe the achievements of each tsar in turn with no direct comparison until the conclusion. It is much better to think of headings under which they can be directly compared and contrasted – for example, political ideas, the circumstances (internal and external) of their reigns and their approach to the peasant problem.

Questions

1 Why was Russian government so conservative, 1881–1905?

Examiner's comments. This question requires knowledge of the 'shift to the right' in Russia after 1881 – for example, the significance of the assassination of Alexander II, the ideas of Pobedonostsev, the security crackdown of the Safeguard System, including stringent censorship and persecution of opposition groups, russification, the limitations on the *zemstva,* and the tight control of secondary schools and universities. However, answers also need to appreciate the rapid economic reform Russia underwent, especially after 1890, which in itself cannot be described as conservative. Better answers will provide detailed information and show an ability to comment on the importance of each factor. The highest level will be reserved for those answers that develop an overall argument supported by precise, detailed material.

2 To what extent can Nicholas II be held personally responsible for the collapse of the Russian monarchy?

Examiner's comments. This question is designed to assess your ability to weigh the significance of Nicholas II's approach to the role of tsar, his political decisions and their consequences as factors in the collapse of the Russian monarchy. Knowledge of the early part of his reign (before 1905), the impact of 1905, the constitutional monarchy (1906–14) and the impact of the First World War will be expected. Better answers will appreciate the contradictions inherent in combining economic modernisation with highly conservative politics and that, under the pressure of international competition and rivalry between the European great powers, Nicholas was faced with difficult choices. The best answers will develop these ideas in a sustained argument, fully appreciating the disastrous impact of the First World War, culminating in a reasoned judgement on 'to what extent'.

A2 SECTION: HISTORIOGRAPHY AND ANALYSIS

Introduction

This section combines the two principal elements that are required in a study of history at A2 level: an awareness of the historiography of (historical writing about) late-tsarist Russia and a capacity for extended analysis of historical issues. The A2 section is therefore divided into a section on historiography and an analytical section.

The section on historiography traces the development of historical writing about late-tsarist Russia, examining the impact of ideologies, politics and other factors on the formation of a number of 'schools' of historical writing.

The analytical section focuses on one overarching question:

Was the tsarist regime bound to fail in an age of rapid and profound modernisation?

To open up this question fully, it is broken down into a discussion of three main topics:

- **Reform in Russia**
- **Opposition in Russia**
- **The wider context.**

To give each of these topics an analytical focus, they are subdivided into a number of separate questions. In this way it is hoped that students will develop an analytical approach in formulating their own answers to the big questions of late-tsarist Russia, covering the key turning points – 1861 and Alexander II's reforms; 1881, Alexander II's assassination and the conservatism of Alexander III; 1905–6, the 'revolution'; 1914, the stability of the empire on the eve of war; 1914–18, the impact of the First World War – and the key factors – the impact of industrialisation, the impact of agrarian problems, the impact of opposition and the impact of strategic and military considerations.

SECTION 1

The historiography of late-tsarist Russia

The history of Russia from the mid-nineteenth century to the 1917 revolution has generated much debate and division. In October 1917 the Bolsheviks seized power, bringing with them a political philosophy (taken from Marx) that was based on a particular analysis of history. Hence, historical writing about the origins of the 1917 revolution became highly politicised in the immediate aftermath of the revolution, and remained so to the end of the Soviet regime in 1991 and beyond. This gave birth to a number of identifiable and often radically differing approaches to Russian history, which are explained in the text that follows.

SCHOOLS OF HISTORIOGRAHY

Two main schools of historical writing have emerged: the Soviet school, and the anti-Soviet western school, usually called the 'Liberal' school. In *Rethinking the Russian Revolution* (1990), Edward Acton also identifies a 'Libertarian' school and a 'Revisionist' school.

Since the collapse of the Soviet system in 1991, labelling historians as belonging to 'schools' has become increasingly difficult. The Soviet school has largely become a thing of the past, as has the Libertarian school. Their demise has also affected the Liberal school, weakening its ideological purpose. The result is the emergence of historical writing that draws on the strengths of all the earlier historical schools and most particularly on the revisionists.

Definitions of schools

Soviet. The 'politically correct' Soviet version of Russian history, written not only to conform to the rules of Marxism-Leninism, but also to project the particular version of Marxism-Leninism popular with the Soviet leaders of the day, be they Lenin, Stalin, Khrushchev or Brezhnev.

Liberal. The anti-Soviet version of Russian history that defended 'liberal' values (the rights of the individual) and saw the Russian revolution as an unfortunate accident. 'Liberal' ideology was not as rigid or all-embracing as Marxism-Leninism. There is, therefore, much diversity among western 'Liberal' historians.

Libertarian. The alternative left-wing view of Russian history that derived from **Trotsky**'s historical works. The Libertarian school comprised

KEY PERSON

Trotsky as historian
Throughout his meteoric political career Trotsky continued to write. After his fall from power and exile (1927) writing became even more important to him. In 1933 he published *The History of the Russian Revolution*, a substantial, carefully researched work with a sharp appreciation of the failings of the tsarist regime, despite the obvious Marxist slant.

KEY CONSIDERATIONS REGARDING HISTORIOGRAPHY

- The Bolshevik regime lasted in one form or another until 1991, holding to its Marxist-Leninist beliefs throughout. These beliefs redefined world politics for over 70 years. With the exception of 1941–5, when Hitler's attack on the Soviet Union brought a shotgun marriage between the USSR and the western powers, Soviet communism caused deep division and hostility between Russia and the West. It is hardly surprising that historical writing on both sides reflects this division.
- This division was reinforced by the totalitarian nature of the Soviet regime. The bitterness caused by the civil war and allied intervention (1918–20) reinforced the 'us and them' mentality of Marxism-Leninism. This was followed by the Stalinist regime, which from 1929–53 aspired to total control of both the present and the past. In this atmosphere it was hardly likely that any scholars, least of all western scholars, would be given free access to Russian archives.
- Marxism and Marxism-Leninism were rooted in a particular analysis of history. The determinism inherent in Marxism-Leninism (the inevitability of key economic and social developments, leading to revolutions) meant that, for the ideologists of Soviet communism from the 1920s to the 1980s, history and the writing of history became an integral part of politics.
- Historical writing about the Russian revolution and its causes was complicated by the forced emigration to the west of Russian historians who could not follow the party line. These scholars naturally gave an anti-Soviet slant to western historical writing about Russia. Although many western historians took this line, there was none of the pressure to conform that affected their Soviet counterparts. Many western intellectuals of the 1930s had sympathy for the Soviet experiment and took exception to the blatantly anti-Soviet stance of the émigré Russians.
- Regardless of political persuasion and where they lived, all historians of Russia have suffered from a lack of reliable source material. After 1917 the politicisation of history, and especially of the history of Russia, deprived all historians of free access to original material in some form or other. More archival material was made available from the late 1950s, but only if it was not politically damaging to the Soviet regime. Since the collapse of the Soviet Union in 1991 this situation has been transformed. New material has substantially altered, and continues to alter, our perspectives on the revolution and its origins.
- Finally, all historians are influenced to some extent by their own personal beliefs, philosophy and culture. Historical investigation and writing is largely an individual pursuit and can be coloured by rivalries and partisanship which are often as much the product of personality and personal circumstances as of politics or historical philosophy.

western historians who reacted against the Liberal and Soviet schools in the 1950s and 1960s. They viewed the revolution favourably but lamented its perversion by Lenin and Stalin.

Revisionist. Western historians, interested in the 'grass roots' of the Russian revolution, who, after 1960, began to react against the ideological pre-conceptions and focus on the 'big events' and leaders that characterised the Soviet, Liberal and Libertarian schools.

Synthesis. After 1991, with a fresh perspective and fresh material, historians both in Russia and the West have taken a broader view of late-tsarist Russia, blending or synthesising elements of earlier schools of historiography.

HISTORIOGRAPHICAL SURVEY

This survey of the historiography of pre-1917 Russia is broken into four parts:
- pre-revolutionary Russian historical writing
- post-revolutionary Russian historical writing
- western historical writing before 1991, and
- western historical writing after 1991.

Leon Trotsky in jail – the Peter Paul Fortress in St Petersburg – in 1905–6.

PRE-REVOLUTIONARY RUSSIAN HISTORICAL WRITING

Before the revolution Russian historical writing was part of a wider European culture. The move away from a literary approach to historical writing towards one that was based on extensive, painstaking research was well established by the late-nineteenth century. Moreover, Russia's leading universities in Moscow and St Petersburg had developed their own schools of historical writing. The Moscow school was concerned with historical theories, explaining the 'broad sweep' of history. The St Petersburg school adopted a precise, more narrowly focused approach. However, to speak of 'schools' of historical writing can be misleading. What made the most impact was the history written by a few outstanding individual scholars.

Vasily O. Klyuchevsky (1841–1911)

The pre-eminent historian of Russia before the revolution was Vasily O. Klyuchevsky. The durability of a number of **Klyuchevsky's works** and his fame in his own time mark him out as one of the great historians of the nineteenth century. Klyuchevsky was Professor of History at Moscow University from 1879 to 1910. He showed an uncompromising insistence on factual evidence. His lectures in Moscow regularly drew audiences of up to 4000. Contemporaries saw him as a cultural figure of similar stature to the novelist Leo Tolstoy.

Klyuchevsky was a hugely influential teacher and became the formative influence on the next generation of Russian historians, notably Pavel Miliukov, Alexander Kizevetter, Matvei Liubavsky and Iurii Gote. The leading historians of Russia at the time of the revolution, these men's lives were turned upside down by subsequent political turmoil.

Klyuchevsky is notable for his original approach to historical study, which in several ways anticipated the **Annales** school of French historians after the First World War. One of Klyuchevsky's most famous sentences, that 'the history of Russia is the history of a nation that colonises itself' encapsulates his innovation. He saw history as an interactive process of man with his environment rather than a linear process centred on politics. In stressing the importance of the environment and hence economic factors there is some overlap between Klyuchevsky and Marxism. However, Klyuchevsky specifically rejected the narrow determinism of Marx's historical analysis. His approach was more broadly positivist, concluding that the historical process was one of constant change in the general direction of improving the lot of the people at large and reducing social inequality. Politically, therefore, Klyuchevsky was a liberal.

Pavel Miliukov (1859–1943)

The political activities of Pavel Miliukov have already been mentioned.

KEY CONCEPT

Klyuchevsky's works Most notable are his *Course of Russian History*, which rapidly sold out its 250,000 copies when reprinted in Russia in 1987–8, and his monograph on Peter the Great.

KEY TERM

Annales An influential school of French historians who moved away from political and military history to adopt a broader approach, stressing geography and social phenomena.

However, before he entered politics, Miliukov was already a distinguished historian, a professor at Moscow university in the late nineteenth century and the author of *Sketches of Russian History* (1895). In the same year as *Sketches* was published, Miliukov was expelled from Moscow University for his liberal political views. He was another **positivist** who, more easily than Klyuchevsky, can be considered a member of the **'statist'** school.

The history written by men such as Klyuchevsky and Miliukov focused primarily on pre-nineteenth century Russia. However, they were very much aware of the dramatic changes that Russia was experiencing in the late-nineteenth and early-twentieth centuries, and of the implications that these changes had for the future.

Miliukov was leader of the Kadet party after 1905 and Foreign Minister of the first Provisional Government from March to May 1917. He became more of a politician than a historian. Swept from office by the street politics of May 1917, he was a marked man after the Bolsheviks seized power in October, and fled to the west.

In 1921–4 Miliukov published his study of the 1917 revolution, *A History of the Second Russian Revolution*. The destruction unleashed by the revolution did not sit easily with Miliukov's positivism. Like many liberals, he explained the revolution as the product of freak circumstances and poor leadership during the First World War. This did not endear him to the Bolshevik leadership, nor to Russian monarchists. In Berlin in 1922 Miliukov was the intended target of Russian monarchist assassins and was saved only by the self-sacrifice of his Kadet colleague Vladimir Nabokov (father of the writer of the same name), who threw himself in front of Miliukov and was killed.

Miliukov continued his academic work in Paris and America, reworking *Sketches*, which was published in a revised edition in 1930. He held to the liberal line that the Bolshevik regime was an aberration and that Russia would return to a more 'normal', western path of development. This view was naturally shared by Miliukov's fellow exiles (such as Kizevetter). However, it became increasingly unfashionable as the Bolshevik regime proceeded to launch a social and economic revolution after 1928 to recast Russia in a Bolshevik-Stalinist image and to create what appeared to be a new society and culture.

Alexander Kizevetter (1866–1933)

Like Miliukov, Alexander Kizevetter was a pupil of Klyuchevsky and in many ways was his natural successor. Kizevetter took over the history department of Moscow University from Klyuchevsky in 1910, and shared his mentor's scholarly and rhetorical gifts.

KEY TERMS

Sketches of Russian History In this book, Miliukov expanded on Klyuchevsky to analyse the rise of Russia from the beleaguered petty states of the tenth to thirteenth centuries to its European great power status of the 1890s.

Positivist Someone who investigates only positive facts or observable phenomena, abandoning 'ultimate', speculative explanations.

'Statist' Those historians of Russia who considered the role of the state the vital ingredient in Russia's progress.

Although he was also involved in liberal politics (having been a Kadet deputy to the Second *duma* in 1907), Kizevetter did not leave Russia immediately the Bolsheviks seized power, but remained at his post in Moscow. As Bolshevik politics began to bite, Kizevetter was arrested three times between 1918 and 1921, banned from Moscow university in 1920 as a 'bourgeois historian' and forced into emigration in 1922 after Lenin's attack on the pre-revolutionary liberal intelligentsia, which soon resulted in 100 forced expulsions. Kizevetter, whose most important works concerned eighteenth-century Russia, spent the rest of his life in one of the main centres for Russian émigrés, Prague.

POST-REVOLUTIONARY RUSSIAN HISTORICAL WRITING

The Bolshevik seizure of power in October 1917 had an immediate impact on intellectual life in Russia. Within days the Bolsheviks had outlawed the Kadet party and introduced harsh press restrictions. Within months Russia was plunged into a civil war with strong overtones of a class war in which the standard term of abuse levelled by the lower classes at the upper, or educated, classes was *burzhooi* or 'bourgeois'. Moreover, the regime soon took steps to assert its intellectual 'legitimacy', especially in historical terms.

Clearly any Russian historians who were anti-Bolshevik and politically active had to leave, as did Miliukov, Kizevetter and, of the next generation, Mikhail Florinsky and Mikhail Karpovich. Those who stayed had a simple choice to follow the Bolshevik line and initiate a revolution in historical studies to match the political revolution that had taken place or to remain apolitical and hope for a measure of tolerance after the crises of revolution and civil war had passed. Historians in the first category were led by the redoubtable Mikhail Pokrovsky, arguably the most influential of all Soviet historians. A number of prominent historians of the Moscow school (for example, S.F. Platonov) and the St Petersburg school (for example, E. Tarle) may be placed in the second category.

Mikhail Pokrovsky (1868–1932)
Mikhail Pokrovsky wrote widely about pre-revolutionary Russia. He transformed the profession of university history teaching and historical writing in the period 1917 to 1932. A student at Moscow University before the revolution, he had the misfortune to have his doctoral thesis failed by Klyuchevsky himself. This may have been a factor in Pokrovsky's speedy conversion to Bolshevism in 1905 and the vendettas he conducted against the likes of Kizevetter, Platonov (1860–1933) and Tarle (1874–1955).

Mikhail Pokrovsky.

KEY EVENT

Academic Affair, or Affair No. 1803
The Academic Affair was one of the series of show-trials. In the Affair, the attacks by Pokrovsky on the likes of Platonov and Tarle were supplemented by primitive 'bugging' by the secret police, the use of informants and blatant falsification and invention of documentary evidence. Although the trial in 1930 was a farce, the sentences were not. Six academics were condemned to death, although their sentences were subsequently commuted to hard labour and exile. Additionally, the historical profession was purged of all prominent historians who did not toe the Pokrovsky line. The Academic Affair was a piece of exemplary 'justice'. Its main purpose was to scare academics into obsequiousness. In this it was predictably effective.

Pokrovsky became a prime influence in Bolshevik education policy, working as Deputy Commissar for Education from May 1918 until his death. He took on the task of transplanting Bolshevik/communist ideals into the study of history and historical writing. He applied to history and historians what politicians like Lenin, Trotsky and Bukharin were advocating for society as a whole. Put simply, he was attempting to bring about a Bolshevik revolution in historical studies and historical writing. He was also inflating the importance of his profession. According to Marxist-Leninist dogma, the 1917 revolution had come about as a result of inevitable historical processes. These historical processes and their 'correct' analysis 'legitimised' the new regime. So in a sense Pokrovsky could claim that historical writing was now of supreme political significance for a regime that had no traditional (religious or cultural) claim to power.

Pokrovsky and his followers set the tone for the rest of the Soviet era (to 1991), even though their particular approach was modified shortly after Pokrovsky's death in 1932.

Pokrovsky's victims

S.F. Platonov. Having been a tutor to the Russian royal family, S.F. Platonov was never going to find life easy under the Bolsheviks. He was denounced by Pokrovsky as 'a well-bred historian', to whom 'the door to the Cheka [the Bolshevik secret police] must always be left hospitably open'. Platonov was implicated in the **Academic Affair** of

1930, imprisoned for eighteen months, then exiled. He died in exile in Samara in 1933.

Tarle. Tarle, whose most famous work analysed the Napoleonic invasion of 1812, similarly fell foul of the prevailing orthodoxy. His apolitical stance drew him into supplementing his work at St Petersburg University with informal gatherings of like-minded university teachers and students. These soon became objects of suspicion. Tarle was also victimised in the Academic Affair and sent into exile. However, in the change of political climate after 1934, he was allowed to return to his work and even to complete and publish his study *The Year 1812* in 1937.

With the outcome of the Academic Affair, Pokrovsky had triumphed. He had brought about his 'revolution' in the historical profession. However, this was not just a personal achievement. It was a triumph for the state and its ideology. After 1930 non-ideological historical writing in Russia was practically impossible. The historical profession had to follow the dictates of the leadership or suffer the consequences.

The impact of Stalin

Pokrovsky died in 1932. Repellent though the consequences of his ideas and actions may have been, most commentators concede that he really believed in the necessity of his revolutionary crusade. Pokrovsky had shown sharp political intuition in the 1920s, backing Stalin's 'Socialism in One Country' slogan, even though it contradicted his own work on the historical origins of international revolution. However, in 1931 he lost his touch.

Stalin, now the supreme leader, published a letter in October 1931 entitled 'About Certain Questions in the History of Bolshevism' as part of his continuing feud with the now exiled Trotsky. In this letter Stalin attacked an article by a member of Pokrovsky's group and began to advance his own views on the importance of Russia's past in explaining the revolution – the past was no longer simply 'accursed'.

In 1934 Pokrovsky's victim Tarle was rehabilitated. Two years later a group of historians was given the task of producing a new official history of the Russian revolution and its causes: *The History of All-Russian Communist Party (Bolshevik), A Short Course* usually known as **The Short Course**.

The impact of Stalin was complex and highly personal. To summarise Alekseeva, one or two individual historians were given considerable personal licence and, providing they kept well away from the revolution, did not have to write 'political' history. Tarle's work on 1812 was a case in point. Others did his bidding – for instance, one of the authors of

---

KEY TEXT

The Short Course
Arguably the most influential single historical text about the late-tsarist and revolutionary period produced in the Soviet era. It merits this status because it established a Marxist-Leninist interpretation of the pre-revolutionary era, which although modified (notably after 1956) held currency until the 1980s. Its main thrust was to establish the links between tsarist industrialisation and the revolution, so that the revolution could be seen to be 'inevitable'; deny any importance to the progressive reforms of tsarist statesmen such as Stolypin; deify Lenin; demonstrate the direct link between Lenin and Stalin, showing that Stalin's radical policies after 1928 were 'Leninist'; remove Trotsky and all other 'Old Bolsheviks' from Russian history, and denounce all non-Stalinist groupings within the party. It praised the efforts at state-building and power of the early Russian tsars.

The historiography of late tsarist Russia

The Short Course (I.I. Mints). Of the remainder, several simply disappeared.

A change of attitude towards history

It was clear that by 1938 a major change in the regime's attitude to history and historical writing had occurred. In 1937–8 Pokrovsky, at the height of the Great Purge, was denounced as 'anti-Russian and pro-fascist'. Instead of Pokrovsky's revolutionary approach to history, more traditional, scholarly methods were encouraged. In particular, national history was restored to its former importance, notably after 1941 and the outbreak of the Great Patriotic War.

Stalin's own views were reinforced by the social changes he had initiated – particularly the much higher levels of education in the country at large. The 'Genius of all times' (a widely used epithet coined by Stalin's admirers) now wanted to give all Soviet citizens pride in a common heritage.

After Stalin, 'the thaw'

The formative period in Soviet historical studies ended around 1938. Thereafter, in the post-war Stalin period and the post-Stalin period to the 1980s, the guidelines for Soviet historians remained essentially the same, although there were two instances when bids for greater freedom were made. The first came in 1955, two years after Stalin's death. The release of some two million political prisoners in these two years clearly signified a change of climate and Soviet historians were among the first to test the water.

Questions of History

The vehicle for a freer approach to historical writing was the journal *Questions of History*. In 1955–6 *Questions of History* published a re-interpretation of the 1905 revolution and then of Stalin's role in 1917. Although Khrushchev had attacked Stalin's 'cult of personality' in his secret speech to the 20th Party Congress in March 1956, *Questions of History* was accused in 1957 of a 'revision of Leninism'. The offending editors were purged.

Political limits of historical investigation

Soviet historical studies under Khrushchev reflected the politics of the leader, just as they had under Stalin. This meant inconsistency. The *Questions of History* conflict determined the political limits of historical investigation. Revisions to *The Short Course* under Khrushchev simply removed Stalin from the story, making Lenin's role even greater. However, much more documentary material was made available in the late 1950s, even if it was politically one-sided. Restrictions on subject-matter for historians to explore became less stringent. There was, in the words of Sidorova, 'a sanctioned freedom'.

The period of stagnation

The demise of Khrushchev in 1964 led to the period of stagnation (*zastoi*) under Leonid Brezhnev and his colleagues. This lasted until Mikhail Gorbachev in 1985. All of the leaders before Gorbachev had made their careers in Stalin's party. They were glad to be rid of Khrushchev's unpredictable and often ill-considered experiments. What ensued, therefore, was a period of stability, often described as **neo-Stalinism**. For historians this meant a new and confusing orthodoxy. Stalin remained a shadowy figure in successive editions of B. Ponamarev's *History of the Communist Party of the Soviet Union* (1960), but his economic achievements were praised. To supplement the deification of Lenin, great stress was put on the sacrifice and heroism of the Soviet people in Peter Tsouras' *The Great Patriotic War*.

> **KEY TERM**
>
> **Neo-Stalinism**
> Stalinism shorn of its extremity of brutality and terror, but just as monolithic and inflexible.

In the 1970s a group of 'new direction' historians who tried to modify the orthodoxy about Lenin were swiftly punished. So were historians who tried to draw on a greater variety of Marxist historical writing, including the work of Trotsky and Bukharin. The academician F.V. Konstantinov denounced such approaches in an article entitled 'Subjectivism in Historical Writing'. It is hard not to conclude that Soviet historical writing was unavoidably sterile from the point at which a Stalinist orthodoxy was established in the late 1930s, because it was an essential part of the ideology that underpinned the Soviet state.

Conclusion

The impact of the Russian revolution on subsequent Russian historical writing is aptly summarised by Alekseeva:

> The 'virus' of serving the party, the state and the leadership squeezed out all other motives and objectives of academic endeavour and altered relationships between the academics themselves, how they regarded themselves and each other. The prestige of learning and sophistication, hard work, impartiality, mutual support and mutual help, which had marked out Russian academics hitherto, disappeared. The appearance of academics driven by different motives and concepts, alien to academic values, was bound to give rise to a struggle for position characterised by enmity, denunciation, envy, intrigue, treachery on the part of teachers and students, cynicism, disregard and conformism. All of this flourished from the 1930s to the 1980s . . .
> (Source: Alekseeva, 1971).

WESTERN HISTORICAL WRITING BEFORE 1991

Western historical writing on pre-revolutionary Russia was also strongly coloured by politics. However, in the West, this was within the context of an essentially liberal, free-thinking consensus of academic and intellectual activity, quite different from the situation in Russia after 1917.

Émigré Russian historians were an important formative influence on western historical writing about Russia. Major figures like Miliukov and Kizevetter fitted in easily with the prevailing western liberal consensus. They helped to popularise the Kadet view of pre-revolutionary Russia and the causes of its revolution. Their positive view of late-tsarist Russia contrasted attractively with tales of the brutality and chaos of the revolution told by other émigrés and popularised in the western press, particularly on the right.

In France, Britain and the USA right-wing or centre-right parties dominated politics. Their beliefs and message were defined by a hostility to Bolshevism. In such a climate the views of the younger generation of émigré historians like **Mikhail Florinsky** had an obvious resonance.

Changing perspective on the revolution

The next development in western historiography of late-tsarist Russia emerged naturally from a changing perspective on the Russian revolution, largely owing to three factors:

- the economic progress the Russian revolution seemed to be making under Stalin
- the contrast this formed with the economic catastrophe visited upon the West in the form of the Great Depression, and
- the emergence of a violently anti-communist Nazi Germany.

This new perspective on Russia encouraged what might be termed a non-dogmatic Marxism among western historians. It seemed, according to Bernard Shaw and other famous western intellectuals, that the Stalinist Soviet regime had 'all the answers', it really did represent the future, and it was a much more attractive alternative to the tribal militarism of Nazism. Hence a reappraisal of the liberal interpretation of the revolutionary and pre-revolutionary period seemed in order.

E.H. Carr

The British historian E.H. Carr exemplified this approach in his authoritative history *The Bolshevik Revolution* (1950). Carr was limited in his source material by the Soviet 'filter', so his views of Lenin and his party correspond in some particulars to Soviet orthodoxy. But his was not a 'closed' interpretation. He gave due weight to Trotsky before and during the revolution. He also conceded that Russia was making economic progress before the war. However, he mediated between the Soviet Marxist and liberal positivist views, stressing the continuity of the revolutionary process in Russia from 1905 to 1917 and playing down the accidental impact of the First World War. He placed Leninist doctrine and socio-political developments at the centre of his interpretation, rather than the actions of individuals or random events. This, and his

KEY PERSON

Mikhail Florinsky His work *The End of the Russian Empire* (1931) reinforced the liberal, positivist views of Miliukov.

conclusion that (on the whole) the Russian revolution represented progress, testifies to the influence of a modified, more flexible Marxist thinking in his work.

Schools of writing in the West

From the 1960s to the 1980s three schools of Russian historical writing developed in the West – the Liberal school, the Libertarian school, and the Revisionist school.

American historians like Adam B. Ulam in his *Lenin and the Bolsheviks* (1969) and Richard Pipes in *The Russian Revolution, 1899–1919* (1990) picked on Lenin's pragmatic re-working of Marxism and tactical opportunism as reasons for Bolshevik success in October 1917. Thus, they played down any continuity with Bolshevik activity before 1914 and essentially reinforced the liberal/positivist view of the revolution of 1917 as a catastrophic accident, brilliantly exploited by Lenin. 'Revisionist' historians from the 1960s concentrated on trying to establish what ordinary Russians, peasants and workers were really like. They were free of the dogma of Marxist interpretation and often concentrated on smaller groups in a particular locality – microhistory.

The microhistorical approach opened up a different avenue. It looked at the behaviour, attitudes and allegiances of specific groups of workers from richer archival material released in the 1970s and 1980s. This was first explored by Soviet historians, but was subsequently available for less dogmatic interpretation in the West. Works by historians such as Evan Mawdsley on workers and sailors and Teodor Shanin on peasants opened up the sheer complexity and confusion of the Russian Empire in the 1900–17 period with numerous regional and local variations, including the non-Russian nationalities.

The overall impact of the study of the diversity of the Russian Empire in this period has been to suggest that the revolutionary parties really were popular in certain closely defined areas. It suggests that these parties naturally possessed the class attitudes that Lenin and other leaders attributed to them. Therefore, revolution was popular – if only with a significant minority.

WESTERN HISTORICAL WRITING AFTER 1985

Gorbachev's *glasnost* after 1985 ushered in a historical revolution in the Soviet Union. Inevitably, this had a major impact on western historiography. Two crucial changes ensued. Soviet historians were encouraged to look to new historical models, and *glasnost* unleashed a spirit of critical enquiry, which demanded that Soviet archives be opened up.

Soviet historians were encouraged to look to new historical models after Gorbachev had declared the Stalinist and neo-Stalinist inheritance bankrupt. At first this resulted in a search for a more liberal version of the revolution, on the assumption that Lenin would not have countenanced Stalinism. However, events soon overtook Gorbachev. His liberalism encouraged the re-evaluation of the whole of the Soviet past, including Lenin. In his quest to fill the 'blank pages' of Soviet and Russian history, Gorbachev had unravelled the entire ideological basis of the Soviet system, with enormous consequences for historians. By implementing *glasnost* he unleashed a spirit of critical enquiry, which demanded that Soviet archives be opened up. Although this has yet to happen in its entirety, by the 1990s enough new material had emerged, revolutionising historical writing, especially in the former Soviet Union.

Revelations about the past accompanied widespread destruction of the historical iconography of the Soviet regime. Statues of leaders, city and street names were removed or replaced. This naturally led to a resurrection of pre-revolutionary symbols, seen most obviously in the changing of the name of Leningrad back to St Petersburg.

A third consequence was the much freer exchange of historical debate that could now take place between former Soviet and western scholars. One of the most important Russian historians to take advantage of this new climate has been **Dmitrii Volkogonov**.

The position of Russian historians in the new climate

In the new climate of the 1990s Russian historians have found that the re-evaluation of the Soviet regime, and the importance of Russia's pre-Soviet past has, if anything, pushed them towards a more conservative stance than many western historians. To bear this out, there is:

- a new respect for tsarist Russia, exemplified by the new power and influence of the Orthodox Church
- the re-burial of the Romanov royal family and approving parallels being drawn between President Putin's policy in Chechnya, and the anti-minority, russification policies of Alexander III.

The work of Marc Raeff. The work of the Russo-American historian Marc Raeff (*Understanding Imperial Russia*, 1984) examines the cultural changes that were sweeping late-tsarist Russia by analysing sociological developments. He stresses the rising level of education of society as a whole and the evolution of what he terms a **'rooted' intelligentsia** as evidence of Russia's potential for stable evolution before 1914. The Russian revolutionary tradition, best exemplified by Lenin after 1905 was, Raeff argues, being marginalised.

KEY PERSON

Dmitrii Volkogonov His biographies of Lenin, Stalin and Trotsky were the first major works to use new archival material and to be free of an enforced Marxist-Leninist historical overview. His explanation of the collapse of the tsarist regime corresponds to the western consensus view: 'Ostensibly the Russian state collapsed suddenly, but its foundations had been eroded long before.' Even so, 'as for the war [1914–17], despite strategic failures, Russia's position was not hopeless'. The chief cause of the tsarist regime's collapse was, therefore, poor government during the war. In Volkogonov's words: 'The regime proved incapable of governing in a critical situation.' Volkogonov's view of Lenin stressed the Bolshevik leader's 'cynicism' and 'anti-patriotism', a far cry from Soviet eulogies.

> **KEY TERMS**
>
> **'Rooted' intelligentsia** A term used by American historian Marc Raeff to describe the educated class that worked within existing social structures, rather than working for their destruction.
>
> **Obshchestvennost** A sense of belonging to society that implies social awareness, education and a desire to get involved in public affairs. The growing *zemstvo* movement is a good example of this.

The work of Ronald Suny. Taking another cultural perspective, the American historian Ronald Suny emphasises the class divide that existed in pre-1914 Russia. This was not an economic class divide in the Marxist sense. It was a more generalised division of Russia based on contemporary attitudes, making a society divided between *nizi* ('lowers') and *verkhi* ('uppers'). Suny has also explored the nationality issue in late-tsarist Russia, emphasising how diverse the Russian Empire was and how inadequate Russo-centric interpretations of this period can be.

The work of Geoffrey Hosking. In Britain Geoffrey Hosking's survey *Imperial Russia, 1533–1917* (1997) takes a different, longer perspective on the evolution of the tsarist state. This includes its restless expansionism, consequent national diversity and sociological peculiarities (notably the persistence well into the twentieth century of the mentality and attitudes of the Russian peasant). Hosking stresses the importance of a long perspective on Russian history and the importance of Russian concepts like ***obshchestvennost***.

The work of Robert Service. Robert Service, whose main interest is in the post-1900 period (*A History of 20th Century Russia*, 1997), has brought together recent western and Russian scholarship. Service again emphasises the importance of Russian society as a force that was evolving and changing rapidly to its own rhythms and at its own speed. Service also stresses the Russian Empire's ethnic and social diversity. It was an empire that 'suffered as much from traditionalism as from modernity'. 'The peculiarity that it was primarily a supranational state' meant that 'loyalty to the tsar and his dynasty was the supreme requirement made by the Russian Empire'. Service concludes that such a state put an enormous premium on the quality of governance. Commenting on 'the decadence and idiocy of Nicholas II's court', which would have been less prominent and important had Nicholas conceded more power to the *duma*, Service asserts that 'some kind of revolutionary clash was practically inevitable'.

The work of Dominic Lieven. Service's harsh judgement on Nicholas II's politics is at odds, at least in tone, with Dominic Lieven's biography of the last tsar (*Nicholas II*, 1994). Lieven sees Nicholas II as dutiful, hard-working and well-meaning. He respects Nicholas II's belief, in the 1906–14 period, that the conservative approach made sense. Both Service and Lieven agree that Nicholas faced a gargantuan task in trying to pilot the Russian Empire through an age of modernisation in competition with Russia's great power rivals.

The work of Orlando Figes. The sheer complexity of Russia's evolution in the revolutionary period has been brilliantly conveyed in *A People's Tragedy* by Orlando Figes (1997). Figes points out that Russia was nothing if not contradictory in this period. In all classes, from peasants to

The historiography of late tsarist Russia

high civil servants and ministers, there were backward-looking and forward-looking elements. The outcome, the revolution of 1917, therefore had to be the result of many causes and pressures. The revolution itself meant very different things to different people.

CONCLUSIONS

Although this survey is unavoidably brief and selective, two conclusions may be drawn. The historiography of late-tsarist Russia has been hugely complicated by the success of Bolshevism in 1917 and its survival in one form or another until the late 1980s. By imposing strict ideological and political imperatives, Bolshevism distorted historical writing, with particular impact on the period 1848–1917. Moreover, Bolshevik success inevitably influenced the perspectives and views of historians writing in the west. The demise of Bolshevism after 1985 has accelerated an established western tendency in historical writing about Russia, as with other subjects, to broaden the canvas, the better to appreciate the sheer complexity and fluidity of Russia in the late-tsarist period.

SECTION 2

Reforming late-tsarist Russia

KEY QUESTIONS

- Was Nicholas I or Alexander II the more effective tsar?
- Were Alexander II's reforms too limited and contradictory to achieve their objectives?
- How effective were tsarist industrial reforms?
- How effective were tsarist agrarian reforms, 1848–1914?

WAS NICHOLAS I OR ALEXANDER II THE MORE EFFECTIVE TSAR?

This question highlights the central theme in Russian nineteenth-century history: was Russia's stability and progress better safeguarded by reactionary conservatism or controlled reform? Both tsars were aware of the underlying dilemma that either approach could lead to the demise of the Russian autocracy.

Reactionary conservatism. This brought with it the threat of backwardness, and the consequent threat of the Russian state compromising its great power status and external security.

Controlled reform. This approach risked a lurch into uncontrolled reform and the possibility of the autocrat losing power.

As a political idea, autocracy acknowledged no other source of earthly authority because it derived its authority from God alone. Therefore, if maintenance of the autocracy was top priority, it was illogical to entertain different political principles such as liberalism. In the longer term liberalism implied the end of autocracy. In the short term it ran the risk of the tsar losing control of the process of reform. Both tsars wrestled with these problems. Nicholas I favoured the more intellectually coherent, conservative approach. Alexander II tried a blend of the two. Judging who was the more effective is hard, because each was confronted with a very different set of circumstances. Furthermore, it is impossible to make a judgement based on the state of Russia at the time of their deaths because both tsars died in special circumstances – Nicholas I as Russia's failure in the Crimean War was becoming a near certainty, and Alexander II as the victim of a successful terrorist campaign.

In Alexander II's case one also has to consider the impact of his policies beyond 1881, as several of his reforms had important long-term effects that are relevant to this question. However, Nicholas I's particular brand of conservatism, denying economic as well as political reform, came to an end in 1855.

Serfdom and its abolition

Serfdom was the most difficult problem facing the Russian monarchy in this period. Fundamental to the economy, the social order and (the ruling classes thought) to the security of the state, it was unlikely to be eroded by economic and social change as it had been in the West. To remove it the state would have to intervene in what would be a fundamental reorientation of Russian society. The enormity of such a change does much to explain why it was so long in coming, although it did anticipate the end of slavery in the USA by four years.

Nicholas's views on serfdom. Nicholas's views were pragmatic rather than principled. Fearing social change and the consequent threat to order seen in revolutionary Europe in the early nineteenth century, he was reluctant to take a step into the unknown. Instead he skirted the fundamental issue of the emancipation of privately owned serfs by concentrating on the easier problem of freeing the 'state' peasants. This was completed in 1837. Committees set up in 1842, 1844 and 1846 to consider extending emancipation to the rest of the Russian peasantry show that, despite his reputation, Nicholas was prepared to countenance change. In fact, he can be credited with preparing the ground for the eventual acceptance of emancipation under Alexander II, not least because there was a direct correspondence of personnel (notably Nikolai Miliutin and the future Alexander II) between the committees of the 1840s and the eventual reforming team of the late 1850s.

Nicholas thought that the condition of the Russian state, compared to its continental European rivals caught up in the revolutionary turmoil of 1848, was healthy – especially in view of Russia's ability to project its power abroad (such as in Hungary in 1849). Nicholas did not live to witness the final debacle of the Crimean War. Had he done so, he would have been forced to consider the emancipation of the serfs as a more urgent priority.

Alexander's views on serfdom. Alexander II had to confront the Crimean debacle, proof of Russia's backwardness. He was, therefore, working in a different political climate. The process of leading Russia, and in particular the Russian nobility, to emancipation was nevertheless hedged by the same practical considerations that had existed in Nicholas's reign. How were the peasants to be kept under control? How was the nobility to be compensated? What should the land transfer arrangements be?

The first consideration had the most immediate impact. Whereas before 1855 serfdom appeared to have kept the peasants under control, after the Crimean War it seemed more likely to incite disorder. In considering the decision to emancipate, therefore, Alexander II's approach was founded on fundamental priorities that he shared with his father, but applied in different circumstances. Alexander II's emancipation statutes of 1861 reinforce this continuity. The 1861 statutes (see page 29) were essentially cautious and conservative. By handing over control of the pace of land transfer to the landowners the government guaranteed that the process would be slow, and that changes in Russian agrarian life would be controlled and evolutionary. This further emphasised continuity from Nicholas to Alexander, again preserving as far as possible the power of the state and the landowning nobility.

The success of emancipation. Emancipation was gradual. Serfs were 'temporarily bound' for ten years and redemption dues were stretched out over 49 years. With hindsight, this seems overly conservative. But it is hard to argue that the emancipation of the serfs had been anything other than successful from the perspective of 1881. Above all, considering the number of people involved (some 22 million families) and the unprecedented nature of the reform, emancipation went ahead with remarkably little social disruption. It was followed by 20 years of rising yields and improved efficiency. Finally, we must be aware of the state's financial limitations with regard to emancipation. Giving vast loans to the peasantry to speed up land transfer was quite unrealistic in the difficult financial conditions that followed the Crimean War.

The press, opposition and 'controlled' liberalism

The major differences between Nicholas I and Alexander II are not to be found in their attitude to serfdom, but elsewhere. One of the most obvious is censorship.

Nicholas and the press. Nicholas regarded the control of the press as essential to the security of the state. After 1848, in the era of the Buturlin committee (page 15), he took censorship to the limit. This persecution of writers and journalists did the tsarist autocracy no favours. For one thing, it did not work. Exiling opinion-formers like Alexander Herzen and Mikhail Bakunin only served to expose them to even more radical western ideas. It also encouraged them to set up free-thinking journals like *The Bell* to disseminate their ideas among Russian intellectuals who frequently travelled to the West. Within Russia the restrictions could be side-stepped by politicising the discussion of literature, a Russian tradition inaugurated in the 1840s by the critic Vissarion Belinsky.

Alexander and the press. When Alexander II began to free the press in 1855–8 this was naturally well received in journalistic and literary circles, but a tradition of lofty criticism from abroad had already been established

Reforming late tsarist Russia 177

by the alienating policies of Nicholas. Once the limitations of the emancipation statutes were known and Alexander's regime had responded repressively to peasant and student unrest, a return to hostile criticism of the regime on the part of the radical press was entirely predictable. The move towards revolutionary extremism was also a natural development.

Opposition, and control of the press. For revolutionary die-hards there was now the real possibility of a tsarist regime that could modernise successfully with its power structure more or less intact. This was the first of several instances when revolutionary theorists feared tsarist success more than tsarist failure (Lenin in 1914 fearing the success of Stolypin's agrarian reforms is another example). Even after 1866 and the appointment of Dmitrii Tolstoy the press was never as severely controlled as it had been under Nicholas, despite the fact that restrictions were much more justified in the more volatile political climate of Populism. To the radical intelligentsia Alexander's milder censorship made no difference. Revolutionary politics had generated its own destructive agenda based on confrontation and hostility. Therefore, it is hard to criticise Alexander II's treatment of the press. The root problem was the alienation of radical critics of tsarism under Nicholas I. By the 1860s this alienation, epitomised by the likes of Chernyshevsky (see pages 53–4), had become a tradition in itself and was a prime factor in the polarisation of Russian politics after 1861.

Alexander II and controlled liberalism. Controlled liberalism was applied more consistently and effectively in Alexander II's post-emancipation reforms. It can be argued that these reforms were simply necessitated by the abolition of serfdom and that any 'liberal' element was purely coincidental. However, in the case of the *zemstvo* (see pages 33–5) reform in particular, Alexander did have other (more traditional) options. But he chose to take a liberal path.

Given the political outlook of reformers like the Miliutins (see page 27), it seems that a genuine change of approach from the sterile politics of Nicholas I had taken place. All the 'liberal' reformers encouraged social mobility. This would make Russian society more capable of coping with its problems rather than relying (as had always been the case) on the state.

The reforms slowed after 1866. But this did not mean that the vision of a more flexible, independent society was abandoned. Rather, it meant that the essentials of what was always a limited reform programme had been achieved and that it was time for the state to exert some discipline to keep the process under control.

To see the assassination attempt of 1866 as the watershed of reform is rather too crude. There were many other changes of political climate in Alexander II's reign that would appear to indicate the regime was trying to find a way to give Russian society more freedom to encourage social and economic modernisation while remaining in control of the process.

The maintenance of autocracy

The underlying consistency between Nicholas I and Alexander II was the maintenance of the autocracy. Alexander II was vehement about not conceding political power, even though doing so was implicit in his reforms. If, as his judicial and *zemstvo* reforms indicated, he wished to create a western-style civil society in Russia, then some form of representative government (and hence the end of a pure autocracy) would have to be considered. However, in 1881 Alexander II modified his stance by approving the Loris-Melikov reforms, so a hard-and-fast assessment of his position is impossible.

Economic and social policies

Unquestionably, Alexander II's policies did have a much more invigorating effect on the Russian economy than those of his father. Economic stagnation under Nicholas I was unavoidable, given the rigidity of his social policies. It was certain that Russia would remain economically stagnant under serfdom. It was equally obvious that the economy would start to modernise and diversify much more quickly after 1861. Once again, the Crimean War is of paramount importance. Nicholas I was dedicated to the strength of the state and its military. It is hardly likely, therefore, that he would have allowed Russia to continue to stagnate after such a humiliating defeat. So with regard to the economy, there was a degree of political continuity between the two tsars. Any differences between them owe more to context than conviction.

Nationality and foreign policy

Continuity was even more evident in nationality and foreign policy. The maintenance of the unity of the Russian state and its role in Europe was arguably more important to tsars and tsarinas than domestic policy. Domestic policy only had pride of place when failure in foreign policy had revealed the state's internal weaknesses, as in 1856.

There is little to distinguish between the approaches of the two monarchs to the Polish rebellions in 1830–1 and 1863–4 or to the faint stirrings of Ukrainian nationalism in the 1840s and 1870s. Neither sought any constitutional compromise. Both reacted with swift repression and russification (see pages 61–6). That said, it could be argued that the Poles and Ukrainians were a special case. They were too much of a threat to the fabric of the Russian state to be allowed autonomy. In his policies towards the Finns, Alexander II was markedly more liberal than his father. In Transcaucasia and Asia both monarchs pursued policies of expansion and colonial imperialism, although opportunities for this were somewhat greater after 1856. Nicholas I and Alexander II both fought wars against the Turks for the same strategic reasons – to give Russia greater control of the Black Sea and to gain better access to the Mediterranean.

It is clear that Alexander II was much more successful than Nicholas. Having said that, he did make diplomatic mistakes (notably in the Treaty of San Stefano). However, the outcome of the Treaty of Berlin (see page 51) was a victory compared with the Treaty of Paris, in which Nicholas's diplomatic errors had resulted in Russia fighting Britain and France as well as Turkey.

WERE ALEXANDER II'S REFORMS TOO LIMITED AND CONTRADICTORY TO ACHIEVE THEIR OBJECTIVES?

The first difficulty in considering Alexander II's reforms is to decide exactly what their objectives were. The emancipation of the serfs conferred on Alexander the grandiose title 'Tsar-Liberator'. However, some contemporaries took Tsar-Liberator to imply that Alexander was a thorough-going liberal, rather than simply the tsar who had liberated the serfs.

There is little doubt that Alexander II's primary objectives were traditionally tsarist – to safeguard the state's (that is, the autocracy's) military capacity and security. This concern highlights the underlying problem of the relationship between state and society in Russia at this time.

In western and central Europe in the nineteenth-century interaction between state and society was more complex than in Russia. This was mainly because most social, economic and (ultimately) political change occurred independently of the mechanisms of government and administration. The latter, therefore, had to react and accommodate change, as in the Reform Act in Britain in 1832. Britain may have been the most economically advanced and socially complex society in the mid-nineteenth century. Nevertheless, social, economic and political change did occur independently of government and administration to some degree in all western and central European states. In Russia, however, change in this sense was conspicuous by its virtual absence.

The autocracy as agent of change

The Russian autocracy had established itself as the sole agent of change. The justification for this was that Russian peasant society was so backward that the only change it could make would be destructive. So the state had to take full responsibility for politics. Until the end of the eighteenth century, Russia's educated classes had also taken this view. This reinforced the unique power of the state, and although there were some dissenting voices from the 1790s, which led to the Decembrist revolt in 1825 and the birth of the intelligentsia under Nicholas I, many

Russian noblemen and state servants remained firm believers in the autocracy and the power of the state throughout Alexander II's reign and beyond. This idea is important because it explains why Alexander II's reforms appear limited and in some ways contradictory. They were enacted in a quite unusual political context, where politics operated according to a set of rules different from those customary in other European states at the time. In Russia it was necessary both for the state to initiate change and, if it saw fit, to call that change to an end.

The emancipation of the serfs

The emancipation of the serfs was a monumental reform. It was immediately appreciated as such by Russians of all classes and foreign observers. In other European countries serf emancipation took place as a consequence of organic social and economic change. It did not have to be forced through by the state and was not on such a vast scale. Thus, serf emancipation in Russia was monumental for two reasons: the immediate change it brought and its long-term potential. By emancipating the serfs, the tsarist regime consciously embraced social and economic modernisation, which (implicitly at least) it had resisted for so long.

The process of emancipation was as important as the statutes themselves in determining the impact and nature of social and economic change. Although the tsarist state had huge power in the essentials of control and political initiative, its power was seriously limited when it came to a wholesale structural change on this scale. First, it had to have the co-operation of the landowning class, without which the reform could not work. Hence the process of consultation in 1856–60. Second, the state's limited financial resources were a key factor in determining the terms of the emancipation settlement, particularly with regard to the land question. With the state indebted after the Crimean War, the process of emancipation would have to be self-financing if possible. The co-operation of the landowners was therefore essential.

The peasants' deal was not the worst that they might have had. In the early years of the emancipation process (1856–8) the idea of transferring any land to the peasants was viewed with alarm.

Criticism of the time it took to achieve emancipation

With hindsight we can criticise the emancipation process for being too slow. Following the two years it took to work out the local details of the settlement, the peasants were temporarily bound for ten years. This meant that the vital process of transferring the land was not fully operational until the reign of Alexander III. However, such criticism takes too short a perspective. It also ignores the practicalities.

- Serfdom had remained in force for centuries.
- Any previous reforms had tended to strengthen rather than weaken it.

Reforming late tsarist Russia

- The upheaval that emancipation was bound to cause required a period of calm to assess its impact and to ensure that the peasants did not indulge in *volya*.

This also explains the other conservative feature of the settlement, its reliance on the *mir* (see page 30) as the main unit of social and economic organisation. This was a logical decision, at least in the first instance. Having removed the power of the landowner, it was common sense to maintain as much of the pre-1861 order as possible.

Criticism of emancipation in halting agricultural progress

The next criticism of the terms of emancipation is that the retention of the commune halted agricultural progress. This explains the poor yields and subsequent agrarian problems that Russia suffered at the end of the century. This criticism is hard to accept unreservedly. Agricultural output was steadily improving in the 1860s and 1870s. So in the short term there was little cause to make fundamental changes to the system. Above all, emancipation and its aftermath had been successfully negotiated. Social peace had been improved and economic progress was discernible, although slow.

Strengths and weaknesses of emancipation

The utter failure of 'Going to the people' in 1873–4 shows just how passive the post-emancipation peasantry was. It is, therefore, reasonable to suggest that, from the perspective of 1881, the emancipation of the serfs was a major success for the tsarist regime.

The weaknesses of Russian agriculture, which can be traced to the emancipation settlement, only became apparent in the 1880s and 1890s when the social and economic climate for Russian agriculture was much less favourable (see pages 72–6). However, this change of climate is vital to the argument. A reform as complicated and difficult to enact as the emancipation of the serfs could not reasonably be expected to prove effective in a different, harsher social and economic climate. The fall in agricultural prices and rapid population growth after 1879 put a premium on efficiency and speedier land transfer, which emphasised the limitations of the 1861 settlement. These limitations could have been tackled more effectively under Alexander III. It is unfair to blame his predecessor.

Other major reforms

The rest of Alexander II's reform package is best explained in terms of the interests of the state.

Reform of the Judiciary. This was the product of a long-standing effort by the Russian state, begun under Alexander I, to modernise its legal practices, although certain details, such as verbatim reporting of cases, would have been inconceivable under Nicholas I. If the origins of the

> **KEY TERM**
>
> **Volya** A Russian word usually translated into English as 'will' or 'freedom'. It also carries the extra meaning of 'wilfulness' or 'abandon'. To a peasant volya meant acting without inhibition or control. The assassins of Alexander II called themselves Narodnaya Volya, or People's Will, to link themselves with this popular peasant concept.

reform were traditional, its effects were not. Setting up an independent judiciary and a court system staffed by full-time professionals who were not servants of the state showed that the autocracy was prepared to concede a basic civil liberty. The fact that subsequent trials of revolutionary defendants, notably the notorious Zasulich case in 1878, did not produce the verdict that the state would have hoped for was proof of the independence and competence of the system.

Although the judicial reforms of Alexander III seen in the Safeguard System (see pages 59–60) compromised the principles of the original judicial reform, we need to take account of the small number of political cases brought under the new regulations. The everyday work of the judiciary in civil and criminal cases unaffected by the new safeguard regulations were a major improvement on what had gone before. As is so often the case in late-tsarist history, the abuses of civil rights, serious though they were, tend to obscure the halting progress being made towards a civil society.

In general, western judicial principles and practices were well established by the turn of the century in Russia, so much so that the regime's abuses of the system were conspicuous. The role of lawyers in the constitutional politics of 1905–6 and in the outcome of the Beilis case (see page 122) is testimony to the legacy of Alexander II's reform of the Judiciary as an important contribution to Russia's social and political evolution.

The *zemstvo* reform. The *zemstvo* (pages 33–5) reform represented a similar departure from tsarist custom with the representative principle entering modern Russian politics for the first time. Like reform of the Judiciary, the *zemstva* took root and developed a political sub-culture of their own in the 1890s. Perhaps this was even more of a contradiction of normal tsarist politics than the reform of the Judiciary. But essentially it had the same aim – to find ways of stimulating the peaceful evolution of Russian society, so that the Russian state could safely negotiate the political dangers of modernisation. The usual criticism levelled against Alexander II is that he refused to take the principle of representative government further when he turned down appeals for a national *zemstvo* in 1865. However, this ignores the Loris-Melikov proposals of 1880 (see page 55), which the tsar took seriously. Naturally, Alexander II wished to defend the principle of autocracy, which had served the Russian state well. However, he did not see a necessary contradiction between this and the establishment of more vigorous consultative and representative bodies to enable the autocracy to function more efficiently, and to reduce its dependence on a monolithic bureaucracy and a declining nobility. Alexander had changed his position between 1865 and 1880 because of the underlying political weaknesses exposed by the activities of the Populists in the 1870s. The Populists' impact on the peasantry was negligible and did not concern the regime. What did, however, was the resonance they struck among a significant slice of Russia's propertied classes, the bulwark of the regime. In his support for the Loris-Melikov proposals, the tsar showed that he was genuinely prepared to co-operate politically in the further evolution of a civil society in Russia, the logical consequence of his earlier reforms.

Alexander II's aims in perspective. It is important to ensure that we take a realistic perspective on Alexander's aims. If we compare the most 'liberal' of Alexander's reforms – the judicial and *zemstvo* reforms – with 'liberal' institutional practice in Britain or France, it is easy to criticise them as half-hearted and contradictory. After all, how can we reconcile autocracy with representative government? However, the more influential model for the future development of the Russian state was Bismarck's (see page 61) Prussia/Germany. This state was successful in both economic and military terms in late-nineteenth century Europe. Yet it had managed to preserve the power of its monarchy and traditional élites.

Bismarck's system may have been somewhat contradictory, but it showed there was a way for conservative states like Russia to modernise without major political upheaval.

In comparison with Alexander's three pivotal reforms – the emancipation of the serfs, and the judicial and *zemstvo* reforms – the remainder of the reform package is less controversial.

Military and educational reform. Military reform, educational reform and the reorganisation of the police were all attempts to update and improve existing institutions so that they meshed better with the more progressive ethos inaugurated by the emancipation of the serfs. Miliutin's military reforms illustrate best of all the influence of the successful model of 1860s Prussia. Cautious improvements to the educational system were not necessarily out of step with a modernising autocratic state. Absolutist Prussia had, after all, set up what was arguably Europe's most progressive educational system in the early years of the nineteenth century, a reform that underpinned Prussia's progress under Bismarck. Properly channelled, more education did not necessarily mean more opposition if the state played its hand cleverly.

After a confusing period of switchback liberalism and repression in the first twelve years of Alexander II's reign, the appointment of Dmitrii Tolstoy as Minister of Education in 1867 brought a period of conservatism. Tolstoy's policies were a response to the assassination attempt of 1866 and the radical tendencies of university students and professors manifested in the early 1860s. However, their impact was to reinforce the alienation of the radical intelligentsia from the state, increase the intelligentsia's appeal and slow down Russia's intellectual progress. Harsh censorship and close supervision of university activity illustrated the arrogance of the tsarist state, which presumed to be able to suppress the ideas that it feared.

In 1878, two assassination attempts on the German Kaiser were blamed on socialist radicals by Bismarck. Yet the response of the German government was confined to politics, not culture. Retribution was targeted at the socialist party and its press, not at educational establishments. Moreover, in the more sophisticated semi-democratic politics of imperial Germany, Bismarck was able to gather much popular support for his conservative policies.

Dmitrii Tolstoy had no such concerns. He was simply acting in the interests of the state. With Alexander II behind him, he must therefore bear heavy responsibility for deepening the divide between the state and the radical intelligentsia in the 1870s, which was to prove so destructive. Its claims that Alexander II was no different from his father, that all tsars were alike and that the whole tsarist system needed to be removed were made to seem plausible.

HOW EFFECTIVE WERE TSARIST INDUSTRIAL REFORMS?

From the emancipation of the serfs to the outbreak of the First World War the tsarist regime made industrial reform a high priority. In 1914 the German general staff were increasingly worried that by 1917 Russia would be too strong for them, industrially and militarily. However, industrialisation brought social and political dangers in the form of an urban working class, feared for decades by Russia's rulers as inherently capable of revolution. In 1905 workers played a leading role in bringing the regime to its knees. There was a further strike wave in 1912–14. Then, in 1917, yet more strikes were the catalyst for the collapse of tsarism.

A judgement of the effectiveness of tsarist industrial reform needs to take into account positive economic achievement set against working-class unrest. Historians' views vary from the 'liberal' view, established by Alexander Gerschenkron, that industrialisation was successful and 'economic modernisation was making revolution more remote', to the Marxist interpretation, stressing the inevitability of revolution as a product of industrialisation, as in Soviet texts such as *The Short Course*. More recent works, such as *The Tsarist Economy* (1986) by Peter Gatrell, suggest a less uniform view, but one that has more in common with the 'liberals' than the Marxists.

The rationale for industrialisation
Russia's defeat in the Crimean War (see pages 19–22) forced the tsars and

their governments to recognise the vital relationship in the second half of the nineteenth century between industrial strength and military power. The wars of German Unification in 1864, 1866 and 1870–1 made this point even more strongly. Prussia's victories owed much to superior organisation and the use of railways and of modern weaponry. After 1871 the two strongest powers in Europe – Great Britain and Germany – had the two best developed industrial economies. Russia had to industrialise to survive as a great power.

Obstacles to industrialisation
Industrialising Russia presented huge problems.

- The country lacked the human and financial resources to undergo a 'self-generating' industrial revolution on the British model. Centuries of serfdom had hindered the development of a substantial middle class, the vital social ingredient for economic change.
- Poor soil (except for the black earth regions) and primitive agriculture meant that Russia was short of funds for investment in industry.
- Foreign trade was also poorly developed, not least because of Russia's awkward size and location.
- Foreign markets were already dominated by Britain and other more developed economies.
- We must also consider Russia's sheer size. With an economically productive land mass some 50 times greater than Great Britain, the investment needed to give Russia an equally efficient railway system would be colossal.

However, industrialising Russia was far from impossible. The country's greatest feature, its size, was an asset as well as a hindrance. Vast natural resources (minerals, timber, oil, precious metals and foodstuffs) and a correspondingly large domestic market, once it had shaken off serfdom, made Russia an attractive proposition for investors.

Industrialisation in practice, 1861–1890
The decision, in principle, that Russia should industrialise was taken by Alexander II's government after 1855, as can be seen in the policies of his Minister of Finances, Reutern (see page 40). What then remained to be decided was exactly how Russia should proceed, and how quickly.

The political considerations that had inhibited Nicholas I were set aside in the early 1860s. The result was a state-inspired railway construction boom from 1868–78, cut short only by the combination of poor harvests and the war against the Ottoman Empire. Although political opposition grew more threatening in the 1870s culminating in the 1881 assassination, it did not deflect the government from its commitment to industrialisation.

The main worry for the government was not a political challenge from the workers but the economic challenge from abroad. After unification in 1871, German industrialisation proceeded at breakneck speed. After 1890 Germany was the leading continental European industrial power and, in the new chemical and electrical industries, the leading power in the world. Despite Russia's best efforts, after 1878 its industrialisation then lost momentum. The critical area was investment. The collapse in agricultural prices in 1879 hit Russia's economic prospects just after its finances had been undermined by the war against the Ottomans in 1877–8. This was the inheritance of Bunge and Vyshnegradsky (see page 68).

Economic expansion continued, although in relative terms Russia was still losing ground to Germany. After 1890 this disparity became much more serious when the young German Emperor, Wilhelm II, set German foreign policy on a new anti-Russian course. This, combined with Germany's withdrawal of investment support for Russia in 1888, pushed Russia into the arms of France, a country eager for a powerful ally against Germany and rich in investment capital.

Industrialisation in practice, 1890–1914

Here we consider the background to Russia's accelerated industrialisation after 1890, superintended by Minister of Finance Sergei Witte (see pages 70–2). Witte's scheme to 'save Russia by rapid and forceful industrialisation' was bold and innovative. He saw rapid industrialisation as a lifeline for tsarist Russia. First, industrialisation was the only way that Russia would maintain its European status. Russian statesmen treated this as a fundamental responsibility. Second, it tied up with Russia's imperial ambitions.

A second phase of intensive railway construction (see page 72) offered the possibility of opening up trade links with the Far East via the Trans-Siberian Railway (see page 71). Exports to China increased in value from 2 million roubles in 1891 to 10 million in 1901 and 30 million in 1914.

Although there was substantial foreign investment (see page 73), it is important to note that the second phase of railway construction in the 1890s was achieved substantially through Russian domestic production. For instance, only 1 per cent of rails and less than 20 per cent of rolling stock were now being imported. The prime suppliers of these two commodities were John Hughes's New Russian Ironworks and the South Russian Dniepr Factory, both in Ukraine.

Despite major progress in this vital area, Russian industry in 1900 was by no means uniformly efficient or modern.

- In 1897 only 35 per cent of the workforce in the mining and metallurgical industries was literate.
- Russian textile mills employed four times as many workers per loom as their equivalents in England, making costs higher despite lower wages.
- There was little standardisation. The main plough factory in Tula produced 30 different models (reduced to three after the 1917 revolution).

Industrial depression. The worldwide slump from 1900–5 ended the railway construction boom. It hit engineering and metallurgical firms, but did not affect progress in other sectors. The response of heavy industry was to form syndicates, starting with Prodameta in the metallurgical industries. Prodameta began with twelve firms in 1902, expanding to 30 firms in 1909.

Industrial boom. After 1909 Russian industry boomed again, this time stimulated by defence production and demand for consumer goods, as well as renewed railway construction. Calico production rose 20 per cent from 1904 to 1913. Another healthy sign was the reduced reliance on foreign investment. In statistical terms it is hard to deny the substantial progress that was being made.

The industrial workforce

The downside to Witte's industrialisation was the creation of a significant proletariat or working class, long perceived by Russia governments to be subversive. The political threat of the proletariat was especially dangerous because it was concentrated in urban centres and on the railway system, the vital organs of state administration. This fear proved abundantly justified in 1905 and again in 1917 when the railway system was sporadically paralysed by strikes. To minimise this threat from the proletariat, tsarist industrialisation began in 'new' towns, notably outside Nizhnii Novgorod and in the Donbass in Ukraine. However, this policy of creating industrial ghettos was only partially successful. The most spectacular urban growth occurred in St Petersburg and Moscow (74 per cent and 70 per cent respectively from 1897 to 1914).

Approach to industrial relations

Witte and police chief Zubatov had an imaginative and surprisingly progressive approach to industrial relations. Both realised the dangers of clashes between employers and workers, especially when the employers called on the state to bring the workers into line. Witte was therefore at pains to improve factory conditions and control labour exploitation. Zubatov was at pains to avoid the growth of hostile trades unions by creating official unions controlled by the police.

It is easy to criticise Witte's failings in this regard. However, the main problem was general poverty and social backwardness. Funding for factory inspectors was poor and workers were often housed in barracks. Although this looks bad, one important reason for the poor social infrastructure was the migratory tendency of most of the early workforce. At least half the so-called proletariat would take seasonal agricultural work in their former villages. In attitudes and customs they could be better described as 'urban peasants'. They saw themselves as outworkers for their village communities rather than as a new urban class.

A migrant, peasant workforce was hardly encouraging for employers. And with more people than jobs, employers took every opportunity to drive down costs. However, a small, genuine proletariat was growing alongside the mass of urban peasants and became important in framing attitudes and political opinions. 'Rooted' urban workers predominated in crafts, skilled factory work, engineering and printing. They were prime targets for early socialist and especially Social Democratic agitation.

The general poverty and social backwardness of the infant working class was cruelly exposed by the slump that hit Russian industry in 1900. It was this and the continuing recession that put pressure on Zubatov's unions, and culminated in the 'Bloody Sunday' tragedy of 9 January 1905.

Industrial unrest

Industrial unrest was a major threat to the regime in 1905. General strikes on the railways in January and October showed that the tsarist administration was losing control. Combined with peasant and middle-class protest and disturbances among the non-Russian ethnic groups, the tsarist regime looked extremely vulnerable. However, the restoration of order was equally dramatic. The rapid progress of the economy after 1909 made the 'anarchic turbulence' (Rogger, 1983) of 1905–6 seem the exception rather than the rule.

Another wave of strikes following the Lena Goldfields Massacre (see page 124) emphasised the confrontational element in Russian labour relations. Such confrontations were not confined to Russia. Between 1907 and 1914 the British, French and German governments all confronted militant unionism with force, although there were no massacres on the Lena Goldfields scale.

HOW EFFECTIVE WERE TSARIST AGRARIAN REFORMS, 1848–1914?

Agrarian reform was the fundamental domestic problem of the later tsarist regime, ranking second only to military and strategic considerations in overall policy making. Without agrarian reform Russia would be unable to modernise and would be threatened by rural unrest. Thus agrarian reform ranked high on the short- and long-term political agendas.

The size of the task
Peasantries tend to be economically and socially static. In Russia this tendency was hugely reinforced by the vast spaces of the Russian plain, the severe climate and, save for the black earth regions, the poor soil.

- Russian villages were peculiarly isolated, needing relatively large acreages to make grain production worthwhile.
- This meant that villages were often 24 to 32 kilometres apart, rather than the three to five kilometres that was the norm in England.
- Isolation reinforced inertia which was, therefore, built into the social and economic structure.

Isolation and inertia meant that very little of the outside world impinged on the lives of the peasants before Peter the Great (in 1718 he conducted a census to enable him to tax and recruit from the peasantry). They were simply left to their own devices. This meant that, in the south and east, flight to avoid taxes or army recruitment was common and hard to prevent. This was the rationale behind serfdom, a crude system for tying the peasantry to the land.

Serfdom then became embedded in Russia because it gave the state stability, regular taxation and an effective recruitment system for the army. The threat of mass revolt, terrifyingly seen in the Pugachev revolt of 1773–5, only served to show that the maintenance of serfdom was essential to the stability of the state. Thus the Russian peasantry, and with it Russian agriculture had taken an evolutionary path opposite to that of peasantries in western Europe. In Russia serfdom was becoming stronger around 1800 rather than weaker. It is important to understand this process if we are to grasp the scale of the task confronting Russian agricultural reformers in the mid- and late-nineteenth century. They were, in a sense, swimming against the tide.

The practicalities of reform: emancipation of the serfs
If the task of diverting the course of Russia's social and economic evolution was daunting, it was made more so by the material and administrative condition of the Russian state. Put simply Russia was too poor to afford an efficient bureaucracy that could reach much beyond the major cities and to fund the modernisation of the peasant masses. Arguably the country was poor because of serfdom. This was a catch-22 dilemma. To break out of it, the only option was to employ the power of the state, the autocracy. Although by 1848 the autocracy is generally perceived to be a sign of Russia's backwardness, ironically it was its best hope of modernising.

KEY TERM
Peasantries
Traditional, inward-looking, rural, agricultural communities.

This is the conceptual background to Alexander II's epoch-making emancipation of the serfs in 1861 and is a classic instance of strength concealing weakness. It is hard to see how emancipation could have turned out differently from the way that it did, given the absolute necessity of the state enlisting the co-operation of the landowning nobility and the fears that too radical a shake-up of peasant life would lead to *volya* (see page 182).

Famine and peasant violence

Over a long perspective to 1914, there can be little doubt that the emancipation of the serfs of 1861 was highly effective.

- It changed the course of the Russian peasantry.
- It enabled more sophisticated farming techniques to become established.
- It opened up the expansion of Russian industry and trade.

However, the progress of Russian agriculture to 1914 was hardly smooth, disfigured as it was by the famine of 1891–2 and the peasant violence of 1902 and 1905–6. These crises have complex origins, which cannot be explained simply by analysing the shortcomings of the emancipation of 1861. Undoubtedly the most important factor was the population explosion after 1861 (74 million in 1861, 164 million in 1913).

The population explosion put the land settlement of the emancipation under increasing strain. It was the chief underlying cause of the crises of 1891–2, 1902 and 1905–6, when first bad weather and, in the latter two instances, the world trade slump exposed the weaknesses of Russia's agrarian development. All three crises were linked to Russia's policy of enforced grain exportation after 1888 (see table on page 192) and, therefore, to the strains of state-led industrialisation.

The shortcomings of conservative agrarian policies

Despite the encouraging production trends, it is possible that the government could have done more for Russian agriculture, especially after 1881 when emancipation had bedded down. The weaknesses of the Russian state continued to be a reason for inertia, but politics also played an important role. Inflexible conservatism was the hallmark of Russian agrarian policy for more than 20 years after the assassination of Alexander II. The traditional stance of the Russian government towards the peasantry was reinforced by the new current of Slavophilism, and by the first unsuccessful attempts by the Populists to bring about a peasant revolution in the 1870s.

Attempts to speed up the transfer of land, such as the Land Banks of 1882 and 1885 or to resettle peasants in Siberia to reduce overpopulation (1896 to 1900) were useful steps but could not cope with the magnitude

GRAIN PRODUCTION, 1851–1914

	Average harvest (1886–90 = 100)	Sown area (1886–90 = 100)	Yield (1886–90 = 100)
1851–5	68	92	75
1856–60	70	94	75
1861–65	71	94	75
1866–70	75	90	84
1871–75	81	98	83
1876–80	84	98	86
1881–85	93	100	94
1886–90	100	100	100
1891–95	109	99	110
1896–1900	120	105	114
1901–05	141	114	124
1906–10	142	117	122
1911–14	156	120	131

Source: P. Gatrell, 1986.

of the population explosion and consequent land hunger. New conservatism really showed its hand in the introduction of land captains in 1887 and the enforcement of the joint payment of taxes by the commune in 1893. Both measures underpinned the traditional view that the peasants should remain a class apart, they needed to be controlled and should not be given the same rights as educated citizens.

The taxation reform was a means of strengthening the commune to prevent social mobility. However, much more important than what the Ministry of Agriculture did in this period was what it did *not* do. The 1891 famine was a graphic failure of Russian agrarian policy. Yet the famine produced no change in policy. The Ministry of Agriculture complacently attributed the disaster to natural causes.

The chances of the Russian peasantry breaking out of a cycle of poverty, especially in the central black earth region, were made worse by the indebtedness of the landowning class who, in most cases, lacked the resources to invest in estates in the hope of making them more profitable. Yet again, Russian agrarian society seemed to be evolving in the wrong direction, as it had done before 1861, and only another dramatic intervention on the part of the autocracy seemed likely to have much effect.

The Stolypin reforms: the second emancipation?
This intervention did come eventually after the peasant revolts of 1902 illustrated the bankruptcy of conservatism. The Imperial Commission on Agriculture of 1902–3 marked the beginning of a dramatic change of course that led to the Stolypin reforms and a new interventionist and progressive spirit in the Ministry of Agriculture under Krivoshein (Minister of Agriculture, 1906–15). Stolypin and Krivoshein pioneered the second emancipation of the peasantry, their emancipation from the commune. If this emancipation was not as dramatic as that of 1861, it was almost as significant. It was the second attempt by the tsarist government to change the evolutionary course of Russian agriculture and, in the short period (1907–15 – after 1915 the war undermined the rural economy) that we have to assess its effectiveness, showed much promise.

Contradictions of tsarist agrarian reform
The grounds for an optimistic assessment of the longer-term impact of the Stolypin/Krivoshein reforms are reinforced by their coincidence with a massive expansion of primary education in rural Russia, and with the greater social mobility and economic diversity brought about by Russia's accelerating industrialisation. This reveals a fundamental contradiction in the tsarist state on the eve of the First World War. In both industrial and agrarian policy the regime was committed to irreversible and fundamental modernisation. Yet, especially after Stolypin, Nicholas II seemed quite unwilling to allow the political system to follow suit, hoping, like his father, that modernisation could go hand in hand with traditional autocratic values.

From 1911 to 1914 (just as in the 1890s) tsarist government pursued simultaneously contradictory agendas. In the 1890s, Witte's progressive industrialisation policy at the Ministry of Finance contrasted with I.N. Durnovo's and Sipiagin's conservatism at the Ministry of Agriculture. From 1911 to 1914, Krivoshein's continuation of the Stolypin reforms, allied to rapid industrialisation and educational reform, did not harmonise with the conservatism of Nicholas II and Maklakov (Minister of Internal Affairs) in the political arena.

CONCLUSIONS

Was Nicholas I or Alexander II the more effective tsar?: conclusions
The reigns of Nicholas I and Alexander II have much in common. This stems from the fact that they were, in different contexts, trying to achieve the same objective – to maintain the internal and external health and strength of the Russian state in an increasingly challenging and competitive European environment. Although Nicholas I's strict, repressive autocracy had greater intellectual and political coherence, it was

bankrupt in 1855. Given the fact that Russia had begun to face the risks of modernisation and had done so with some success by 1881, one must conclude that Alexander II, for all his inconsistencies was the more effective ruler of Russia.

Were Alexander II's reforms too limited and contradictory to achieve their objectives?: conclusions

Alexander II's reforms *were* limited and contradictory. But on closer inspection, they were more coherent than they may at first appear. If one takes Alexander's prime objective to be the defence of the key interests of the state, and therefore the autocracy, then a common thread is discernible. Alexander was trying to set the Russian state on course for modernisation without losing control of the political situation. Of Russia's last three rulers, he had the most flexible approach. There may have been contradictory elements in this, but his was arguably the most important and successful strategy for modernisation. Without his reforms, Witte's industrialisation and the evolutionary political and agrarian reforms of 1905–10 would have been impossible.

How effective were tsarist industrial reforms?: conclusions

In 1861 Russia, emerging from serfdom, was undeniably backward. By 1914, in the fast-moving, competitive economic environment this was no longer the case. Russia was on the threshold of becoming a major industrial power, moving into self-sustaining industrial growth. The statistics relating to growth, investment, consumer demand and foreign trade all indicate that Russia was following the pattern of industrialisation of its European competitors.

It is reasonable to conclude that the tsarist regime, taking agrarian reform in isolation, was on the right track immediately before the First World War. The Stolypin/Krivoshein approach had helped to produce organic, evolutionary modernisation in agriculture for the first time in Russian history. These policies were so effective that they showed signs of working again in entirely different political circumstances in the 1920s. When one couples the Stolypin/Krivoshein reforms with the colossal preparatory step of peacefully emancipating the serfs in 1861 and acknowledges the limited administrative capacity of the Russian state, one is forced to recognise that, although patchy, tsarist agrarian reform was ultimately effective in this period.

SECTION 3

Opposition in later-tsarist Russia

KEY QUESTIONS

- How significant was the national problem in tsarist Russia?
- How extensive and effective was opposition to tsarism, 1848–1914?
- Why did opposition to tsarism develop an extremist tendency?

HOW SIGNIFICANT WAS THE NATIONAL PROBLEM IN TSARIST RUSSIA?

The national problem was a major political concern for the tsarist regime throughout the period 1848–1914. Although suppression of the Poles had been severe under Nicholas I and Alexander II, the national problem became most acute after 1881 when the government embarked on an uncompromising policy of russification (see pages 61–6). Russification, in turn, created more widespread discontent among non-Russians, contributing significantly to the unrest of 1905–6. The national problem was at the root of a number of political crises in the *duma* period from 1906 to 1914, notably:

- the radicalism of the first two *dumy*
- the western *zemstvo* crisis, and
- the Beilis affair (see page 122).

By 1914, the national problem had become a governing issue in the politics of the Russian Empire. It was deeply divisive, a real threat to Russia's internal stability and an indirect cause of Russia's forceful foreign policy.

What is meant by the 'national problem'

Before the significance of the national problem can be more precisely established, we need to clarify what we mean by 'national problem' in this particular context. Six key points must be considered.

- During the period 1848–1914 national consciousness spread throughout central and eastern Europe. National groups that had little sense of national identity in 1848 considered themselves fully fledged nations in 1914.

- The Russian Empire was Russian-dominated. Although in absolute terms the Great Russians did not constitute a majority of the Empire's inhabitants in this period (44 per cent in 1897), they were the largest single national group, dominating the Russian state politically, culturally and historically. However, as a group, the Russian nationalities (Great Russian, Ukranian and Belorussian) made up 67 per cent of the population.
- Before 1881, or perhaps even 1905, the tsarist state could not consider itself a national state in the usual sense (a state in which the majority of the inhabitants feel a sense of common cultural identity). This was mainly because (by 1900) 'national consciousness among Russians was only patchily developed' (Service, 1997). There was little sense of a mass common identity except among the educated classes.
- After 1881, and especially after 1905 with the formation of the Union of the Russian People (see page 103), the government and other right-wing politicians attempted to create this identity by playing on xenophobia.
- Although a sense of Russian national identity may have been weak, xenophobia was deeply rooted in parts of the Russian and Ukrainian peasantry, as can be seen in the vicious pogroms of 1903–6 (see pages 65–6).
- In several cases national tension and violence did not directly involve Russians at all, as shown by the violence between Azeris and Armenians in Baku in 1905 (see page 102).

Special characteristics of the 'national problem'

Putting the six key points together, it can be seen that the national problem in the last decades of the Russian Empire had two special characteristics. First, like all national problems in this period it was dynamic. The nature of the problem changed, especially as the population expanded and became more mobile after the emancipation of the serfs in 1861. Second, the national problem in the Russian Empire was extended by Russian imperialism, by the territorial expansion of the empire in the Caucasus, Central Asia and the Far East.

It is a mistake to consider Russian nationality policy as defensive, simply because the Russians were not a majority of the population. The vital factor was the small size and disparate nature of the non-Russian nationalities. This invited the Russian state to take a high-handed, aggressive approach to the national problem.

The national problem under Nicholas I and Alexander II

The defining point of the treatment of the national problem under Nicholas I and Alexander II came early in Nicholas I's reign in the form of the suppression of the Polish revolt of 1830–1. Nicholas I took his pro-Russian imperial strategy even further by helping his allies, the

Austrians, to suppress the Hungarian revolution in 1849, and by strengthening censorship and university activity.

The universities, in which research into ethnic origins and local cultures was becoming increasingly fashionable, could be seed beds of national consciousness. The arrest and imprisonment of the Ukrainian poet Taras Shevchenko in 1847 is the most famous example of Nicholas's repression in this regard.

Under Alexander II, Poland was again the defining feature. Although Alexander's freeing of the press after 1856 heralded a more liberal approach, the Polish revolt of 1863–4 (see pages 41–3) brought the traditional interests of the Russian state (to maintain its unity and territorial integrity) to the fore. After 1864, the Poles were the guinea pigs for russification, the two most prominent assaults being made on the use of the Polish language and the Catholic Church.

Further stirrings of Ukrainian nationalism in 1876 also brought a harsh response in the suppression of the Geographical Society of Kiev University, prohibition of the importation of books in Ukrainian, and prohibition of the use of Ukrainian in the theatre.

Alexander II's policy towards the Finns was in sharp contrast to the repression of the Ukrainians. In 1863 the Finns were given a Parliament, the *diet*, which passed laws for the Finnish provinces, granting freedom of worship, creating a separate currency and even a separate army. Geoffrey Hosking (1998) explains this as a policy of '"divide and rule" – setting the Finns against the Swedes to dominate both'.

Policies under Alexander III and Nicholas II

After 1881 Alexander II's divide and rule approach was replaced by a more uniform policy of russification. The policies adopted for the Poles after 1863 were made universal throughout the empire. This uniform policy provoked uniform resistance, which in turn meant more forceful repression and violence. In the case of the Jews russification also played on local anti-Semitic violence in the form of the pogroms.

Nationality policy became more complicated after 1905. First, the creation of the first and second *dumy* moved the national minorities from the fringes of imperial politics to its centre. The left and left-centre majority in the first two *dumy* made loud demands for major concessions for national minorities. Second, Prime Minister Stolypin attempted to exploit Russia's new political arrangements to create a unitary Russian Empire with representative institutions – a policy that was both conservative and forward-looking. Finally, the tsar and Russia's new right-wing Populist movement, the Union of the Russian People, gave new impetus to the old russification policy.

Stolypin's attempts to direct the national problem
What started as a three-cornered battle in 1906 became a simple struggle between Stolypin and the extreme right after 1907 when the 3 June reform (see pages 107–9) made the third *duma* more conservative and prepared to support Stolypin.

Re-integration of Finland. Although Finnish autonomy had been restored in 1905, in 1908 Stolypin proceeded to reduce the Finnish *diet* to what was roughly the status of another *zemstvo*. However, it should be remembered that the political context had changed entirely. With the creation of the *duma*, Stolypin could argue that Finnish interests and those of all the other minority nationalities were now properly represented and that there was no need for separate national Parliaments. Additionally, the October Manifesto heralded much greater freedom of the press, so that restrictions on the circulation of non-Russian publications were less effective.

The western *zemstva*. Stolypin's next step was consistent with his plan to create a unitary empire with representative institutions. In 1911 he proposed the extension of *zemstva* to Russia's western provinces, an area of mixed population, including Ukrainian, Belorussian and Lithuanian peasants, many Jews in the towns, and an influential Polish landowning class.

An elaborate electoral system was designed to prevent the Polish landowners dominating the new *zemstva*. Although this anti-Polish provision was enough to ensure that the bill passed the *duma*, the upper house (the State Council) threw it out after the tsar himself had indicated his opposition to the reform. Stolypin then used Article 87 to make the bill law, a tactic so arrogant it cost him much of his support in the *duma*.

Stolypin's downfall and the consequences
In effect, the western *zemstvo* crisis ended Stolypin's ability to direct the course of Russian politics. It must be emphasised that the cause of his fatal alienation of both tsar and *duma* was, at root, the nationality issue. Stolypin's loss of power and subsequent assassination meant the end of his redirection of nationality policy. The shift to the right that occurred after 1911 was exemplified by the Beiliss affair in which government ministers and, at one point, the tsar made their anti-Semitism plain.

HOW EXTENSIVE AND EFFECTIVE WAS OPPOSITION TO TSARISM, 1848–1914?

In the West, we are used to politics being founded on rivalry, either between competing ideologies or parties. 'Opposition' as a political concept and practice is part of the system. But in nineteenth-century and early twentieth-century Russia, this was not the case. 'Opposition' was instinctively seen as alien to the system. This is because the only 'system' that Russia had had was the all-embracing autocratic state. Of course, there were shades of difference within the 'system', seen in the political arguments between liberals and conservatives in Alexander II's reform era, and again from 1905 to 1914. But it would be a mistake to confuse this variety of opinion within the state structure with genuine 'opposition'.

Definition of opposition as a threat
The autocratic state of Nicholas I, Alexander III and Nicholas II would not countenance 'opposition'. It was characterised as an alien threat and therefore had to be crushed. Such a definition of opposition had a fundamental bearing on its development and future characteristics. It also defined its extent.

Confusion of 'opposition' with 'resistance'
One must not confuse 'opposition' with 'resistance'. The tsarist state encountered a lot of resistance at many times and in many forms. Falling into this category are:

- the peasant dispute at Bezdna (see page 31) in 1861
- subsequent peasant disturbances at Chigirin in 1875, and
- the more extensive peasant upheavals of 1902 and 1905–6.

In each case, the peasants were showing their resistance to particular aspects of tsarist rule, but could not be classified as opponents of the regime. The fact that these events were caused by misunderstandings or economic hardship, or both, means that their political importance should not be overestimated. Much the same could be said for the urban protest that faced the tsarist regime after 1900. There were some links with genuine political opposition among the striking rebellious workforce. In Georgia, for instance, the Menshevik Social Democrats had a real grip of popular politics by 1914. But, in the main, urban protest was resistance rather than outright opposition. This can be seen in the collapse of the strike movement after 1906 and its largely economic nature in 1912 and 1914.

Collapse of tsarism through urban resistance
The tsarist regime eventually collapsed in 1917 when another wave of urban resistance struck. The regime's means of control had been chronically weakened by the war. Nicholas II had made such a poor job of wartime politics that not even his generals would support him. Thus the regime collapsed in the face of resistance on the streets. It was not overthrown by opposition.

The peculiar character of opposition and the impact of Nicholas I
What constituted opposition to the tsarist regime? The most obvious starting point is the Decembrist tradition (see pages 10–11). The Decembrists defined Nicholas I's political outlook and set a pattern for the future. In his reaction to the Decembrists, Nicholas I epitomised the attitude of the autocratic state to opposition. He saw the Decembrists as traitorous and hugely dangerous, and developed a mania for security and control of the press, which was reinforced in 1848. The persecution of the politically trivial Petrashevsky Circle (see page 15) in 1849 is the best illustration of this.

If Nicholas's policy of rooting out opponents was essentially successful, his treatment of the press is less easy to assess. By interfering so extensively and personally with freedom of speech, Nicholas reinforced some peculiar characteristics of Russian opposition to tsarist rule.

First, he forced all serious opponents of the regime underground or into exile. This had the effect of disconnecting opponents of tsarism from Russian realities, exposing them directly to western European ideas and politics, and giving their political thought an abstract, theoretical quality. Russian political thinkers from Herzen to Bakunin to Lenin all thought 'big', in international terms. This was surely a product of their alienation from Russian reality. By coupling the alienation of opposition with censorship, Nicholas virtually ensured that opposition in Russia would cultivate ideas rather than popular support.

Another quirk resulting from Nicholas's alienation of opposition was the influence that Russian exiles were able to exert on western opinion. In the West a negative view of the tsarist regime became common, not only among fellow western liberals and socialists, but also among conservatives. This is one obvious explanation of the tendency of western historians in the wake of the 1917 revolution to see tsarist Russia as doomed to succumb to opposition. This was, in Russian terms, a 'westerniser' view, which saw Russia's future as essentially western European.

The growth of opposition: nihilism and populism
The growth of opposition to the tsarist regime is hard to assess. Opposition did not follow a linear course of development. Rather, it went through a series of phases, most of them ending in failure and repression. Because of the lack of coherence of opposition to the tsarist regime, it is perhaps dangerous to talk of growth without some qualification. But opposition was undoubtedly considerably more extensive in 1914 than it had been in 1848, even if it took several different forms. This growth can be measured in two ways: numerical growth and organisational growth. Although numerical growth is hard to pin down because of the sporadic nature of opposition, it is reasonable to argue that opposition by 1914

was much better organised and more deeply rooted than it ever had been before.

Phases in the growth of opposition

There were three main phases in the growth of opposition:

- reactions to the 'thaw' after 1858
- the growth and decline of Populism
- the growth of the Social Democrats and the Social Revolutionaries.

Each of these is studied in more detail in the following pages.

Phase 1: reactions to the 'thaw' after 1858

The first phase in the growth of opposition came with the lifting of censorship in 1858. Debate was possible in Russia and critics of the regime made the most of this in journals such as Chernyshevsky's *The Contemporary* (see page 48). In the wake of the emancipation of the serfs sympathy for critics of the regime was extensive among Russia's student population, but this numbered only 5000 at the time. After 1865, the regime's reforming impulses weakened. Censorship was extended under Dmitrii Tolstoy (Minister of Education, 1867–82). The reaction of the regime's opponents was predictable:

- acute frustration, and
- a return to the established intellectual abstraction and alienation that had been fostered by Nicholas I.

To grow and be more effective, critics of the regime had to become more practical. Two strategies suggested themselves: either they could convert Russia's disaffected (so they thought) peasant masses to their cause or they could adopt conspiratorial techniques to try to overthrow the Russian state. Already, as can be seen in the use of the word 'overthrow', the abstract, intellectualising traditions of the opposition were evident. Root and branch, utopian solutions were the order of the day. The popularity of scientific nihilism (see pages 51–4) in the 1860s had much to do with this.

These alternative paths of development were typified first by the ideas of Pyotr Lavrov (see page 54), and second by Sergei Nechaev, Mikhail Bakunin (see page 53) and Pyotr Tkachev.

Lavrov advocated the conversion of the peasantry to the revolution by 'Going to the people' – in other words, living among the peasants and converting them to revolutionary ideas by persuasion and example. Nechaev, Bakunin and Tkachev advocated the conspiratorial approach. Nechaev and Bakunin's terrifying blueprint, the *Catechism of a*

Revolutionary, assumed that the tsarist state would be filled with potential revolutionary sympathisers and that it would be unnecessary to drum up popular support. In fact, more open support, according to Nechaev's thinking, compromised security and could only weaken the movement. The catechism did not bear fruit. It is more important as a testimony to the radicalism of the extreme wing of Russian revolutionary thought, a radicalism that always had a few adherents due to the failure of more conventional methods.

Phase 2: the growth and decline of Populism

Populism was the second phase in the development of opposition to tsarism. It was also the first attempt by the Russian intelligentsia to stage a popular revolution. Additionally, it was the first movement to experience the failure of conventional methods.

'Going to the people.' The first failure was the 'Going to the people' (see pages 54–5) in 1874, in which 3000–4000 students immersed themselves in rural Russia in the hope of converting the peasantry to their political ideas. The 'Going to the people' was inspired by the ideas of Pyotr Lavrov. Its failure vanquished hopes that the peasants were ready for revolution and Lavrovism fell victim to Populist impatience in the form of terrorism. Lavrovism was never entirely abandoned, as can be seen in the ideology of the Socialist Revolutionary party, formed in the late 1890s.

Minority revolution. A rival to Lavrov, **Pyotr Tkachev**, built on Nechaev's conspiratorial idea to produce a fully fledged programme for a minority revolution, taking account of Russia's social and economic development. His influence on the Populists of the late 1870s was minimal, but his influence on Lenin was profound.

'Land and Liberty.' Instead of following Tkachev, active Populists formed 'Land and Liberty' (1875) to promote Lavrov's ideas by living among the peasants for longer periods so that they could be educated and politicised. 'Land and Liberty' then drifted into terrorism, which was more or less an admission of Populism's unpopularity as a political movement.

Sympathy for populism. The dramas of assassination attempts culminating in the murder of Alexander II in 1881 and the subsequent arrest of the People's Will seemed to sound the death-knell for populism. Beneath the surface, however, the story is not quite as simple. During the 'Going to the people' in 1874 the Minister of Justice, Count Pahlen, had compiled a secret report cataloguing the police operation against the Populists. He was surprised not by the scale of the subversion, but by the sympathy that the Populists aroused among local landowners. Despite this sympathy, populism lost momentum in the 1880s. The conspiracy to

> **KEY PERSON**
>
> **Pyotr Tkachev (1844–86)** Forced into exile in Switzerland for his association with Nechaev. He was more scholarly and less brutal than his mentor.

assassinate Alexander III in 1886 was symptomatic of Populism's weakness and its inability to find an effective way of putting its ideas into practice.

Phase 3: the growth of the Social Democrats and the Socialist Revolutionaries

Populism's revival came in the third phase in the development of opposition in the late 1890s. By this time the economic reforms of Witte (see pages 70–2) were making an impact, and pointing the way to profound and rapid socio-economic change in the future. A Russian urban working class was beginning to emerge, giving extra appeal to the socialist doctrines of Karl Marx. At the same time, land hunger among the peasantry, caused by the rural population explosion, was becoming acute. Thus, for the first time, Marxist socialists and Populist socialists had real hope of generating popular support.

This third phase in the development of opposition saw both of them found political parties:

- the Russian Social Democratic Workers' Party (RSDWP) in 1898, and
- the Socialist Revolutionary (SR) party in 1900.

Both of these parties became major political forces in 1917 after the collapse of the Romanov dynasty.

Confrontations

The birth of opposition political parties was accompanied by a series of bitter confrontations between the Ministry of Education and the universities, beginning in 1899. In 1902 the SR Combat Detachment succeeded in assassinating Interior Minister Sipiagin, further raising the political temperature. A sequence of protests, closures, dismissals of staff and arrests continued to 1905 and deepened the dangerous alienation by the government of the educated classes that Count Pahlen had observed 30 years earlier.

Even more important in the short term was the emergence of liberal opposition. The work of Shipov's *zemstvo* liberals and Struve's 'Liberation' movement had begun to shift the political agenda in 1904. In 1905, in an improvised alliance with protesting workers and peasants, the liberals managed to score a major victory over Nicholas II and end the autocracy in all but name and habit.

Political activity during the third phase of opposition

This third phase of opposition produced an explosion of political activity in 1905. Urban strikes and protests, some of which involved crowds of over 100,000, afflicted all of Russia's major cities and most of the non-

Russian cities as well. In non-Russian cities economic grievances played second fiddle to national grievances sharpened by the government's clumsy russification (see pages 61–6) policies. Peasant unrest reached epidemic proportions in early 1906.

The distinction made earlier between 'opposition' and 'resistance' becomes blurred in 1905–6, such was the scale of protest and unrest. Even so, the first steps towards political organisation were discernible in both worker and peasant protest. From January 1905 the workers had a programme that included parliamentary democracy and an eight-hour day. In June, a peasant congress endorsed these demands, adding comprehensive land redistribution and the end of redemption dues.

Opposition was so extensive in 1905–6 that the tsarist military was hit by mutinies, most famously in the Black Sea fleet in Odessa in June 1905 when the sailors of **Battleship *Potemkin*** sailed to Constanza in Romania. Early in 1906 there were moments when the tsarist regime seemed close to collapse. However, what is as remarkable as the extent of opposition in 1905–6 is the rapidity of its decline.

The decline of opposition

First, we should acknowledge that this was not a freak storm that simply blew itself out. A better analogy would be a fire that was at first allowed to get out of control but was then brutally extinguished. The key personnel were Witte, Durnovo and Stolypin.

- Witte forced Nicholas to concede the October Manifesto, which ended the liberals' opposition, or at the very least, brought it within the system.
- Durnovo restored order in 1906–7.

KEY TERM

Battleship *Potemkin* The story of the *Potemkin* was made into a silent film in 1925 by Soviet director Sergei Eisenstein. It is widely recognised as the single most influential film ever made. It tells the story of the Black Sea mutiny of 1905 from a Bolshevik viewpoint. Eisenstein's most famous scene, the Odessa Steps, portraying the massacre of all classes of ordinary people by tsarist troops, is pure fantasy but great cinema. The film was appreciated as a work of genius in the West, although in Britain it was banned for its political content until the 1950s.

Battleship *Potemkin*, lying in anchor at Constanza, July 1905.

- Stolypin introduced essential agrarian and political reforms to ease rural unrest and stabilise the contradictory political outcome of 1906 by a shift to the right in 1907.

Thus, opposition appeared to evaporate after 1906, not because it had been weak, but because it had been successful.

Two strands of the third phase
The third phase of opposition, from the late 1890s to 1914 can, therefore be split in two around 1905–6.

- Liberal, student and peasant opposition had been successfully appeased or repressed.
- Worker opposition had been mainly repressed and less successfully appeased.

However, working-class opposition after 1906 was never as threatening as it had been in 1905 when it was in temporary alliance with the liberals and peasants. The Lena Goldfields Massacre and subsequent strikes, including the brief attempted general strike in St Petersburg in July 1914, lacked the clear political challenge of the strikes of October 1905. Moreover, the tsarist regime had its means of coercion (the police and the army) operating in 1912–14. There was no danger of mutiny, as there had been in the aftermath of defeat by Japan in 1905.

A new era of politics
Although the 1905 crisis had a significant impact on the revolutionary opposition parties, including a redefinition of ideology in the case of the Bolsheviks (see page 9), in absolute terms it is hard to argue that their utopian goals were any nearer in 1914 than they had been around 1900. As late as January 1917, Lenin wrote that he 'would not live to see the decisive struggles of the coming revolution'.

The ideological crisis over aims and means, which had already split the Social Democrats (SDs), and remained a permanent (if better concealed) feature of the SRs, could not be resolved. In both cases it came down to the extent to which revolutionary socialist parties were prepared to co-operate with Russia's new liberal constitutional regime, which, although heavily compromised in the form that it took from 1907 to 1914, could not be ignored.

What is clear is that the extremist tendency, despite continuing terrorism, was no closer to success. From a 1914 perspective, therefore, it is reasonable to suggest that the revolutionary opposition parties had been thrown badly off balance by the new, more sophisticated politics of the *duma* era. They undoubtedly lost support after order was restored in

1906–7. The case of Pyotr Struve is instructive but by no means unique in this context. One of the leading Russian intellectuals of his day, Struve was a founding member of the RSDWP in 1898, had dropped Marxism for liberalism by 1904 and was a mild conservative by 1909. He represented a shift among the Russian intelligentsia away from strict Marxism towards a less doctrinaire, freewheeling, often mystical political philosophy. While it is fascinating and important to establish Lenin as the torch-bearer of the Nechaev/Tkachev/Chernyshevsky revolutionary tradition it is arguable that the extremist tendency, if it had not had its day, was probably losing ground after 1905.

WHY DID OPPOSITION TO TSARISM DEVELOP AN EXTREMIST TENDENCY?

In attempting to answer this question we need to consider two things:

- the importance of the extremist tendency, and
- the origins of extremism.

The importance of the extremist tendency

The extremist tendency in Russian opposition is important not just as a peculiar political phenomenon, but because of its impact on the thinking of the tsarist regime, before, and especially after, 1881.

Extreme opposition (acts of terrorism and the like) was not confined to Russia in this period. From 1878 to 1914 there was a spate of assassinations in many European states. Even the sober politics of Britain was not immune, as could be seen from the activities of the suffragettes from 1910 to 1914. However, most states did not allow extremists and terrorists to dictate major policies. Tsarist Russia did, in significant ways, for much of the period after 1848.

The origins of extremism

The extremist tendency in opposition to the tsarist regime emerged in the early years of Alexander II's reign. The circumstances of the early 1860s were ideal for breeding extremist ideas, including:

- interference with the press so soon after it had been almost freed
- unrest in the universities
- disappointment with the conservatism of Alexander II's reforms, and
- (above all) the Russian intelligentsia's fascination with utopian socialism.

The revolutionary tradition. The championing of violent, revolutionary methods by Marx and the advocacy of conspiratorial tactics by Blanqui both found a ready audience among Russian intellectuals confounded by Russia's political inertia and the tsarist regime's strength. The earliest Russian political extremists (for instance, Mikhail Bakunin) saw themselves as part of this European revolutionary tradition, much would the later generation of Marxists like Lenin.

The persistence of extremist opposition. Pride of place in explaining the persistence of extremist opposition must go to the tsarist regime itself. *The Catechism of a Revolutionary* by Nechaev and Bakunin is a prime example of this. Nechaev (the principal author) sought to fight fire with fire. To overthrow a bureaucratic, cynical police state a tightly organised, cynical organisation was needed. He sought to compensate for lack of numbers by the sheer ferocity and single-mindedness of the members of his organisation.

The key players. Nechaev's approach was reinforced by Chernyshevsky's belief that the mass is simply the raw material for diplomatic and political experiments. 'Whoever rules it tells it what to do, and it obeys.' Such views and methods were taken up by Tkachev, the People's Will and (later) by the SR Combat Detachment. Indirectly they influenced Lenin, although Lenin's arguments for a tightly knit revolutionary party sprang mainly from internal disputes among German and Russian Marxists about revolutionary strategy.

By the turn of the century the hard-liners had rejected much of the core liberal values of the earlier generations of Russian opposition typified by Herzen.

Reasons for the persistence of extremism

After the assassination of Alexander II in 1881 the extremist tendency among the regime's opponents was sustained by persecution. The Safeguard System could have been invented with the specific purpose of driving the revolutionary movement underground and reinforcing its extremism. The harsh punishments meted out to political dissidents and the sheer scale of the *okhrana*'s efforts had the effect of building camaraderie and deepening bitterness towards the regime among revolutionaries, many of whom were imprisoned in Siberia. As the tsarist regime relaxed somewhat after 1905 one might have expected the extremist tendency to diminish. By 1914, however, there was not much sign of this happening.

Two reasons can be suggested for the persistence of extremism. First it could be argued that the weakness of the *duma* meant that the tsarist state was as strong as ever, justifying a hard-line approach. The 1907–14 political arrangements had, if anything, a tendency to push the regime to the right. Second, a tradition as deeply rooted as that of the revolutionary

Opposition in later tsarist Russia

The *okhrana*, Russia's secret police, in 1905.

extremists would take some time to weaken, although some historians, like Marc Raeff (1984) have discerned signs of relative weakness – for example, the growth of more moderate politics among the intelligentsia and even a shunning of politics altogether.

The impact of repression

Over the course of the nineteenth century the Russian state gained an unenviable reputation for arbitrariness and brutality. The Marquis de Custine, perhaps the most influential foreign observer of Russian political and administrative culture under Nicholas I, wrote in 1839 that, in the state administration, 'fear replaces, that is, paralyses thought' and that: 'If ever your sons should be discontented with France, tell them to go to Russia. It is a useful journey for any foreigner: whoever has well examined that country will be content to live anywhere else.'

Nicholas I, with his Third Section (1826) to spy on officials and the Buturlin committee after 1848, amply justified de Custine's views. The Third Section became the justification for Nechaevism and it is no surprise that the then head of the Third Section, General Mezentsev, was the first victim of the Populist terrorist campaign in 1878.

Alexander II's liberal minister Loris-Melikov reformed the police in 1880, abolishing the Third Section and transferring its duties to the police department of the Ministry of the Interior. This made little difference to the role of the police, whose powers, after the assassination of 1881, were once again expanded by the Safeguard System.

The Safeguard System, always in force in some part of the empire after 1881 and universal in 1905–6, gave further weight to the Marquis de Custine's analysis. According to retired police chief Alexander Lopukhin writing in 1915, it made 'the entire population of Russia dependent on the personal opinions of the functionaries of the political police'.

Tsarists versus revolutionaries

The drama of a violent struggle between an interfering police force with overwhelming power and revolutionary opponents with none was too attractive for western intellectuals to resist. Both sides developed ideologies to justify their views. However, it is dangerous to assume that Russia before 1914 was confronted with a simple choice between two rival autocracies: tsarist and revolutionary.

This thesis fails to acknowledge other possibilities for Russia's future and, in particular, that the evolutionary course that Russia was taking after 1905 was both softening the tsarist autocracy and marginalising the extremists.

Russias distorted political development

Unfortunately, the extremist tradition distorted the political development of the Russian state, especially after 1881. Its main effect was to weaken the development of the forces of political moderation. This had little direct impact before 1914 but was to prove highly significant in October 1917 when Russia's deep-rooted extremist tradition emerged, in the form of Lenin and the Bolsheviks, to seize power from the moderates in the **Provisional Government**.

> **KEY TERM**
>
> **Provisional Government** The caretaker liberal government that took over from the tsarist regime in March 1917 but was forcibly overthrown by Lenin's Bolsheviks in October 1917 before it could establish a liberal-constitutional regime.

CONCLUSIONS

In this section, we have covered three questions. The conclusions to each of these are listed below.

How significant was the 'national' problem of tsarist Russia?: conclusions

Unfortunately, the net effect of the national problem was to entrench Nicholas II's conservatism while it simultaneously strengthened opposition to the regime. Even so, the national problem was far from bringing the tsarist regime to its knees in 1914. Perhaps, as in 1905–6, it was only a serious threat to stability when the regime faltered.

How extensive and effective was opposition to tsarism, 1848–1914?: conclusions

True opposition to the regime, as opposed to protest and resistance, had been sporadic throughout the period and only coalesced properly and threateningly in 1905–6. However, the government, in the form of its ministers rather than its sovereign, showed considerable skill in handling this wave of opposition so that opposition became more confused and divided in the years before the First World War.

Perhaps the greater danger to the regime came not from opposition, but from the lack of it. This emboldened Nicholas II to attempt a thinly disguised return to autocracy during the First World War. As the war went badly this meant that he succeeded in putting together all the ingredients that had brought Russia to its knees in 1905–6, except that the First World War was hugely more damaging than the Russo–Japanese war and very much harder to end.

Why did opposition to tsarism develop an extremist tendency?: conclusions

Opposition to the tsarist regime developed an extremist tendency as a result of the interplay between tsarist repression and utopian, socialist ideologies from the West. Some historians, such as Geoffrey Hosking and John Roberts, have seen older, deeper influences in Russian history at work here. They have pointed out that the extremism and the messianic zeal of the revolutionary tendency shared these qualities with the Orthodox Church in an earlier age.

As the tsarist regime became less autocratic and repressive after 1905 the extremist tendency had, in terms of opposition, less of the field to itself. It is important, therefore, not only to understand why Russian opposition had an extremist tendency, but to put this extremism in context and not exaggerate its significance in hindsight.

SECTION 4

The wider context

KEY QUESTIONS

- In what ways did strategic and military considerations determine economic change in Russia?
- In what ways are broader cultural developments in late-tsarist Russia important for an understanding of Russian history in this period?
- Why did the tsarist regime collapse in 1917 and not earlier?

IN WHAT WAYS DID STRATEGIC AND MILITARY CONSIDERATIONS DETERMINE ECONOMIC CHANGE IN RUSSIA?

KEY PLACE

Muscovy Medieval Russian state (c.1400–1700) that eventually grew into Russia.

The tsarist regime was founded on a strategic and military rationale. Controlling a defensible territory had been its overriding task since the growth of **Muscovy** in the fifteenth century. However, defensible frontiers were impossible to find until the Russian state controlled much of the Eurasian land mass, hence tsarist Russia's relentless expansionism. This policy had been pursued with particular success by Peter the Great and Catherine the Great. Peter's defeat of Sweden and the demise of Poland made Russia the strongest power in eastern Europe after his death. The subsequent partitions of Poland (1772–95) and victories over the Turks under Catherine fed the Russian state's appetite for expansion into the richer and more strategically significant lands to the south and west of Muscovy. In a military sense tsarist Russia reached the peak of its power in Europe in 1814 with the defeat of Napoleon.

Keeping with military tradition?

Such a tradition of almost unbroken military success and expansionism was a heavy burden for the nineteenth-century and early twentieth-century Russian state to carry, and proved too much on several occasions. Nevertheless, it was a tradition that was hard to break, reinforced as it was by Nicholas I's interventions in Poland (1830–1) and Hungary (1849), and a revival of Russia's historical national mission as a Christian Slav state in the Pan-Slav era of the 1870s.

Of the four rulers under consideration here, only one – Alexander III – managed to avoid major war. Of the wars that were fought, one, the Russo–Turkish war of 1877–8, was disappointing from a Russian point of view. The others in the Crimea (1854–6) and against Japan (1904–5) were military disasters. Two of Russia's First World War campaigns in 1914–15 were also disasters. This indicates that during the nineteenth century Russia's ambitions in foreign policy were no longer as practical as they had been. The main reasons for this were the spread of industrial revolutions through western and central Europe, and the sudden rise of Germany after 1866, which fundamentally altered the European balance of power, leaving Russia far behind.

Russia's weakness and its importance for foreign policy, 1856–1914

The defeat in the Crimea (see pages 19–22) was a major shock to the tsarist system. Not only did it lay bare Russia's backwardness, it also forced the government to intervene and direct modernisation, as the prospects of organic self-generating modernisation were negligible. From this follows the argument, advanced by A.J. Rieber (1971), of the emancipation of the serfs being the direct product of military failure. This point can be extended to explain all of Alexander II's reforms in that they were designed to create a Russian social and economic system that would be able to project Russian power more effectively.

Once the major reforms were in place, a forward foreign policy was high on the agenda. The restrictions made on Russian activity around the Black Sea in the Treaty of Paris (1856) were removed by negotiation in 1871 and Russia went to war with Turkey in 1877 during the First Balkan Crisis (see pages 49–51). The outcome of the Russo–Turkish war was, in a sense, similar to that of the Crimean War in the 1850s.

- Russia defeated Turkey, not without difficulty.
- Russia was then forced to climb down from the bold Treaty of San Stefano after concerted diplomatic and military pressure from the other great powers, notably Britain.
- However, in 1878 Germany lined up with Britain and France to pressure Alexander II and his foreign minister Gorchakov into accepting the Treaty of Berlin (see page 51), emphasising how Russia's diplomatic and military position was becoming more precarious.

The Three Emperors' League

In 1881 Russia re-established a conservative foreign policy with a new Three Emperors' League signed with Germany and Austria-Hungary. Gorchakov was succeeded by Nikolai Giers as foreign minister in 1882, but there was little change in policy. Both Gorchakov and Giers recognised the importance of maintaining good relations with Germany while Russia combined repression with industrialisation.

This conservative approach did not prevent Russia becoming involved in the Second Balkan Crisis when Bulgarian nationalists in Eastern Rumelia overthrew Ottoman rule in Plovdiv and signed a union with Bulgaria. Russian interventionism produced the anti-Russian Mediterranean Agreements of 1887, signed by Germany, France, Britain and Austria-Hungary guaranteeing the *status quo* in the Balkans.

The move from Germany to France

Giers, keen to repair any damage that the Bulgarian affair had done to Russo-German relations, then negotiated a three-year Reinsurance Treaty with the Germans in June 1887. In November, however, Bismarck forbade the German *Reichsbank* to accept Russian securities as collateral for loans. This action, which remained in force for seven years, had serious consequences.

- Russia was forced to look elsewhere for financial support for industrialisation.
- It found a willing partner in France.
- Bismarck's resignation after his differences with the young Kaiser Wilhelm II made Giers's pro-German policy even more difficult as the Reinsurance Treaty was coming up for renewal.
- Giers's entreaties fell on the deaf ears of Wilhelm II and his foreign policy adviser Friedrich Holstein.

Cast adrift by the Germans, Russia moved into a closer relationship with France, underpinned by French loans in 1888 and 1892. The net result was the Franco-Russian Alliance of 1894, a defensive treaty, which became the unlikely cornerstone of Russian foreign policy until 1917.

Links between foreign policy and industrialisation

The Franco–Russian alliance was the natural product of Russia's strategic weakness, seen in its failure in the Balkans and slow industrialisation before 1892. The importance the tsarist regime gave to this can be judged from the fact that the foreign ministry and the tsars were prepared to withstand vehement attacks from such influential politicians as Pobedonostsev (see page 59) and Pavel Durnovo (see page 75).

It is hard to deny that the Franco-Russian alliance was a crucial determinant of the last 23 years of the tsarist regime. It illustrated Russia's priorities, its weakness and the pragmatism of its politicians. The loans that were linked to the alliance were an essential component of its industrialisation and, just as important, a vital prop to the regime when anarchy threatened in early 1906 and Witte managed to secure another timely French loan.

There is no doubt that the pattern of Russia's industrialisation reflected its military and strategic priorities. Railway building was the first consideration. Witte's railway boom of the 1890s had an obvious strategic dimension in the Trans-Siberian project which gave Russia much enhanced diplomatic and military leverage in the Far East. The aggressive policy towards Japan, and the work of Captain Bezobrazov and others, would not have been possible without the Trans-Siberian Railway, largely complete in 1903.

The defeats that Russia suffered in Japan were proof that it had overestimated the strength of its military in the wake of the Witte boom. Witte's strategic industrialisation policies had not been taken far enough to give Russia the military power to make it secure in an increasingly competitive militarising Europe. Worst of all was the state of the Russian navy, which had been humiliated just as warship construction was entering a new era with the launch of **HMS *Dreadnought*** in 1906. Nicholas II sought to turn this to Russia's advantage by insisting on a hugely expensive (760 million rouble) *Dreadnought* construction programme for 1911.

Whether the *Dreadnought* construction programme was the best use of Russia's military budget is open to question. What is not is the fact that rearmament, most notably naval rearmament, was central to the second industrialising boom of 1908–14, just as railway building had been in the 1890s.

Although Russian foreign and military policy before 1914 seemed to be

KEY TERM

HMS *Dreadnought*
This battleship revolutionised naval warfare. Its 'all big gun', uniform heavy armament, heavy protective armour and high speed meant that it easily outclassed every other warship afloat. It was also roughly twice as expensive as its predecessors and much more technologically demanding to build. Relatively backward powers with limited technological and financial resources, like Russia, were immediately threatened with second-class status in world power terms as the '*Dreadnought* race' in naval construction took place between Great Britain and Germany, 1906–14.

Battleship *Dreadnought*, pictured in 1909.

KEY TEXT

Durnovo's Memorandum: an extract 'The vital interests of Russia and Germany do not conflict. There are fundamental grounds for a peaceable existence of these two States. Germany's future lies on the sea, that is, in a realm where Russia, essentially the most continental of the great powers, has no interests whatever … It should not be forgotten that Russia and Germany are the representatives of the conservative principle in the civilised world … If the war ends in victory, the putting down of the Socialist movement will not offer any insurmountable obstacles … But in the event of defeat … social revolution in its most extreme form is inevitable. Source: B. Dmytryshin (1967)

following a logical course in view of Russia's commitments to France and Germany's aggressive stance, there were some important dissident voices. The most significant was that of the repected former Minister of the Interior, Pavel Durnovo (see page 75). In a **memorandum** to the tsar of January 1914, Durnovo questioned the whole orientation of Russian foreign policy. He argued that Russia had much more in common with imperial Germany than republican France or the British Empire. With the French calling the tune, Russia could easily be dragged into a disastrous war with effects similar to, or worse than, 1905. Like Stolypin, Durnovo appreciated Russia's vulnerability to internal unrest and thought it essential for it to have an extended period of peaceful development.

IN WHAT WAYS ARE BROADER CULTURAL DEVELOPMENTS IN LATE-TSARIST RUSSIA IMPORTANT FOR AN UNDERSTANDING OF RUSSIAN HISTORY IN THIS PERIOD?

So far, this book has concentrated on political and economic history. For the student to have more of a feel for the complexity of late-tsarist Russia it is helpful to take a broader view of the development of Russian culture. Several important figures in Russian culture have already found their way into the text so far, as have socio-cultural developments such as the use of languages, the growth of national self-awareness and education. Here we will attempt to pull these together to fill in the cultural background.

High culture: the arts

Nineteenth and early twentieth-century Russia produced artists of world

A scene from Igor Stravinsky's *The Rite of Spring*.

The wider context   215

stature. Their works offer a special insight into the paradoxes of a Russia that was European and yet non-European, and that was static and yet changing. It is important to note that the arts were generally exempt from censorship in late-tsarist Russia, making them, and literature in particular, a rich resource. Three themes stand out when looking at the distinguishing features of Russian culture:

- Russia's combination of backwardness and sophistication,
- the degree to which Russia was European or Asiatic, and
- the slow development of a 'bourgeois' culture.

Contrasts

Russian culture in this period is a culture of astonishing contrasts. Russian society still rested for much of this period on the medieval concepts of autocracy and illiterate peasantry. Yet it produced some of the world's most influential and innovative artists in the years before the First World War. Sophisticated art is generally seen as proof of sophisticated culture, yet in Russia this was not really the case. It simply showed how, over the course of the nineteenth century, Russia had acquired a

Leo Tolstoy in 1906, inspecting his estate after a bathe in the lake.

sophisticated European culture that had little impact on the lives of the mass of the population. The paintings of Mikhail Larionov, Natalya Goncharova or Vasilii Kandinsky would mean as little as the music of Igor Stravinsky to a peasant starved of land in Tambov province. However, there were some links. Russian high culture – literature, music, painting and architecture – was very much Russian, and like many art movements at the turn of the century, Russian art was keen to rediscover national roots. In Russian peasant culture, unchanged in many respects for centuries, Russian artists found a peculiarly rich resource.

Leo Tolstoy (1828–1910)

Author Leo Tolstoy's respect for the peasant and peasant society would at first sight seem to classify him as a Populist. In fact he was the enemy of all western-educated Russians who thought that they knew better than the peasants. After a spiritual crisis in 1878, Tolstoy became even more anti-western and anti-materialist, advocating a simplified Christianity, stressing non-violence and self-denial. His brilliance and authority as a writer and the sincerity of his convictions ensured that he was taken seriously.

Anton Chekhov (1860–1904)

Anton Chekhov, the playwright and short story writer, was also fascinated by the contrast between peasant Russia and the European world of the educated classes. Unlike Tolstoy, Chekhov had no didactic philosophical-religious mission. He saw the peasants objectively, through the clinical eye of a doctor (Chekhov's profession) and failed to discover the spiritual truths that Tolstoy claimed to have found. Chekhov could not ignore the baseness of the peasants, their willingness to swindle one another, their cruelty and their superstition. Writing in the late 1880s and 1890s, Chekhov saw the Russian peasantry struggling in an agricultural crisis as government policy and over-population conspired against them. Despite these extenuating circumstances, it is hard to see that either Chekhov or **Maxim Gorky** saw much merit in the peasant way of life in Russia at the turn of the century.

Fyodor Dostoevsky (1821–81)

Fyodor Dostoevsky, one-time liberal activist turned conservative enthusiast, had yet another take on Russia's social contrasts. His answer to Russia's identity crisis was to be found in the spiritual teaching of the Russian Orthodox Church. Dostoevsky delved deeply into the contradictions of contemporary urban life, and the philosophical problems of alienation and free will that beset modern man. But he also understood the cruelty of the ill-educated peasant. Additionally, he was very conscious of Russia's extra-European dimension, accentuated as the tsarist empire spread deeper into Asia in the late nineteenth century. He wrote, 'In Europe we are Asiatics, but in Asia we, too, are Europeans'.

KEY PERSON

Maxim Gorky
Realist novelist from humble origins who came to literary prominence with his brutal account *My Childhood*.

The impact of education
Russia's peculiarities of culture and cultural orientation were compounded by its comparative lack of a mainstream 'bourgeois' culture, the norm in western Europe by 1914. Some of the reasons for this are obvious, for example, the longevity of serfdom, the government's attempts to control social, and economic change after 1861 and the widespread lack of education. Although these explanations hold good for the earlier part of the period, after 1881 they begin to fade. As the culture and attitudes perpetuated by serfdom receded, the government's attempts to control social change faltered during the industrialisation of the 1890s. It then failed completely in 1905–6. At the same time momentum was building to spread education. Therefore, in the period after 1905 it is fair to say that Russia had developed its own bourgeois culture.

By 1914 some Russian newspapers had circulations approaching 100,000. To quote Dominic Lieven (1994):

> Although urban, educated, Westernized Russians still made up a relatively small part of the empire's population, in absolute terms they were a large and rapidly increasing group ... equal in size to the town population of one of the bigger Western European states.

Bourgeois culture had always been looked on with a certain disdain by several influential social groups:

- by the ruling élite who saw in bourgeois Russia the end of their monopoly of power and status
- by Slavophiles, and moralists like Dostoevsky and Tolstoy, who feared the corrupting influence of bourgeois materialism on the Russian soul, and
- by the radical opponents of the regime who, influenced by western socialist thought, condemned the Russian bourgeoisie before it had properly come into existence.

In 1880 the People's Will described the tsarist state as 'bourgeois', more because it was a fashionable term of abuse than because it had much relation to reality. In the revolution of 1917–18 the standard denunciation of any educated person by a Bolshevik sympathiser was *burzhooi,* or 'bourgeois' in Russian.

Russian culture as a reflection of modernisation
Russian culture illustrates the main dilemmas facing the Russian state and Russian society in this era of modernisation. These dilemmas were in some ways unique. Russia's size and location gave it a special world role. This resulted in difficult internal problems, its European/non-European identity crisis, and its peculiar social and economic development. All of

these factors contributed to the idea of an all-powerful state, which in itself created further peculiarities.

WHY DID THE TSARIST REGIME COLLAPSE IN 1917 AND NOT EARLIER?

Three characteristics of late-tsarist Russia have been established.

- The tsarist regime had to modernise and evolve, economically and militarily, to maintain its European status.
- The Russian Empire was extraordinarily diverse, socially, ethnically and economically.
- The Empire was changing and modernising more and more quickly through this period as Russia's European competitors and the Russian government forced the pace.

The political situation

The over-riding concern of the tsarist regime, as modernisation unfolded after the emancipation of the serfs, was to minimise the political impact of this process. This was a difficult challenge. Ending serfdom and gradually encouraging social mobility and urbanisation was bound to promote education. In turn, this would undermine the passive acceptance of the tsarist system by the bulk of the population. The protests and political demands of opposition groups in 1905–6 are clear evidence of the risks this process presented to the tsarist regime. However, the regime survived 1905–6 by a mixture of force and concession, emerging 'healthy and strong enough' according to Leon Trotsky. Trotsky's words are at the heart of the problem. Before 1905 opposition to the regime, although dramatic and extreme, had not posed a concerted threat. It was hard to see any grounds for expecting the regime to collapse, the aftermath of the assassination of the tsar in 1881 testifying to the regime's overwhelming strength. However, in the crisis of late 1905 as the empire was hit by a wave of strikes, peasant anarchy and mutinies in the armed forces, collapse suddenly became a very real possibility.

The *duma* monarchy period

The *duma* monarchy period held the key to the long-term future of the tsarist regime. By 1907 the empire had stabilised, although an important concession in the form of the new constitution (see page 104) had been granted.

The political history of the period of the third and fourth *dumy* (1908–1914) would indicate that concerted opposition on the scale of 1905–6 had ceased to exist, the revolutionary parties were in decline and the liberal parties were having difficulty putting down roots. From this, it may be fair to conclude that political opposition to the tsarist regime was unimpressive, especially as the regime had moved to the right with the 3 June coup (1907) and that, if the regime's freedom of action was not quite what it had been before 1905, it was still very considerable.

Power remained concentrated in the monarchy and the bureaucracy, an arrangement that was not really challenged after 1907, hence the validity of Trotsky's 'healthy and strong enough' comment.

The regime's internal problems: the move to the right

Perhaps the greatest political problem facing the regime came not from the obvious source of liberal or revolutionary opposition but from within its own ranks. Nicholas II drew the painful conclusion that the October Manifesto had compounded rather than solved his problems, and that the autocracy needed to claw back as much power as possible. At first Nicholas was aided in this by Stolypin, who had greatly impressed the tsar. Indeed, Nicholas once referred to Stolypin as 'my Bismarck'. However, Stolypin's star waned after 1909 when he ran up against a political obstacle, partly of his own making.

As Dominic Lieven (1994) has pointed out, the tsarist regime experienced the same paradoxical result of introducing limited representative government as Prussia (see page 36) had after 1848. Rather than weakening the regime's conservative tendencies, it strengthened them. The limited franchise after 1907 brought a new party, the United Nobility, to prominence, backed by Russia's most effective political lobbying group, the Union of Nobility. The Union of Nobility was determined and well positioned to pursue unambiguously conservative goals. Widespread rural anarchy in 1905–6 had made the plight of the indebted landowner even more precarious, and the new institutions of the representative system, especially the upper house or State Council, gave the Union of Nobility real political power.

The impact on Stolypin. Stolypin was the first to suffer from this new conservatism. His agrarian reforms were stalled and obstructed in 1909–10. But their momentum was too great to stop them completely. The State Council then obstructed the government's Naval Staffs Bill (1909), wrecking relations between the State Council and the *duma*. This rupture fractured Stolypin's power base, the consequences of which were seen in the crisis over the western *zemstvo* bill. At this point, the strength of the noble lobby coincided with the innate conservatism of the sovereign to resist further social and political change.

A change of prime minister

Under Prime Minister Kokovtsov (1911–14) the government began to fragment. Kokovtsov did not have a close relationship with the tsar. He was also vulnerable to ministerial intrigue and rivalry, notably between Minister of War Sukhomlinov, who was close to the tsar, and Minister of Agriculture, Krivoshein, who was adept at defending his ministry's budget and cultivating powerful allies – not least the empress, Alexandra.

The appointment of Nikolai Maklakov, very much Nicholas's and not Kokovtsov's candidate, as Minister of Internal Affairs in 1913 marked the prime minister's continuing loss of influence and in February 1914 he was replaced by the aged Goremykin, whom Krivoshein thought he could control.

Nikolai Maklakov epitomised the rightward shift in Russian politics after Stolypin. He employed the Safeguard System to clamp down on revolutionary activity, shutting down *Pravda*, the Bolshevik newspaper, in July 1914. At the same time he was considering a further revision of the Fundamental Laws to curb the *duma's* power.

The economic and social situation
The state of Russian politics from 1907 to 1914 is hard to assess because it falls into two parts:

- the progressive Stolypin era, and
- the drift to the right thereafter.

However, Russia's economic and social progress was less ambiguous. Statistics concerning growth, investment, agricultural productivity indicate that between 1907 and 1914 Russia was fast becoming a major economic force in European terms. The country was industrialising and urbanising at high speed. Peasant agriculture was beginning to free itself from its restrictive traditions. Additionally, literacy was spreading more quickly than ever before, the proportion of illiterate army recruits falling from 73 per cent in 1900 to 37 per cent in 1913. The years 1905–6 had shown Russia's potential for anarchy if the regime failed, but by 1914 the concessions of 1905–6 had greatly reduced the possibility of a serious internal challenge to the regime.

RUSSIA'S OVERALL PROSPECTS FOR STABLE EVOLUTION AFTER 1905

It is at this point that different historians' perspectives become most apparent.

Historical perspectives
- The 'liberal/positivist' view saw the First World War and its consequences as derailing Russia's stable evolution.

- Soviet historians took a longer perspective, seeing 1905 as the beginning of a revolutionary era that culminated in 1917.
- The war was seen as integral to the development of world revolution (not just revolution in Russia), mainly as a consequence of Lenin's 1916 thesis *Imperialism, the Highest Stage of Capitalism*.
- Lenin saw world war as the latest stage in the struggle for markets between capitalist powers, dismissing entirely the importance of strategic, national considerations as sufficient motives for war.
- Because of the political straitjacket that was applied to historical writing in Russia/the Soviet Union after 1917, Lenin's interpretation could not be challenged by Soviet historians. Of course, his thesis was politically rather than historically motivated.

In the West and in Russia after the collapse of communism our understanding of the question of Russia's evolutionary potential in 1914 has been deepened and stretched. Historians such as Orlando Figes (1997) concentrate on the narrative of events rather than theoretical explanation. However, he is sceptical of Stolypin's efforts to modernise rural Russia in particular and of Russia's post-1905 reforms in general: 'The land enclosure movement [Stolypin's agrarian reform], like every other reform of the tsarist regime, came too late.'

Nevertheless, his analysis of the breakdown of Russian society, politics and the economy emphasises how the 1917 revolution was essentially produced by the war. As Dominic Lieven (2000) puts it: 'The war destroyed the Russian Empire not because the army was defeated but because the home front collapsed.'

Lieven distinguishes clearly between Russia's military prospects in 1917 and its grave domestic situation: 'Ironically, in February 1917 the Russians had every likelihood of victory'; 'Churchill's comment that "with victory in our grasp she [Russia] fell to earth" was actually correct.'

Would modernisation stay on course?

Of the three fundamental steps towards modernisation (in industry, agriculture and politics) the first two seemed the most likely to stay on course. Russian industrialisation had generated real momentum after 1908 and was approaching the take-off point which would lead naturally to the completion of the process. Stolypin's reform of the peasantry, although uneven in its effects, looked unlikely to be reversed in normal economic conditions. It was, of course, undone by the war. That leaves politics. In 1905–7 Russia had made spectacular progress in founding a new constitutional system after centuries of autocracy. However, autocratic traditions and habits were not easy to uproot or soften when the new system threw up new political problems – for example:

- competing parties with new political philosophies
- rival interest groups in the *duma*, the State Council and at ministerial level, and
- a more conscious struggle to court public opinion.

The potential for success

Stolypin was the difference between the new system working constructively and losing its way, as it did after Stolypin's death. This was because in Nicholas the new regime had a chief executive whose conservative, Slavophile convictions and indecisiveness were poorly suited to the complexities of constitutional politics and tended towards right-wing escapism. It would be wrong, however, to anticipate revolution on the strength of Russia's problems in 1914. If anything, these problems were diminishing.

- Peasant unrest was minimal.
- Industrial unrest was short-term and mostly economically, rather than politically motivated.
- Russia's middle class was growing fast and, since 1905, 'most educated Russians had turned their backs on revolutionary socialism' (Lieven, 2000).

The evolution of the social and political system had at last begun to catch up with economic evolution, so the prospects of controlled and relatively stable modernisation were rather better than they had been before 1905.

The remaining problems

Two problems remained: a repeat of Russia's military adventurism that had been at the root of crises in the 1850s and in 1905–6, and the perils of short-sighted leadership.

As Durnovo's Memorandum (see page 216) pointed out, war against Germany in 1914 was a dangerous gamble. As the nature of the war became apparent, the Russian Empire found itself locked in a conflict that remorselessly exposed its weaknesses. Not the least of these weaknesses was poor leadership.

Nicholas II was not solely to blame for Russia's entry into the First World War, nor for the poor quality of many of his commanders – arguably the crucial factor in the Russian war effort. But his peculiarly backward-looking politics restricted Russia's options in the period after the death of Stolypin. It is revealing that the politicians and generals who eventually forced Nicholas to abdicate in 1917 only sought a change of leader, not a change of regime.

The wider context

CONCLUSIONS

In what ways did strategic and military considerations determine economic change in Russia?: conclusions

It is fair to conclude that military and strategic considerations were the key factor in determining Russia's pattern of economic and social change. They illuminate the underlying continuity of tsarist government and are at the root of any explanation of tsarist domestic policy. They also emphasise the unique importance of geo-politics in Russian history – how the physical characteristics of Russia have shaped its evolution.

In what ways are broader cultural developments in late-tsarist Russia important for an understanding of Russian history in this period?: conclusions

It could be maintained that, on the eve of the First World War, Russia's cultural and social development was tying it ever more closely to Europe. Economic change was the driving force. The rise of industry and the middle class, the beginnings of modernisation in agriculture and the spread of education meant that Russia was changing much more quickly than ever before. Even in politics Russia was beginning to evolve into a western European constitutional state after 1905. The First World War undid all these evolutionary trends, which were crucified in the growing anarchy after the March revolution. This left Russia open to extremists who were determined to end Russia's natural Western evolution and to use it as a test bed for a revolutionary ideology that itself had been russianised: Lenin's version of Marxism.

A2 ASSESSMENT

This section offers examples of the main types of source-based and essay questions used by examiners at A2 level and guidance on how best to answer them. In most cases examined assessment at A2 will consist of two distinct units, one a study in depth ('Historical Investigations' for OCR) and the other a synoptic 100-year topic ('Themes in History' for OCR). The study in depth is assessed by source-based questions, for which an element of historiographical knowledge is required, and the synoptic topic is assessed by essay writing.

SOURCE-BASED QUESTIONS

Historiography

A consideration of different historical approaches to topics is an important skill for the historian to develop. As will have become clear from the section devoted to historiography you need to know the wider context of influences on historical writing that often fall outside the period you are studying. For example, interpretations of opposition to tsarist rule have been heavily influenced by the course of the Russian revolution after March 1917 and its consequences both within Russia and in the rest of the world. Historiography adds another level to our understanding of history, and the awareness that historians differ in their views and that the way they approach the past is changing all the time makes history especially exciting.

Evaluating historical perspectives

As a student of history you will be expected to consider the views of historians, to compare and contrast their arguments and assess their value. It is useful to think about the following questions when you read extracts from the works of historians.

- What is the main *thrust* of the source (that is, what is it saying)?
- What *evidence* is being used by the author to develop the argument? (For example, does the author rely on letters, conversations and personal accounts?) How is the evidence being used?
- What *angle* does the author take (that is, does the author focus on one particular angle and neglect others)? It is worth remembering that two historians with the same ideology and approach may very well look at the same issue from different angles.
- What is the *background* of the author (that is, have the nationality, social origin or other background factors affected the way in which the author sees the issue)?
- What is the *perspective* of the author (that is, which line of interpretation does the historian seem to be taking and to what school of interpretation does he or she belong)?

How have the underlying principles of this perspective affected the way in which the author has approached the topic?

Explaining *how* historians agree/differ should be seen as a first step before considering *why*. This is what will usually be expected in high quality answers. Most of the questions you will be working on will revolve around these points. Answers should always make close reference to the extracts you are asked to consider and this is best achieved by direct quotation of short phrases to support the points you wish to make.

Using historiography in essays

An understanding of historiography can be used to support and develop standard essays as well as more specific tasks. History is a subject that, by its very nature, involves extensive reading and, in order to make maximum use of the material you have studied, it is important to consider the issues of historiography that are reflected in it. This will deepen your understanding of the topic and make you a more competent historian.

When writing an essay it can be useful to refer to different historiographical perspectives and approaches. This shows an awareness of different interpretations and can demonstrate that you have engaged in wider reading. For essays specifically geared to historiography an awareness of historiographical issues will be essential. Whatever the task in hand, there are several pitfalls to avoid.

- Try to avoid a seemingly endless list of historians' names and their books. 'Name-dropping' in itself is of limited use and examiners are well aware that students have often never read the books themselves but are merely regurgitating learnt lists of names. It is more important that you show an awareness of different historiographical perspectives even if you have never read the books themselves and cannot even remember the names of their authors. Showing an understanding of the perspectives is a higher skill more likely to score marks.

- Take care in quoting from historians. A statement by a historian can be useful in summing up a relevant point or illustrating a factor, but such statements should be used sparingly. It is never advisable to use long quotations, especially in exam answers, as the reward rarely compensates for the effort involved in learning quotations or copying them out. Short, sharp quotations are preferable, but think carefully: are they fact or the historian's opinion?

- Referring to different interpretations by historians can often result in a lapse into description rather than using them as a tool of analysis to develop your argument. For example, the answer that falls into outlining what historian A states and then goes on to what historian B states is not using the material effectively. It is much better to state and justify your own view in relation to those of other historians. Writing historiographical essays usually requires you to explain the different perspectives and to assess their value. Ensure that you evaluate the different approaches by relating historians to their wider context and philosophical views. For example, consider the evidence they have used, the period they were writing in and the values that have influenced them. This will enable you to show your skills in evaluation and assessment and therefore gain more marks than you would by offering a merely descriptive answer, however well detailed.

QUESTIONS WITH EXAMINER'S COMMENTS IN THE STYLE OF OCR

Source A
After hardly three months of war the greater part of our regular, professional officers and trained men had vanished, leaving only skeleton forces which had to be hastily filled with men wretchedly instructed who were sent to me from our depots … . From this period onwards the professional character of our forces disappeared, and the army became more and more like a sort of badly trained militia … . The men sent to replace casualties generally knew nothing except how to march … . many could not even load their rifles and, as for their shooting, the less said about it the better … . Such people could not really be considered soldiers at all.

General Brusilov assesses the state of the Russian army at the end of 1914. Adapted from Alexei Brusilov, *A Soldier's Notebook, 1914–1918*, 1930.

Source B
With the beginning of the war … the revolutionary elements found themselves isolated, and quieted down. In the course of the war the situation began to change, at first slowly, but after defeats faster and more radically. An active discontent seized the whole working class. To be sure, it was to an extent patriotically coloured, but it had nothing in common with the calculating and cowardly patriotism of the possessing classes, who were postponing all domestic questions until after victory. The war itself, its victims, its horror, its shame, brought not only the old, but also the new layers of workers into conflict with the Tsarist regime.

Trotsky's interpretation of Russia's war effort. Adapted from Leon Trotsky, *The History of the Russian Revolution*, 1936.

Source C
The war of 1914 was destined to serve as the forcing-house for the seeds of revolution. The immediate effect of its outbreak was to complicate immensely the task of the revolutionaries and to break up such rudimentary organisation as they possessed … . The February revolution of 1917 which overthrew the Romanov dynasty was the spontaneous outbreak of a multitude exasperated by the privations of the war and by manifest inequality in the distribution of burdens.

A British interpretation from the 1950s. Adapted from E.H. Carr, *The Bolshevik Revolution*, 1950.

Source D
The war destroyed the Russian Empire not because the army was defeated but because the home front collapsed. Before the Revolution of 1917 Russia's military record was no worse

than that of its Western allies. If the Russian army was on the whole inferior to the German, the same was usually true of the French and British. In 1916 Russia's economic and military performance was often spectacular. The Brusilov offensive inflicted major defeats on the Austrians and Germans, and had a good claim to be the most successful allied offensive of the war before 1918. Meanwhile, against the Ottomans the Russians had done far better than the British, who had been defeated in Gallipoli and Mesopotamia in 1915. By contrast the Russians had defeated the Ottomans in every engagement and were driving deep into Anatolia (Asiatic Turkey) when revolution came. It came partly because of a complete collapse of faith in the tsarist regime among most Russian elites and the Russian urban masses.

A modern British interpretation. Adapted from Dominic Lieven, *Empire*, 2000.

Questions

1 Analyse the differences between the judgements in Sources A and D about the military competence of the Russian army in the First World War. (15)

Examiner's comments, based on OCR mark schemes
Focus: Comparison and evaluation of two sources
In Source A, Brusilov notes the immediate circumstances of the army in late 1914 after the crushing losses of the early months of the war; in Source D Lieven takes an overview of the whole Russian war effort from 1914 to 1917, combining this with an international perspective. Hence Source A explains military failure whereas Source D, while not denying the weaknesses of the Russian army early in the war, points out that, overall the Russian army was relatively successful. A good quality of evaluation in explaining the differences, including a relevant discussion of bias, can be awarded Band A, especially if the evaluation is supported by appropriate contextual knowledge. Band B answers will demonstrate some unevenness. Band E is suggested for explanation of the obvious differences, Band D if accompanied by limited evaluation. A more thorough explanation of several differences would merit Band C.

2 Using Sources A to D, explain why the impact of the First World War on tsarist Russia has been an issue of debate among historians. (30)

Examiner's comments, based on OCR mark schemes
Focus: Evaluation of the sources in the context of the continuing historical debate on the impact of the First World War on tsarist Russia
Band A and B answers should make some positive use of all four sources. The weaknesses of the Russian army and the despair of one of its commanders in Source A gives weight to the view that the Russian army simply could not cope for the remainder of the war. Although a reliable source in some ways, Brusilov's comments are so negative that it is hard to understand how Russia was able to survive for another three months, let alone another two years. Source B takes a Marxist analysis, discounting purely military considerations and concentrating on economic factors and class politics, although Trotsky does see 'defeats' as a catalyst in this process. Source C essentially takes the same line as Trotsky and is interesting

from a historiographical standpoint. Carr was not a Russian revolutionary but his perspective is clearly Marxist and typifies the historical writing of the western post-Second World War Marxist school. Source D, written after the collapse of the Soviet Union, if not entirely dismissing some elements of the Marxist analysis, takes a less obviously ideological approach, conceding some successes to the tsarist regime after 1917 while still, at the end, acknowledging its political failure. Band E can be awarded for initial description of the four sources, Band D for more thorough analysis. Band C will show some evidence of historiographical analysis, more developed for Band B. Answers in Band B and Band A will show some distinct understanding of the reasons for the continuing debate. Band A answers will contain a thorough evaluation of the sources, shaped by some own knowledge.

Essay question

> To what extent, and for what reasons, can the reforms of Alexander II be considered a failure?

Examiner's comments, based on OCR mark schemes
Focus: Evaluation of an interpretation of an historical development
A discussion of the impact of the reforms over an extended period of Russian history will look at their short-term impact (releasing Russia from the relative stagnation of Nicholas I), their medium-term impact (accelerating economic and social change combined with a reversal of the initial liberalising direction of the reforms) and their longer-term relationship to the *duma* monarchy and revolutionary upheavals of the early twentieth century. Candidates may well conclude that the reforms were contradictory in their purpose to modernise Russia yet strengthen the tsarist autocracy and that this contradiction explains their mixed fortunes. Vague assertions about the impact of the reforms without any sense of development or understanding will be awarded Band U. Band E will require some basic understanding and knowledge of one key development, perhaps the impact of the emancipation of the serfs. The answers in Bands D and E will have little success in making synoptic links with later tsarist history. Band C will usually combine a highly descriptive or narrative approach with some success in making the synoptic links and connections between the different eras under review. Band A answers will be aware of the extent to which any argument – success or failure – can be pushed over the extended period. They will deal with several aspects of the reforms and their economic, social and political dimensions, even if briefly in the time allowed. Band B answers will show a good ability to organise an answer across a long period but will miss some possible lines of discussion.

SELECTED BIBLIOGRAPHY

E. Acton, *Rethinking the Russian Revolution* (Edward Arnold, 1990)

E. Acton, *Russia* (Longman, 1995)

A. Adams (ed.), *Imperial Russia After 1861* (D.C. Heath, 1965)

R. Auty and D. Obolensky (ed.), *An Introduction to Russian History* (Cambridge University Press, 1976)

D. Christian, *Imperial And Soviet Russia* (MacMillan, 1997)

N. Davies, *Heart Of Europe* (Oxford University Press, 1986)

A. Davydoff, *Russian Sketches* (Hermitage, 1984)

B. Dmytryshin (ed.), *Imperial Russia* (Holt, Rinehart and Winston Inc., 1967)

N. Ferguson, *The Pity of War* (Penguin, 1998)

O. Figes, *A People's Tragedy* (Pimlico, 1997)

P. Gatrell, *Government, Industry and Rearmament in Russia* (Cambridge University Press, 1994)

P. Gatrell, *The Tsarist Economy* (Batsford, 1986)

A. Geifman (ed.), *Russia Under The Last Tsar* (Blackwell, 1999)

M. Gorky, *My Universities* (Penguin, 1979)

C. Gray, *The Russian Experiment In Art* (Thames and Hudson, 1986)

A. Herzen, *From The Other Shore* (Oxford University Press, 1979)

A. Herzen, *The Russian People and Socialism* (Paris, 1851)

G. Hosking, *Russia: People and Empire* (Fontana, 1998)

G. Hosking, *The Russian Constitutional Experiment* (Cambridge University Press, 1973)

G. Katkov (ed.), *Russia Enters The Twentieth Century* (Methuen, 1973)

V.O. Klyuchevsky, *The Course of Russian History* (Moscow, 1908)

L. Kochan and R. Abraham, *The Making of Modern Russia*, 2nd edn (Penguin, 1983)

D. Lieven, *Empire* (John Murray, 2000)

D. Lieven, *Nicholas II* (Pimlico, 1994)

D. Longley, *Imperial Russia* (Longman, 2000)

J. Lubowski and H. Zawadzki, *A Concise History of Poland* (Cambridge University Press, 2001)

K. Mochulsky, *Dostoevsky* (Princeton, 1971)

D. Moon, *The Russian Peasantry 1600–1930* (Longman, 1999)

R. Pipes, *Russia Under The Old Regime* (Penguin, 1977)

R. Pipes, *The Russian Revolution, 1899–1919* (Collins Harvill, 1990)

S. Pushkarev, *The Emergence of Modern Russia* (Holt, Rinehart and Winston, 1963)

M. Raeff, *Understanding Imperial Russia* (Columbia University Press, 1984)

A.J. Rieber, *Alexander II: A Revisionist View* (Journal of Modern History, Vol. 43, 1971)

H. Rogger, *Russia, 1881–1917* (Longman, 1983)

D. Saunders, *Russia in the Age of Modernisation and Revolution, 1801–81* (Longman, 1992)

H. Seton-Watson, *The Russian Empire* (Oxford, 1967)

H. Seton-Watson, *The Decline of Imperial Russia* (Methuen, 1952)

R. Service, *A History of 20th Century Russia* (Harvard University Press, 1997)

N. Stone, *The Eastern Front* (Penguin, 1998)

T. Szamuely, *The Russian Tradition* (Fontana, 1988)

A. Ulam, *Lenin and the Bolsheviks* (Fontana, 1969)

A. Ulam, *Russia's Failed Revolutions* (Weidenfeld & Nicholson, 1981)

D. Volkogonov, *Lenin: Life and Legacy* (HarperCollins, 1995)

P. Waldron, *The End of Imperial Russia* (MacMillan, 1997)

J. Westwood, *Russia Against Japan* (MacMillan, 1986)

D. Warnes, *Chronicle Of The Russian Tsars* (Thames and Hudson, 1999)

INDEX

Academic Affair 166–7
agriculture 73–6
agriculture reforms 110
Alexander I, Tsar 10, 23–57, 183
Alexander II, Tsar
  achievements 55–6
  assassination 52–3, 55, 59, 78–9, 202–3, 207
  assassination attempts 47, 53
  comparison with Nicholas I 175–80, 193–4
  Crimean War 20–2
  economic policy 39–41
  effectiveness 175–80, 193–4
  failures 55–6
  industrialisation 67
  personality 24
  political legacy 56
  preparation for the throne 23
  'Tsar Liberator' 23
Alexander III, Tsar
  assassination attempt 203
  succession 58
Alexandra, Tsarina 144–7
Alexeyev, General 132, 133, 134, 135, 137, 148–9
Alexis, Tsarevich 145, 149
All-Russian Peasants' Union 99
Alma, Battle of 20
anti-semitism 65–6
Armenia 62
arms race 116–8
army 115–6
army reform 35–6, 184–5
arts 215–7
assassinations and assassination attempts
  Alexander II 48, 52–3, 59, 78–9, 202–3, 207
  Alexander III 203
  Bobrikov 64
  Kaiser 185
  Mezentsev 56
  Miliukov 164
  Nabokov 164
  Nicholas II 150
  Plehve 96
  Rasputin 103, 144
  Sipiagin 78, 203
  Stolypin 121
Austria 13, 15, 109
Austria-Hungary 114–5
autocracy
  agent of change 180–1
  maintenance 179
  move to constitutional monarchy 105
  serfdom 5, 7
Azev, Evno 122

Baku 77, 102
Bakunin, Mikhail 53, 201, 202, 207
Balkan Crisis, First 212
Balkan Crisis, Second 213
Balkan league 116

Balkan War, Second 116
Balkans 50 (map)
Baltic provinces 28, 63
banking system 41, 67
Beilis (Mendel) affair 121–2, 198
Bell, The 27, 28, 48
Belliustin, Ivan 38
Bem, General Josef 14
Berlin, Treaty of 50, 51, 180, 212
Beseda 85
Bezdna 31, 199
bicameral legislative 101, 102
Bismarck-Schönhausen, Otto von 61, 213
Black Hundreds 78, 102, 103
black repartition 74, 76, 112
Blanqui, Louis-Auguste 53, 54
Bloody Sunday 97–9, 189
Bobrikov 64
Bolsheviks 9, 82–3, 101, 150
Bosnia-Herzegovina 49, 114–5
Boxer rebellion 87
Brusilov, General Alexei 135–7
Bulgaria 49, 134, 213
Bulygin, Alexander 98, 99–100
Bunge, Nikolai 68
Buturlin Committee 15, 27

calendar 88
Canning, Stratford 19
Catechism of a Revolutionary 53, 202, 207
Catherine the Great, Empress 10, 17
Caucasus 44–5, 62, 63
censorship 15, 177–9, 201–2
Charter of the Nobility 17
Chekhov, Anton 110, 217
Chernov, Victor 122
Chernyshevsky, Nikolai 53, 54–5, 80, 207
Cherry Orchard, The 110
Chigirin 199
Church reform 38
coal and steel industries 40
Combat Detachment 84, 122, 203, 207
Commission on Agriculture 76
Constituent Assembly 100
constitutional monarchy 104–9
Cossacks 65
cotton industry 40
Crime and Punishment 15–16
Crimean War 12, 13, 19–22, 21 (map), 66, 212
Custine, Marquis de 208, 209

Danilevskii, Nikolai 49
Decembrists 10, 11, 13, 42, 200
Dmowski, Roman 64, 105
Dolgorukaya, Ekaterina 58–9
Dostoevsky, Fyodor 15–16, 217
Dreadnought, HMS 214
duma 34–5, 104–8, 198, 220
Durnovo's Memorandum 216, 224
Durnovo, I N 75
Durnovo, Pavel 102–3, 204, 213, 215

Ecclesiastical Commission 38
economy
   agriculture 141–2
   foreign investment 73 (tables)
   French loans 118
   growth index 71 (table)
   progress breakdown 139–42
   Stolypin's strategy 111
   strategic and military considerations 211–5
   strategies 1880s 66–8
   First World War 130, 137–9
education 218
education reform 37–8, 184–5
Eisenstein, Sergei 204
Elena Pavlovna, Grand Duchess 28
Engels, Friedrich 53, 54
Estonia 28
Evert, General Alexei 135, 136, 137
Extraordinary Safeguard 59–60
extremist opposition 206–9

famine 69–70, 75, 191
Figes, Orlando 174
Finland 43–4, 63–4, 102, 198
First World War 128–39
Florinsky, Mikhail 165, 170
foreign policy 113–4
France 109
Franco-Russian Alliance 213
French loans 103
Fundamental Laws 104, 105

Gapon, Father 97, 99
Georgia 62
Germany 14, 109, 116, 130, 134, 187, 213
Giers, Nikolai 212
gigantism 120, 121, 121 (table)
glasnost 171–2
Gogol, Nikolai 12, 26
'Going to the People' 54–5, 202
gold standard 72
Golitsyn 146
Golovnin, Alexander 31, 37, 47
Gorbachev, Mikhail 169, 171, 172
Gorchakov, Alexander 49, 212
Goremykin, Ivan 146, 221
Gorky, Maxim 122, 217
Gorlice-Tarnow offensive 144
grain production 192 (table)
grain shortage 142
Grand Plan, The 116
Great Retreat, The 133–4, 144

Herzen, Alexander 27
histiography 160–74
   key considerations 161
   Liberal school 160, 171
   Libertarian school 160, 162, 171
   Revisionist school 160, 162, 171
   Soviet school 160
   Synthesis school 160, 162
historical writing
   Marxist 94
   Russian 1990 onwards 172–4
   Russian pre-revolutionary 163–5
   Russian post-revolutionary 165–9
   Western before 1991 169–71
   Western after 1985 171–4
History of the Russian Revolution, The 162, 164

Holy Places 19
Hungary 10, 14–15, 196, 211

industrial reforms 185–9
industrialisation 8–9, 68–73, 70–3, 76–8, 111, 117–8, 214
industry 119 (map)
inquisitorial system 32
intelligentsia 15
Iskra 82
Italy 134
Ivanov, General Nikolai 132
Izvolsky, Alexander 115

Jewish people 44, 64–5, 65–6, 102, 197
'Jewish Witch Hunt' 122
judiciary reform 32, 182–3

Kadets 147, 165
Karakozov 47, 48
Karpovich, Mikhail 165
Katkov, Mikhail 48, 49, 62
Kazakhstan 62
Kazan University 31
Khlysts 145
Khrushchev, Nikita S 168, 169
Kiev 43, 67
Kishinev 66
Kizevetter, Alexander 164–5, 170
Klyuchevsky, Vasily O 163
Kokovtsov 221
Kravchinsky, Sergei 54, 56
Krivoshein 147
Kuropatkin, Alexei 135, 137

Lake Naroch offensive 135
'Land and Liberty' 54, 56, 202
Land banks 74, 191
land captains 60
landless proletariat 19, 111
Lavrov, Pyotr 53, 54, 201, 202
Lena Goldfields Massacre 123–4, 189, 205
Lenin 53, 80, 81–3, 113, 122–3, 150, 206, 207
Leningrad *see* St Petersburg
Lermontov, Mikhail 12
liberalism 85–6
Lieven, Dominic 173, 222–3
local government reform 33–5
Lodz 102
Lopukhin, Alexander 209
Louis-Melikov, General M 48, 54, 59, 183
Lvov, Prince 35

Maklakov, Nikolai 147, 221
Makorov, Nikolai 123
Malevich, Kasimir 5
manufacturing industries 40
Martov, Julius 122
Marx, Karl 52–3, 81, 203, 206–7
marxism 80–3
Masurian Lakes, First Battle of the 129
Mediterranean Agreements 213
Mensheviks 82–3, 122
Menshikov, Prince 19
Mezentsev, General 56, 208
Mikhail, Prince 149
Miliukov, Pavel 86, 98, 147, 163–4, 170
Miliutin, Dmitrii 27, 28, 30, 35, 36, 47
Miliutin, Nikolai 27, 28, 30, 42, 115

Index 233

mir 30, 76, 110
Moltke, General Helmuth von 116
Moscow 8, 31, 68, 101
Moscow News 48
Mukden, Battle of 90
Muscovy 211
mutinies, naval 99
Myasoyedov (Colonel Sergei) Scandal 133

Nabokov, Vladimir 164
Napoleon III, Emperor 19
Napoleonic Wars 10, 11
national debt 140
national problem 195–6
Nazimov, General 28
Nechaev, Sergei 53, 80, 201, 202, 207
neo-Stalinism 169
New Russia Company 40
New Russian Ironworks 187
Nicholas I, Tsar
  comparison with Alexander II 175–80, 193–4
  death 20
  effectiveness 175–80, 193–4
  succession 10–12
  Third Section 208
  threats to his reign 13–20
Nicholas II, Tsar
  abdication 148–50
  assassination 150
  Beilis Affair 121–2
  conservatism 100
  dangers to the regime 124
  October Manifesto 101–2, 204, 220
  power struggle with *duma* 143, 144
  succession 57
  traditional views 126
  victory hopes 147–8
nihilism 52, 200–1
Nikolai, Grand Duke 133
Nizhnii Novgorod 188
nobility, decline of 110–1

Obshchestvennost 173
October Manifesto 101–2, 204, 220
Octobrists 121, 133
Odessa 77
okhrana 65–66, 122, 207–8
opposition 78–80, 120–1, 195–210
Orthodox Christianity 11
overpopulation 75, 84, 113, 191

Pahlen, Count Konstantin 47, 202–3
pan-slavism 42, 43, 49–51
Panin, Count Victor 28
Paris, Treaty of 21, 180, 212
Peking, Treaty of 45, 91 (map)
People's Will, The 52–3, 56, 59, 79–80, 182, 207
Permanent Revolution concept 95
Peter the Great, Emperor 8, 10
Petrashevsky Circle 15–17, 42, 200
Petrashevsky, Mikhail 15–17
Petrograd *see* St Petersburgh
Petropavlovsk 89
Platonov, S F 166–7, 168
Plehve, Vincheslav von 78, 88, 96
Plekhanov, Georgii 81
Plevna, Siege of 51
Pobedonostsev, Konstantin 59, 60–1, 213

Pokrovsky, Mikhail 165–6
Poland
  defence 115
  deputies 107–8
  emancipation statute 42
  national uprising 1830: 11
Pale of Settlement 65
partitions 211
Polish Circle 105
political parties 64, 65
  revolt 1830–31: 14, 196
  revolt 1863: 41–2
  russification 64–5, 197
political pluralism 69
Polivanov, Alexander 133, 134, 146
population explosion 75, 84, 113, 191
populism 52, 80, 200–1, 202–3
populists 54, 78–9
Port Arthur, Battle of 89–90, 97
Portsmouth, Peace of 90–2
Potemkin 99, 204
Pravda 123, 221
press freedom 27, 31, 48, 60, 97, 177–9, 200
profiteering 141
Progressive Bloc 144
prohibition 139–40
Protocols of the Elders of Zion 65–6
Protopopov, Alexander 146
Provisional Government 149–50, 209
Prussia 13, 15, 36
Pushkin, Alexander 12

Raeff, Marc 172–3
railway construction 18, 70–2, 72 (table), 118, 186, 187, 188, 213–4
railways 39–40
Rasputin, Grigory Efimovich 103, 144–7
rearmament 117–8
reforms
  agrarian 110–3
  army 115–6
  Electoral coup 106–8, 120, 220
  Stolypin's 110–3
Reinforced Safeguard 59–60
Reinsurance Treaty 213
religion 11, 38
Reutern, Mikhail von 40–1, 47, 67, 68
revisionism 82
revolution 1905: 94–6
Riga 102
Rodzianko 148–9
Romania 21, 134, 136–7
Roon, General Albrecht von 36
Rostov 77
Rostovtsev, Yakov 28
rouble value 68
Russia
  Asiatic orientation 8
  culture 215–9
  diversity 1–2
  eastern Russia (map) 46
  European orientation 17
  frontiers 2
  geography 6 (map)
  industrialisation dilemma 8–9
  modernisation dilemma 8–9
  national groups 4 (map)
  nationalism 44
  nationalities 1897: 3 (table)

234   Russia 1848–1917

poverty of land 2
situation 1848: 9–10
size 1–2
Russian Courier 32
Russian Social Democratic Workers' Party 203
russification 61–6, 102, 195, 197
Russo-Japanese War 5, 71, 84, 87–92, 91 (map), 96, 115–6, 212
Russo-Turkish Wars
1853–56: 5, 19
1877–78: 5, 49–51, 68, 211–2
Ruzsky, General Nikolai 148–9

Safeguard System 59–60, 69, 183, 207, 208–9, 221
St Petersburg
capital 8
names 148
soviet 101, 102, 103
University 31, 37, 79–80, 98
Winter Palace 7, 97
St Petersburg, Treaty of 91 (map)
Sakhalin 45
San Stefano, Treaty of 50, 51, 180, 212
Schlieffen Plan 116
Serbia 114–5
serfdom
abolition 176–7
autocracy 5, 7
economy 17–19
emancipation 25–31, 177, 181–2, 190–1
emancipation statutes 29
Peter the Great 10
reform aims 29–30
Sergei, Grand Duke 78
Service, Robert 173
settlement of 1815: 10
Sevastopol, Siege of 19, 20
shell shortage 132–3, 135
Shevchenko, Taras 42, 197
Shipov, D N 85–6
Short Course, The 167
Shuvalov, Pyotr 47
Siberia resettlement 11, 191
Sinope, Battle of 19
Sipiagin, Dmitrii 78, 203
Sketches of Russian History 164
Skhod 110
slavophilism 26, 74, 191
social Darwinism 66
Social Democratic Workers Party 81–3, 101, 203–4
social policies 72
Socialist Revolutionary Party 83–5, 120, 122, 203–4
South Russia Dnieper Factory 187
Stalin, Josef 123, 167–8
Stavka 132
Stolypin, Pyotr 30, 60, 76, 103, 108, 110–3, 121, 141, 192–3, 197–8, 204–5, 221, 223
'Stolypin' peasants 112
Stravinsky, Igor 41
strikes
1902–1903 various 77
1905 general 98, 100
1905 railway 100
1905 widespread 205

1905–06 industrial unrest 189
1912 May Day 123–4
1914 general 124
1914 St Petersburg 205
1916 St Petersburg 141
Struve, Pyotr 86, 96, 206
Stürmer, Boris 146
Sukhomlinov, Vladimir 116–7, 132, 133, 221
Suny, Ronald 173
Svyatopolk–Mirsky 86, 96, 97, 98

Tannenberg, Battle of 129, 131–2
Tarle 167
tax farming 40–1
Tchaikovsky, Piotr 41
Third Section of Imperial Chancellery 11, 16, 37, 56, 208
Three Emperors' League 212–3
Timashev, Alexander 47
Tkachev, Pyotr 201, 202, 207
Tolstoy, Dmitrii 38, 47, 184–5
Tolstoy, Leo 47, 216, 217
trades unions 77–8, 82
Trans-Siberian Railway 71–2, 75, 88,
Trepov 146
Trotsky, Leon 95, 103, 150, 162, 167
Trudoviki 105
Tsarist regime collapse 128–50, 159, 199, 219–22
Tsu-shima, Battle of 90, 98

Ukraine 41–2, 43, 62, 187, 197
Ulyanov, Alexander 80
Ulyanov, Vladimir *see* Lenin
Union of Liberation 96, 97
Union of Nobility 220–1
Union of the Russian People 102, 103
Union of Unions 98, 100
United Nobility 220–1
Universities 76–8, 196–7
urban resistance 199
Uvarov, Sergei 11

Valuev, Pyotr 31
Vilna 134
vodka tax 40–1
Volkogonov, Dmitrii 172
volya 182
Vyborg Manifesto 106, 108
Vyshnegradsky, Ivan 68–9, 75

Weltpolitik 113
Western *Zemstvo* 121, 198
What is to be done?
Chernyshevsky 53
Lenin 82
Wielopolski, Marquis 42
Witte, Sergei 70–3, 100, 103, 124, 187, 204–5
worker–peasant alliance 123

Yellow Sea, Battle of the 89
Young Turks 113, 114
Yusupov, Prince Felix 147

Zamyatrin, Dmitri 31
Zasulich, Vera 54, 56, 183
zemstva 33, 34–5, 85, 183–4
Zubatov, Sergei 77–8, 188–9

To help you get the grades you deserve at AS and A-level History you'll need up-to-date books that cover exactly the right topics and help you at exam time. So that's precisely what we've written.

How to pass AS Modern World History
0 435 32752 6

- What your exam board is likely to ask you - and how to do it!
- What you need to know to pass your exam.
- Confidence-boosting preparation that really works.

THE HEINEMANN ADVANCED HISTORY SERIES

16th/17th/18th Century

Spain 1474-1700
0 435 32733 X   Autumn 2002

The English Reformation: 1485-1558
0 435 32712 7

The European Reformation: 1500-1610
0 435 32710 0

The Reign of Elizabeth
0 435 32735 6

The Coming of the Civil War: 1603-49
0 435 32713 5

England in crisis: 1640-60
0 435 32714 3

France in Revolution: 1776-1830
0 435 32732 1   Autumn 2002

19th/20th Century: British

Britain 1815-51: Protest and Reform
0 435 32716 X

Poverty & Public Health: 1815-1948
0 435 32715 1

The Extension of the Franchise: 1832-1931
0 435 32717 8

Liberalism and Conservatism 1846-1905
0 435 32737 2

European Diplomacy 1870-1939
0 435 32734 8

19th/20th Century: European

Russia 1848-1917
0 435 32718 6

Lenin and the Russian Revolution
0 435 32719 4

Stalinist Russia
0 435 32720 8

Germany 1848-1914
0 435 32711 9

Germany 1919-45
0 435 32721 6

Mussolini and Italy
0 435 32725 9

20th Century: American and World

Civil Rights in the USA 1863-1980
0 435 32722 4

The USA 1917-45
0 435 32723 2

The Cold War
0435 32736 4

**Call Customer Services
01865 888068**

Heinemann

F582

S999 ADV 08